T0329816

ATLANTIC STUDIES ON SOCIETY IN CHANGE

NO. 103

Editor in Chief, Béla K. Király

Associate Editor in Chief, Kenneth Murphy

Editor, László Veszprémy

EVOLUTION OF
THE HUNGARIAN ECONOMY
1848-1998

Volume II.

Paying the Bill for Goulash-Communism

János Kornai

Social Science Monographs, Boulder, Colorado
Atlantic Research and Publications, Inc.

Highland Lakes, New Jersey

Distributed by Columbia University Press, New York

2000

EAST EUROPEAN MONOGRAPHS, NO. DLVII

The publication of this volume was made possible by grants from
the Soros Alapítvány [Soros Foundation], Budapest

All rights reserved, which includes the right to reproduce this book
or portions thereof in any form whatsoever, without the written
permission of the publisher.

Copyright © 2000 by Atlantic Research and Publications, Inc.
ISBN 0-88033-455-X
Library of Congress Control Number 00-131495

Printed in the United States of America

Table of Contents

Chapter III
Adjustment without Recession:
A Case Study of Hungarian Stabilization

Preface to the Series and Acknowledgments

The present volume is a component of a series that is intended to present a comprehensive survey of the many aspects of East Central European society.

The books in this series deal with peoples whose homelands lie between the Germans to the west, the Russians, Ukrainians and Belorussians to the east and north, and the Mediterranean and Adriatic seas to the south. They constitute a particular civilization, one that is at once an integral part of Europe, yet substantially different from the West. The area is characterized by a rich diversity of languages, religions and governments. The study of this complex area demands a multidisciplinary approach, and, accordingly, our contributors to the series represent several academic disciplines. They have been drawn from universities and other scholarly institutions in the United States and Western Europe, as well as East and Central Europe. The author of the present volume is a prominent Hungarian expert of his theme.

The editors are responsible for ensuring the comprehensiveness, cohesion, internal balance, and scholarly quality of the series they have launched. We cheerfully accept this responsibility and intend this work to be neither justification nor condemnation of the policies, attitudes, and activities of any person involved. At the same time, because the contributors represent so many different disciplines, interpretations, and schools of thought, our policy in this, as in the past and future volumes, is to present their contributions without major modifications.

The Biographies of Key Personalities and the Selected Bibliography were compiled by Julianna Parti.

Ms. Andrea T. Kulcsár gave extensive help in arranging, refining, type-setting of the text, and preparing the appendices. I wish to express our gratitude to her.

Budapest, March 15, 2000

Béla K. Király
Editor in Chief

Foreword

The first paper in this volume was written in 1985 and the last in 1995.[1] The ten years in between the two years produced a political change of historic importance, which replaced the one-party system in Hungary and the other communist countries in Europe with a multi-party system: dictatorship gave way to democracy. It is true though that the period of brutal Stalinist dictatorship in Hungary had ceased well before 1989–90: the system's adversaries were suppressed with a softer hand. Furthermore, there is still friction in the way democracy operates today, so that efforts towards political centralization and curbing the scope of opposition appear time and again. Nonetheless, 1989–90 can be said to mark a watershed in the *political* history of modern Hungary.

While the political change was sudden, the transformation of the Hungarian *economy* shows continuity in many respects. To put it more precisely, there is a kind of mixture of continuity and discontinuity in the economic sphere, with the former having a large share—larger than in the political sphere. This mixture is apparent in the three studies included in the volume. Here, in the Foreword, let me point to just a few aspects.

Hungary serves as a prime example of what is known, in the discourse on post-socialist transition, as the "gradualist" strategy of transformation. This ties in with the fact that structural transformation in Hungary started as early as 1968, so that it had a longer time to run its course. The reforms before 1989–90 and after the change of system had a gradualist character. Although some measures or packages of measures—abolition of the system of planning directives in 1968, the introduction of bankruptcy legislation in 1992, or the adjustment and stabilization package in 1995—had an extensive and lasting influence on the economy, the process of replacing the socialist system with the capitalist system involved hundreds and hundreds of small steps.

In many countries of the post-socialist region, the transformation of property rights hardly started until the political change. However, there were some exceptions, where the process had begun much earlier. Hungary had been in the vanguard in this respect, so that the private sector showed significant development in the second half of the Kádár era. To quote the first study in this volume, written in 1985, "The most spectacular trend of the Hungarian reform process is the growth of the private sector."[2]

The same study suggested that the reform process would certainly come to a standstill if the political, ideological and legal barriers to further development of the private sector remained.[3] Overcoming these barriers and speeding up the development of the private sector only became possible with the political turning point, the change of system. The governments and economic agents of post-socialist Hungary alike refrained, in a traditional spirit of gradualism, from the course taken, for instance, by the Klaus government of the Czech Republic, whose actions were aimed at distributing the wealth of the state free of charge, and speeding up the process of privatization spectacularly and artificially. Instead, the course taken in Hungary encouraged and created the conditions for an organic growth of the private sector. State assets were sold and an inflow of foreign capital was permitted and encouraged. This led to a growth in productivity unequalled anywhere in the post-socialist region except Poland.

However, insistence on continuity and gradualism had harmful effects as well. The second study in the volume analyses in detail the policy of "goulash communism" that came about in the Kádár era. The dictatorship was "soft". The regime could not or dared not keep the people down by repression. Instead it strove to win their benevolent support or at least to render them politically passive. It preferred to run up foreign debt rather than take unpopular restrictive measures at home.

This attitude survived after the political turning point as well. Successive governments refrained from introducing the strict measures that would protect or restore the country's internal and external economic equilibrium.

Only with the stabilization package of 1995 was there a radical departure from this lenient, and in many respects populist macroeconomic strategy. It was a painful operation, causing much public suffering, but it succeeded in correcting the severely distorted proportions of the macroeconomy. It also set out to cut the burgeoning state expenditure and thereby reform the role played by the state.

The last study in the volume, assessing the initial visible results of the adjustment package, was written in 1995. Since then, these results have become all the more apparent: economic growth has accelerated, and the restoration of the internal and external equilibrium has proved sustainable. The temporary acceleration of inflation entailed in the package has been steadily slowing down; the disinflation too is taking place in a gradualist fashion. However, any exaggerated or overconfident attempt to extrapolate from all this into the future could easily be a serious mistake.

The struggle for macroeconomic stability is by no means a battle that can be won at a stroke. It is a constant war, demanding vigilance and perseverance against populism, and eschewing cheap promises. There is always a danger of expanding the paternalist state again, that the government may loosen financial discipline and decrease efforts at efficiency. The warnings contained in these three studies remain timely in Hungary and in the other post-socialist countries.

Budapest, Hungary, and Cambridge, MA, January 2000
János Kornai

Notes

1. Many people change their view of the world during great turning points in history. That happened in Hungary in the 1990s. Indeed, some people did so several times, and if they expressed their momentary opinions in writing, they may feel ashamed to publish them again.

   My interpretation of socialism and capitalism, the command economy and the market, dictatorship and democracy remained the same after the change of system in 1989–90 as they had been before. I present my present-day readers with my previous writings in good faith, because I believe their message remains valid to this day.

2. This view of mine remained fairly isolated in the literature of the time, in Hungary and abroad. Most analysts in those days considered the most significant gain of the reform to be the market orientation assumed by state-owned firms.

3. I use deliberately the phrase "the study suggested". It should be remembered that it was written in 1985, under the legal publishing constraints of that time. So the final part of the study expressed the author's negative opinion in the form of questions, not statements.

   I am sure that readers understood the author's real message in those days, when the art of "reading between the lines" was widely practiced. I trust that in that sense readers today will be able to empathize with the style of the period.

Chapter I

The Hungarian Reform Process: Visions, Hopes, and Reality[1]

I. INTRODUCTION [2]

The Hungarian economy has undergone major systemic changes in the last 30 years. The impact of the reform is felt by every Hungarian citizen. The influence of the Hungarian experience, however, does not stop at the borders of this small Eastern European country. At least the temptation to follow a similar road appears in other socialist countries. The leaders of the Chinese economy are studying the Hungarian situation carefully in an effort to learn from its successes and failures. In the Soviet Union and in a few smaller Eastern European countries, where a genuine reform has not yet begun, the advocates of more far-reaching changes frequently refer to Hungary. It is probably not an exaggeration to say that the Hungarian reform has some global relevance.

According to a widely held view, the Hungarian economy has become or is close to a system of 'market socialism'. Referring to Oscar Lange's [3] famous model of socialism, Paul R. Gregory and Robert C. Stuart [4] write: 'In a general way, NEM (the New Economic Mechanism of Hungary) bears a close resemblance to the Lange model'. [5] I am convinced that this interpretation of the Hungarian reform is erroneous and the purpose of this paper is to support my rejection of this view. At the end different 'visions' of market socialism will be reviewed and confronted with Hungarian reality. But before this confrontation of 'vision' with reality, a positive description is needed. I will try to answer the following question: if it is not 'market socialism', what is the true nature of the present Hungarian system? For an answer, we have to go into some detail in reviewing the Hungarian situation, so as to avoid oversimplification.

This paper addresses the general reader, not only the specialist in comparative systems and socialist economies; therefore it cannot avoid including information known to the experts. The approach is largely 'institutional'; data are used for illustration. There is no attempt to support rigorously formulated hypotheses with econometric analysis. Many important questions remain unanswered; the paper stops at the present frontier of research in Hungary and elsewhere.

There are dozens of books and hundreds of journal articles about the Hungarian reform.[6,7] The paper is not an utterly mechanical compilation of every treatment. It recognizes and presents the principal alternatives, but, in the end, it describes and appraises the Hungarian reform in the light of my own views. It is best to say at once: This is a *subjective* description and appraisal of the Hungarian reform, its intellectual background, and its real development. Another personal remark is in order. Although my writings are not without some intellectual influence in my country, I do not claim to be regarded as one of the 'architects' of the reform. I was not and am not a government official or a member of any decision-making body, or a formally appointed adviser. In other words, I am accountable neither for the great results of the reform, not for its shortcomings. At the same time, I was and still am a firm supporter and a critical observer of the reform process. It is hoped that this special position gives me a certain closeness to the events, but also the necessary distance for a frank and fair appraisal.

Subjectivity is not identical with originality. The paper contains some ideas originating in my own writings but also the ideas of other economists whose contributions will be acknowledged. In some cases the originator cannot be traced, because the thought or formulation has been generated anonymously and now belongs to the folklore of the Hungarian economics profession. In some respects this paper reflects a rather wide consensus shared by a larger group of Hungarians. That does not imply that something like a universally accepted 'Hungarian view' exists. Economists in Hungary are no less divided in their opinions than their colleagues in any other country.

The review is not impartial; my own set of desiderata will become clear to the reader as he or she goes through the paper. Yet the article will remain in the domain of positive analysis and discuss a few intellectual currents; there is no attempt to present my own updated blueprint of an 'ideal' socialist system.

Because this paper deals with institutional changes, it inevitably touches on problems in the fields of sociology, social psychology, political science, and political history. Nevertheless, this is the work of an economist concentrating on economic issues without aiming at a thorough analysis of their political aspects.

The Hungarian reform was not a sudden action, but a slow process. Its intellectual history started with papers of György Péter[8] presenting a penetrating criticism of the old system and a draft of the reform.[9] The history of practical reform measures began in 1956-57 with the abolition of compulsory deliveries in agriculture, although the dominant feature of the period 1957-64 was the conservation of the old bureaucratic economic mechanism. An important milestone was reached in 1968, when a whole package of substantial changes was introduced. Further steps came later. But the reform process did not follow a one-way road even after 1968: phases of progress were followed by reversals. After the great reform wave of the late sixties the years 1972-79 again represented a period in which anti-reform forces could break through. A new wave of reform measures started in 1979 and has been going on since. Apart from consecutive ups and downs, proreform and counterreform tendencies have been manifest side by side continuously.

Unfortunately, limitations of space do not allow a discussion of the historical evolution of the reform. This paper focuses on phenomena that prevailed throughout the 1968-85 period and characterize the present state of affairs, with only occasional backward glances.

The Western reader will recognize many issues familiar to him or her from his or her experience in his or her own economy or, at least, in the public sector and administration of his or her own country. It would certainly be instructive to discuss similarities and differences between different socio-economic systems. There is also an extended theoretical and empirical literature on certain issues, which are the Western counterparts of problems discussed in this paper for the Hungarian case. For example, there are many valuable studies on taxation, price and wage control, regulation, privatization, and the relationship between government- and state-owned firms in non-socialist economies. Except for a few occasional hints, such comparative study and a survey of the Western literature on the analogous issues go beyond the limitations of the present paper.

II. CONCEPTUAL CLARIFICATION

There are a few general concepts that represent key building blocks in our thought, concepts that are not unambiguous. We do not pretend to arrive at generally applicable exact definitions. The purpose of this section is more modest: to clarify in a rather pragmatical manner the meaning of certain concepts in the context of the present paper.

1. Economic systems

We use the term *economic system* to mean not only 'grand' systems, like 'capitalism' or 'socialism', which could rather be regarded as system 'families', but also the particular members of such a family. Contemporary Czechoslovakia, Hungary, and Yugoslavia, for instance, have different systems, although all three are socialist countries.

Instead of an abstract definition, I give a summary list of the main components of an economic system:

* The organizations functioning in the economy: for example, administrative organs, non-profit institutions, firms, households, associations;
* The distribution of the various forms of ownership and property rights;
* The distribution of decision-making power;
* The information structure: types of information flowing between organizations;
* Incentives motivating the decision-makers;

11

* The role of political organs and the government in economic affairs;
* Laws and governmental resolutions, that is, the formal legal regulation of the economy's operation;
* Informal 'rules of the game': routine behavioural patterns enforcing, hindering, or complementing the formal legal regulation.

The list is not exhaustive.[10] The components are interdependent; they cannot be chosen arbitrarily.

In the Hungarian literature the terms *economic mechanism* or simply *institutional circumstances* are used more or less as synonyms for *economic system*.

We contrast the concept of *policy* with the concept of *system*. The former is the determination of certain variables by policy makers within the framework of a given system. In this respect we follow the usage of Hungarian discussions, which consistently apply the distinction between issues of economic policy and issues of the economic mechanism.

2. Bureaucratic and market coordination

A system coordinates the activities and interactions of its members, i.e. individuals and organizations. For the sake of our study we distinguish two pure types of coordination.[11]

a) *Bureaucratic Coordination*.[12] There is a *vertical* relationship between the coordinating individual or organization and the coordinated individuals or organizations. Control is exerted by a microlevel hierarchy. Administrative coercion and legal sanctions compel individuals and organizations to accept orders and prohibitions from above. The vertical relationship is lasting and institutionalized; it is mutually acknowledged both 'above' and 'below'. The transactions are not necessarily monetized, but if they are, the subordinated individual or organization is financially dependent on the superior. The bureaucracy is active in the allocation of resources and in the redistribution of income.

b) *Market Coordination.* There is a *horizontal* relationship between the buyer and the seller individual or organization; the two participants are equal from the legal point of view. The individuals or organizations are motivated by financial gain. In its pure form market coordination takes place at prices based on agreement between buyer and seller. The transactions are monetized.[13]

Some writers prefer a wider definition; the present paper, however, will apply consistently the narrow definition outlined above. We refer to market coordination only if money, prices, and profit are at work.

The debate over the reform of socialist systems can be translated into the language of the above classification: the participants suggest alternative combinations of the basic forms. Systemic changes in the real world can be described as new combinations of the two basic forms with shifts of relative weights and new linkages between them.

3. Reform

Reform is a notion widely used by many parties and political movements all over the world. The present paper will apply a narrow definition designed especially for our discussion. We reserve the term *reform* for the change in a socialist economic system, provided that it diminishes the role of bureaucratic coordination and increases the role of the market.

The modernization of a highly bureaucratic regulation of the economy with the aid of computers is not 'reform'. Nor do we give this name to efforts aimed at tighter labour discipline. Useful as these policy measures might be, they do not imply change of the system; they do not lead to a reduction in the role of bureaucracy and to an increase in the role of the market.

In this sense there are only three countries where a genuine reform process is in progress: in the order of inception these are Yugoslavia, Hungary, and China. There are signs that perhaps Poland will follow suit.

III. THE STATE SECTOR

We divide the economy into two main *social sectors*: organizations working with capital owned by the state and the rest of the economy, that is, the non-state sector. (The adjective *social* will be used throughout to refer to the sectors distinguished by ownership.) Systemic changes associated with the state sector are discussed in Section III and with the non-state sector in Section IV.

Table 1: Share of social sectors in employment and national income (percentage distribution)

	Distribution of active income earners				Contribution to national income		
	1966	1975	1980	1984	1975	1980	1984
1. State sector	65.0	70.9	71.1	69.9	73.3	69.8	65.2
2. Non-state sector							
a Cooperatives	30.7	24.9	25.5	25.9	17.8	19.8	20.6
b Household farming	-	-	-	-	4.0	3.2	2.8
c Auxiliary production of employees	-	-	-	-	3.0	3.7	5.9
d Formal private sector	4.3	4.2	3.4	4.2	1.9	3.5	5.5

Sources: Column 1: CSO, 1967, pp. 52-53; Column 2: CSO, 1976, pp. 92-93; Columns 3-4: CSO, 1985a, p. 23; Column 5: CSO, 1976, p. 58; CSO, 1982, p. 87; CSO, 1983b, p. 93; Columns 6-7: CSO, 1985a, pp. 55, 60; CSO, 1982, p. 85; CSO, 1983b, p. 98; CSO, 1985c, p. 77.
Data broken down according to our classification are not available for the contribution to national income in 1966.
Note: The non-state sectors are discussed in Section IV. 'National income' is a net output concept within the framework of the 'Material Product System' (MPS), the accounting system used in socialist countries. Except for sectors 2b and 2c, the table does not cover the informal private sector.

The state sector, it must be emphasized, was and still is the dominant sector of the Hungarian economy. As shown in *Table 1*, about two-thirds of officially recorded total national income is produced by state-owned firms.[14]

1. The abolition of mandatory plans

We begin with a brief description of the *command economy* by which the state sector was administered in the pre-reform period.[15] Usual synonyms are the traditional centrally planned economy or classical socialist economy, economy of the Soviet type, or simply, the 'old' economic mechanism contrasted with the reformed 'new' one.

The national plan is elaborated by the Central Planning Board and approved by the highest political bodies. After that, the plan is strictly mandatory. The economy is governed by a bureaucracy, organized in a multilevel hierarchy.[16] The plan indicators at the top are successively disaggregated from higher to lower levels. At the bottom, the state-owned firm gets hundreds or thousands of mandatory plan indicators each year, containing four sets. Firstly the set of output targets, whenever possible, in physical terms or in aggregate real terms expressed in base-year fixed prices. A multiproduct firm may get as many output targets as it has products or groups of products. Secondly, input quotas, again in physical or real value terms. This set contains the rations of centrally allocated materials and semifinished products, indicating not only quantity and quality, but also the supplier obliged to deliver. There are also labour quotas and wage funds. Thirdly, mandatory financial indicators concerning production costs, profits, credit ceilings. Fourthly, a list of certain actions to be taken by the firm: introduction of new technologies or products, investment projects, and so on. Although all plan indicators are compulsory, certain 'priority indicators' are enforced more strictly. Typically this is the case with at least one indicator of aggregate output, with some ceilings on wage expenditures, and also sometimes with a few specific export targets.

The flow of information is not unidirectional. The firms submit proposals in the course of plan elaboration and they report results during and after the plan period. The more important flow, however, is the flow downward: commands given by the higher level to the lower level of the hierarchy.

One of the most tormenting properties of the command system is rigidity. Commands once given are hard to change. Any change must go through a multistage process of approval in different sections and different levels of the hierarchy. The system of detailed plan indicators is, of course, interdependent; it is a kind of a 'general equilibrium' image of future economic processes. It is required that the spillover effects of any significant change should be followed in all other segments affected and appropriate adjustment should be made. Planners understandably are not fond of such extra work. As a consequence, response to unexpected shifts in supply, demand, or technology is slow and incomplete.

Top planners seek to assure 'taut planning'.[17] The plan must have a 'mobilizing' effect, extracting maximum output from given resources. This is one more reason for rigidities: there are no easily accessible reserves left to be used for quick adjustment. Furthermore the plan leads to defensive tactics on the part of subordinates. It is in the interest of the firm's manager to hide the genuine capabilities of the firm and to fix a more law target that can be fulfilled comfortably even if supplies do not arrive on schedule. Of course the staff of the higher authorities knows this. 'Plan bargaining' evolves: the superior planner wants more output out of less input, the subordinate wants the opposite. In the course of realizing the plan, the manager's motivation is to achieve target, perhaps even to exceed target slightly, but this must not be overdone. Otherwise the exceeded target of this year will be incorporated into the mandatory target of the next year. As a consequence, a restrictive practice is common.[18]

Input-output combinations are distorted. The direction of distortion depends on the exact nature of the 'priority' indicators. If,
for example, gross output in aggregate value terms is enforced rigorously, the manager's interest is to produce goods containing large
quantities of expensive material. If the output target is given in tons
or, as in textile industry, in metres, the manager is motivated to produce heavy goods or thin textile. Output plans must be fulfilled at
any price, neglecting all other 'non-priority' objectives or those the
authorities are less able to check, like the improvement of quality,
the introduction of new products, reduction of costs, and proper
maintenance of machinery and buildings.

The abstract model of the command economy operating in the
state-owned sector is a strictly vertical bureaucratic control, executed by a disciplined bureaucracy in a consistent way. Real command economies are not as 'pure' as the model; some horizontal
coordination exists too. This proceeds partly on a non-pecuniary
basis: informal agreements of reciprocal help are made between
cooperating producer and user firms, complemented by some
incentives in money terms to the suppliers for the sake of more reliable deliveries (i.e. a half-tolerated, half-forbidden 'market' relationship). In any case, the system in the Hungarian state sector in
the early fifties was rather close to the model of a pure command
system.

There were minor changes introduced in the late fifties and
early sixties, for example, some limited forms of profit sharing for
employees. When the dispute over reform revived in the mid-six-
ties, there were discussions about how far the country should go in
the abolition of commands. Finally, the leadership opted for a radical solution. After careful preparation, the whole short-term command system was completely abolished in one stroke, beginning
with the first of January, 1968. The state-owned firms were formally declared to be autonomous regarding short-term output and input
plans.

Orthodox economists in Eastern Europe had been afraid that the socialist system would collapse without mandatory planning. It turned out that they were wrong. This paper will make many critical comments about the Hungarian reform, but this must not overshadow one of the most impressive and undeniable conclusions concerning the Hungarian systemic changes: the radical abolition of short-term mandatory planning is viable even without a fully developed market mechanism.

2. Dual dependence

What replaced the command system? A state-owned firm of the reformed Hungarian economy operates in a condition of *dual dependence*. It depends vertically on the bureaucracy and horizontally on its suppliers and customers. A brief look at the life of a state-owned firm will illustrate how the system of dual dependence works.

Entry. The creation of a state-owned firm is the result of a lengthy bureaucratic process. It may be initiated by an individual or a group, but the very active support of bureaucratic organs is needed for success.

Recently the legal conditions for establishing small state-owned enterprises have been eased. Existing firms can 'branch out' and create subsidiary enterprises half subordinate to and half independent of the founder. There is also some possibility of entry by non-state producers as potential competitors of the state-owned firm, but this is subject to severe restrictions.

Exit. There are state-owned firms that go out of business, but their number is rather small and the exit (both final liquidation and absorption by another state-owned firm) is decided by bureaucratic producers. 'Death' is not the outcome of a natural selection process on the market. No substantial positive correlation can be found between exit and persistent loss-making or insolvency.[19]

Selection and appointment of top managers. This remained the most important vertical linkage. Until some changes in the mid-eighties the leading executives of a firm were appointed by a superior authority. A successful manager will be promoted either by moving upward within the same firm or by transfer to another firm or to some state agency. Similarly, a successful official in a ministry may be appointed to the directorship of a large firm. There is no genuine 'job market' for managers; their career depends to a large extent on the opinion of the top bureaucracy. Therefore, it is understandable that one of the main objectives of managers is to please their superiors.

In 1985 new regulations were introduced. The top managers in the majority of state-owned firms are no longer appointed by the higher authority, but elected, directly or indirectly, by the employees of the firm. The administrative and political organizations have formal or informal veto powers over both the preselection of the candidates and the outcome of the election. It is too early to appraise the results of these arrangements.

Determination of output. The firm's autonomy has increased a great deal in this respect. Short-term annual plans are determined by the firm. The superior authority does not set aggregate output targets and that is an important change. It still puts forward, however, informal 'requests' telling the firm what is 'expected' from the managers. Typically, certain deliveries are urged for export or for a customer who is a protégé of the intervening official or for the elimination of certain pressing shortages. In any case, the management of the firm will usually be willing to comply.

Determination of inputs. The all-encompassing system of formal material rationing and allocation has been dissolved, though a few goods are still centrally allocated. There are, however, informal quotas, licenses, or other restrictions.[20]

Horizontal linkages between state-owned firms in their capacities as sellers and buyers certainly have becomestronger than they were before the reform. The linkages are mixtures of genuine market contracts following business negotiations about prices, quality standards, and delivery dates, and of 'gentlemen's agreements' based on reciprocal favours. But the horizontal linkages are still not insulated from the decisive influence of vertical regulation. In case of disagreement or contract violation, complaints are addressed to the bureaucracy, which is asked for judgment and intervention.

Choice of technology. Administrative intervention occurs, but it is not wide-spread. The firm's autonomy has increased substantially in this respect.

Determination of prices. Prior to the reform, the price of almost all goods produced by state-owned firms was set arbitrarily by administrative organs. The relative prices were grossly distorted. The rules have changed several times in the course of the reform process. Some prices are still determined administratively, although usually under some influence and in quite a few cases under strong pressure on the part of the firms. The majority of prices ceased to be administrative, at least nominally, after 1968. Most of such prices have still not become genuinely free market prices, either. Bureaucratic price control has different ways and means to exert strong, in some cases, decisive influence on price formation.

Firstly, for many goods strict rules prescribe how to calculate the price. Regulations determine the cases in which a 'cost-plus' principle must be implemented. For such calculations there are strict instructions as to how costs should be calculated and what are the permitted profit margins. In some other cases the application of the so-called competitive pricing principles is mandatory. Profit margins for goods sold on the domestic market must not exceed the profit margins achieved on export markets. Similar correspondence is prescribed between price increase for domestically sold and exported goods.[21] There are many exceptions to the declared calculation principles, again determined by a long sequence of bureaucratic rules.

Secondly, many of the changes nominally decided within the firm must be reported in advance by the producer to the price authority, which may or may not intervene, formally or informally.

Thirdly, there are laws against 'unfair profit' and 'unfair price'. These are, of course, vague concepts; much depends on interpretation and arbitrary judgment. Because firms are audited frequently, there is always the concern that their pricing practice may be condemned.

Unfortunately, there is no study available that would give a clear appraisal of how the present Hungarian relative price system compares with a rational one, reflecting relative scarcities more or less correctly. Some authors argue that prices have come much closer to rational proportions than they did before the reform, mainly because the main raw materials, energy, and many tradable goods are closer to relative prices on the world market.[22] Others, the author among them, accept these results but maintain that a large degree of arbitrariness still prevails, because of the widespread and bureaucratic interventions mentioned above. In an interdependent price system each arbitrary aspect spills over and leads to further distortions. As we shall see later, an arbitrarily differentiated system of positive and negative taxation exists, which inevitably leads to price distortions. An indirect piece of evidence supporting the views of the critics is provided by a study of László Halpern and György Molnár,[23] who calculate a 'cost-plus' shadow price system based on uniform profit rates with the aid of an input-output table. The calculation[24] shows a strikingly wide dispersion of the shadow-price/actual-price ratios.

The impact of prices on firms' decisions has become somewhat stronger in the wake of the reform, but it is still not decisive; we will discuss that later. But even if firms eagerly watch prices, they may still give the wrong signals.

Determination of wages and employment. An important change: absolute ceilings on the total wage bill that had been one of the most powerful target figures in the prereform era were completely abolished. There are still several bureaucratic instruments of interference in wage formation. The instruments have changed several times since the beginning of the reform process. To mention just a few: progressive taxation of the firm linked to average wages or to wage costs or to the increase of wages; wage policy guidelines associated with strong pressures to follow them.

As a result of the reform, mandatory employment quotas were abolished, but formal and informal restrictions on hiring labour reappeared in the seventies, as a reaction to growing labour shortages.[25]

Credit. Hungary has a highly centralized monetary system. There is permanent excess demand for credit. The banking sector, except for new institutions to be discussed later, acts as a credit-rationing administrative authority and not as a genuine bank following commercial prinicples.[26] It is strongly connected with the planners' and the other authorities' supervision of the state-owned firms. Granting or denying credit is almost uncorrelated with the past or present profitability and credit worthiness of the firm. To some extent, the opposite relationship is true. The credit system is used frequently to bail out firms failing on the market. Perhaps a more market-oriented practice will evolve soon following recent changes in the financial sector. We return to this issue in Section V/3.

Taxes and subsidies. Before the reform firms had to pay all gross profits, except for a minor profit retention, to the central budget. The introduction of taxation, which leaves the post-tax profit with the firm, is an important change. The tax system is, however, extremely complicated. The total number of taxes and subsidies of different sorts to be paid by or to state-owned firms is between 290 and 300.[27] Few of them are based on rules that affect all firms uniformly. Many tax or subsidy regulations appear to be general, but a closer look shows that they are calibrated to affect only a small targeted group, in many instances only a few dozen out of 1,600-1,700 firms. These are 'tailor-made' rules. In addition, *ad hoc* tax exemptions are granted or payments due are postponed to help firms in financial trouble. Firms suffer from the unpredictability of taxation. Any time that the central authorities feel that firms have 'too much money', tax rates may be arbitrarily increased or new taxes introduced or firms might be forced to save (for example, by prescribing mandatory deposits or reserves).

The total of all subsidies for the entire state-owned sector is about equal to the total gross profit before taxation; the total taxes are even larger than total gross profit because the state sector is a net tax payer. This means that a huge reshuffling of gross profits goes on taxing away and handing out money through hundreds of channels.

Investment. Investment decisions and financing were highly centralized before the reform. As a result of the reform, the firm's discretion has increased; a substantial fraction of profit can be retained for investment purposes. Nevertheless, central power is still very strong. For major projects the firm needs additional capital either from the bank or from the governmental budget. Only a small part of state sector investments, about one-fifth of the total, is really decided at the firm's level and financed exclusively form the firm's own savings. As for the rest, the firm must come to an agreement with those who give external assistance; consequently the bureaucracy can have a decisive influence on the allocation of investments.[28] Another form of intervention is to freeze the firm's savings originally reserved for investment purposes.

The central allocation of investment resources is not based on profitability criteria. Almost the opposite is true. Redistribution assists the losers with money taxed away from firms making large profits. A closer look at the financial data of firms in the study of Kornai and Matits,[29] Matits and Temesi[30] and Várhegyi[31] shows that there is no substantial correlation between pre-or post-tax profitability in a certain year and investment activities in later years (no effect of past and present profitability). And there is no substantial correlation in the opposite direction, either, namely, between investment activity in a certain year and pre- or post-tax profitability in later years. Thus, expected future profitability has no effect, assuming that there is substantial correlation between expected and actual profitability.

The situation is eased to some extent by recent developments. New financial intermediaries have been created, and new ways of raising capital are permitted. We shall come back to that in Section V/3.

3. Soft budget constraint and weak price responsiveness

In official declarations, profitability is the main criterion in appraising the performance of a firm. The bonus of the managers is profit-linked and there is also profit sharing for employees.[32] It was hoped that these measures would transform the firms into genuine profit maximizers. This has not happened. The situation is illustrated in *Table 2*.

First let us look at the losers. Loss, even if long term, can be compensated for by different means: *ad hoc* or permanent subsidies, *ad hoc* or permanently favourable tax conditions or bail-out credits. Price authorities can be permissive, allowing increase of the administrative price or deviation from certain interventionist price rules. The author[33] coined the term *soft budget constraint* to describe this phenomenon. The financial position of the state-owned firm is not without influence. Although there *is* a budget constraint that forces some financial discipline on the firm, it is not strictly binding, but can be 'stretched' at the will of the higher authorities. In principle, the firm should cover expenditures from revenues made on the market. In practice, earnings from the market can be arbitrarily supplemented by external assistance.

Table 2: Transition probabilities due to fiscal redistribution in the state
sector of manufacturing in 1982

From original profitability	To final profitability			
	Loss-maker	Low profitability	Medium profitability	High profitability
Loss-maker	.233	.500	.122	.145
Low profitability	.038	.853	.103	.006
Medium profitability	.000	.734	.206	.060
High profitability	.008	.394	.515	.083

Source and detail: Matits (1984a, p. 48).
Note: The research background of this table is indicated in note 19.
Transition means the proportion of firms in any given original profitability class that became members of a given final profitability class as a result of fiscal redistribution. The transition from 'original' to 'final' profitability means the transition from the pre-tax and pre-subsidy position to the post-tax and post-subsidy position.

The crucial issue is the fate of the chronic loss-makers. Their fate will clearly show whether profit is something 'dead serious' or only an illusion. The state bureaucracy exhibits a paternalistic attitude toward state-owned firms. This is understandable, for they are creations of the state, and the creator cannot let them down. There are strong social and political pressures to keep ailing firms alive for many reasons, for example, for the sake of job security[34] or of import substitution. But many observers ask the following question. If the firm is in deep financial trouble and for socio-political reasons it cannot be closed down, why at least are the managers not fired? Such harsh treatment would—so these observers say— increase the influence of the profit motive. In fact the managers may either stay or are transferred to another job without significant loss in income and prestige. The reason is simple. Because of the thousands of bureaucratic interventions, the manager does not have full responsibility for performance. In case of failure he can argue, perhaps with good reason, that he made all crucial decisions only after consulting superiors. Furthermore, many of the problems are consequences of central interventions, arbitrarily set prices, and so on. Under such circumstances, the bureaucracy feels obliged to shelter the loss-makers.

At the other end of the spectrum are firms making large profits. Table 2 shows that there is a peculiar egalitarian tendency operating to reduce larger profits. The budget constraint is not only soft, but also perverse. Because of the ceaseless and unpredictable changes of financial rules, taxes, and subsidies, firms feel insecure and exposed to the arbitrary improvisations of the bureaucracy.[35]

There are differences in terminology, but in substance a large group of Hungarian economists agree: financial discipline is lax, and there is no strong market coercion to enforce the search for profits. This 'soft budget constraint' syndrome has many negative consequences. Only one will be mentioned at this point, namely, weak responsiveness to prices, especially on the input side. If a wrong adjustment to relative prices does not entail an automatic penalty through a well-functioning selective market process, the firm does not have a strong stimulus for quick and complete adjustment. There are some studies, unfortunately not many, that show the firms' weak response to relative prices. Judit Szabó and Imre Tarafás,[36] with the aid of multiple regression analysis, demonstrate that changes of the foreign exchange rate have only a weak impact on producers' choice of the output and still less of inputs.

We are facing a vicious circle between the arbitrariness and irrationalities of the relative price system on the one hand and the soft budget constraint syndrome on the other, as argued by Halpern and Molnár,[37] Antal,[38] and Kornai and Matits.[39] Because prices are arbitrary and distorted, firms have legitimate reasons to ask for compensation. And when external assistance is granted, it leads to the preservation of the wrong price.

4. Size distribution, monopolies

The size distribution of firms in Hungarian production is much more skewed in favour of large units than in developed capitalist economies[40] as illustrated in *Table 3*. In 1975 in Hungarian industry the three largest producers supplied more than two-thirds of production in 508 and 637 product aggregates.[41] The extremely high concentration weakens or eliminates potential rivalry and creates monopolies or oligopolies in many segments of production.

Table 3: Size distribution of firms in manufacturing

	Hungary	Sample of capitalist economies
Average number of employees per firm	186	80
Percentage distribution of employees by size categories:		
10–100	14	35
101–500	26	33
501–1000	19	13
more than 1000	41	19

Source and detail: Ehrlich (1985b, p. 92).
Note: The figures refer to averages of various years in the seventies. The right column covers the following sample of countries: Austria, Belgium, France, Italy, Japan, and Sweden.

There are quite a few organizations that have the legal status of a 'state-owned firm', but are practically playing the role of a state authority. Their number now is smaller than before the reform, but still not negligible. They have the power to determine the rationing of the goods or services they supply to customers. For example, this is the situation with the monopoly company delivering automobiles. There is a monopoly bank with the exclusive right to grant consumer credit and mortgage loans.

In the last few years, there have been serious efforts to break up monopoly positions and to partition large entities into several smaller ones. The size distribution has become somewhat less extreme, shifting a little toward smaller units. But the process is slow and meets with strong resistance.

There is a peculiar disparity in the treatment of large and small state-owned firms. On the one hand, large firms are much more successful in lobbying for favours, particularly for investment resources. Some of them are in great financial trouble; nevertheless large credits or subsidies are granted to them.[42] On the other hand, smaller units count for less in the eyes of the supervisors. They suffer less form frequent inspections, and it is easier for them to evade certain rigid regulations than it is for large firms.[43]

5. Summary: from direct to indirect bureaucratic control

The reform has improved the performance of the Hungarian state sector. Firms now have more room for manoeuvre; they have become less rigid and more adaptive. They respond in a more flexible way to changes in demand and pay more attention to quality improvement and technical progress. These achievements become even more visible if one compares Hungary with the unreformed socialist economies.

This appreciation notwithstanding, the reform went only halfway. Hungarian state-owned firms do not operate within the framework of market socialism. The reformed system is a specific combination of bureaucratic and market coordination. The same can be said, of course, about every contemporary economy. There is no capitalist economy where the market functions in the complete absence of bureaucratic intervention. The real issue is the relative strength of the components in the mixture. Although we have no exact measures and, therefore, our formulation is vague, we venture the following proposition. The frequency and intensity of bureaucratic intervention into market processes have certain critical values. Once these critical values are exceeded, the market becomes emasculated and dominated by bureaucratic regulation. That is exactly the case in the Hungarian state-owned sector.[44] The market is not dead. It does some coordinating work, but its influence is weak. The firm's manager watches the customer and the supplier with one eye and his superiors in the bureaucracy with the other eye. Practice teaches him that it is more important to keep the second eye wide open: managerial career, the firm's life and death, taxes, subsidies and credit, prices and wages, all financial 'regulators' affecting the firm's prosperity, depend more on the higher authorities than on market performance.

In the course of the reform the bureaucracy itself has changed: it has become less tightly centralized. It is a peculiar complex of partial multilevel bureaucracies that often act in an inconsistent manner; it is more polycentric than before the reform. The head of each branch has his own priorities and performs his own intervention, granting favours to some firms and putting extra burdens on others. The more such lines of separate control evolve, the more they dampen each other's effects.

The 'rules of the game' are not generated in a natural, organic way by economic and social processes; rather they are elaborated artificially by the officers and committees of the administrative authorities. They are, of course, never perfect: they do not produce exactly the results expected and are therefore revised time and time again. Hence they are unable to provide stable guidance for the behaviour of the firm. Once the reactions of the firms become manifest, the rules are revised again.

The role of the state is not restricted to determining or influencing a few important macro-aggregates or economy-wide parameters like the exchange rate or interest rate. As we have seen, there are millions of micro-interventions in all facets of economic life; bureaucratic *microregulation* has continued to prevail.

The firms are not helpless. Every new tactic of the higher organs evokes new countertactics. First of all, bargaining goes on about all issues all the time. This is a bargaining society, and the main direction is vertical, namely bargaining between the levels of the hierarchy, or between bureaucracy and firm, not horizontal, between seller and buyer. All issues mentioned in Section III/2—entry, exit, appointment, output, input, price, wage, tax, subsidy, credit, and investment—are subject to meticulous negotiations, fights, lobbying, the influence of open or hidden supporters and opponents. The Hungarian literature calls this phenomenon 'regulator bargaining'; it has taken the place of 'plan bargaining' which had prevailed in the command economy. Firms had quite a bit of bargaining power even in the classical command system and their bargaining position improved substantially in the new system, especially in the case of large firms.

If bargaining does not succeed, there is one more instrument in the hands of the firm: to evade the regulations preferably not in an explicitly illegal way, but by using some tricks, seemingly following the letter of the law, but violating its intentions. And then, when the lawmaker recognizes that there are loopholes, he tries to create a new, more perfect decree—and the game starts again.

Let us sum up. For future reference we need a short name for the system that has developed in the Hungarian state-owned sector. We propose calling it indirect bureaucratic control, juxtaposing it with the old command system of direct bureaucratic control. The name reflects the fact that the dominant form of coordination has remained bureaucratic control but that there are significant changes in the set of control instruments.

IV. THE NON-STATE SECTOR

1. Digression: the reform in agriculture

Sections III and IV proceed generally by reviewing the various social sectors based on different types of ownership. Here in this section we digress to take a closer look at all ownership types in one particular branch, agriculture. This is perhaps the most successful area of the reform. It is therefore instructive to discuss agriculture as a whole.[45]

Contradictory tendencies have developed in the last 25-30 years. The share of state-owned farms remained rather stable. There were two big waves of 'collectivization', that is, the forced formation of agricultural cooperatives: the first in the early fifties and the second in 1959-61. The latter brought more than two-thirds of arable land from private ownership into the hands of the cooperatives. Members of the cooperatives were allowed to hold only a small private plot and a few animals. The present shares of the various types of ownership are shown in *Table 4*. Still, in spite of dramatic changes in the direction of collective ownership, Hungarian agriculture is different from the prototype 'collectivized' organization of agricultural production.

Cooperatives. This has remained the largest social sector in agriculture. Many important changes have occurred in their functioning. In the prereform system the position of a cooperative was not far from that of a state-owned farm. It was tightly fitted in the framework of a command economy; it received detailed mandatory plan targets like state-owned firms. As a result of the reform process, the system of mandatory plans was abolished in 1966, just

32

as in the state sector two years later. Frequent informal interventions, however, remained.

Even in the old system leaders of the cooperatives were elected and not appointed; that was the essential legal difference between a state-owned and a cooperative enterprise. In practice, however, elections were manipulated and there was only a formal approval of the preselected managers by the membership. This practice has not been rooted out, although the participation of the members in the selection and appointment of managers has become more active; the word of the membership carries more weight than it did.

In the cooperatives of the early fifties material incentives were weak. Compulsory delivery quotas at very low administrative prices absorbed the largest part of production. In other words, the peasantry carried a heavy tax burden. In years of poor harvest even seeds for the next year and foodstuff for the farmers' own consumption were barely left in the village. In the expression coined during those times, the attics of the farmers' houses were swept clean by compulsory deliveries. The sale of surplus on the market was legally permitted, but little or no surplus was left to sell.

There have been substantial changes in this respect. Some (though not all) price distortions, both on the output and on the input side, have been eliminated. Material incentives are strong. As has been mentioned, the compulsory delivery system was abandoned as early as 1956-57. The cooperatives can sell to state trade organizations on a contractual basis, but they are allowed to do their own marketing if they prefer. The cooperative as a whole is motivated to earn more income and more profit. The cooperatives have more autonomy in deciding how to use their own profit. In many areas a special kind of decentralization is applied within the cooperatives: working teams or individuals are in charge of a certain line of production and get their own share of their production line's net income.

Table 4: Contribution of social sectors to total agricultural gross output
        (percentage distribution)

Sectors	1966	1975	1980	1984
State-owned farms	16.4	18.0	16.8	15.3
Cooperatives	48.4	50.5	50.4	51.1
Household farming	23.7	19.0	18.5	18.4
Auxiliary production and private farms	11.5	12.5	14.3	15.2

Source: Columns 1, 2, and 3: CSO, 1983b, pp. 28, 37 and 116; Column 4:
CSO, 1985c, p. 73.

Before the reform, agricultural cooperatives were prohibited
from engaging in any but agricultural activities. In the reform
process non-agricultural activities have developed. The cooperatives have engaged in food processing, in the production of parts
for state-owned industry, in light industry, in construction, in trade,
and in the restaurant business. The share of non-agricultural production in the total output of agricultural cooperatives was 34 per
cent in 1984. In this way profits have increased and seasonal
troughs of employment can be bridged more easily.[46]

Private household farms of cooperative members. Here one
finds the most dramatic changes. Whereas the legal limitations on
the size of the household plot have remained unchaged,[47] much
more family work is devoted to this special kind of private agriculture. Restrictions on keeping animals and on owning machinery
have been lifted. Household farms produce a large percentage of
meat, dairy and other animal products, fruits and vegetables. With
few exceptions, there is no legal restriction on selling output, and
prices are determined by supply and demand on the free market for
foodstuffs; hence the peasants have a strong incentive to work hard
and produce more. The attitudes of both the cooperative and of the
agricultural administrative apparatus towards the householdfarm
are now very different from what they were. In the old system the
cooperative was hostile; private household farming was regarded as

a 'bourgeois remnant' that should be replaced soon by collective forms of production. Now private household farming is declared a permanent component of agriculture under socialism. Cooperatives render assistance in different ways: They provide seeds, help with transport, lend machinery, give expert advice, and assist in marketing. A remarkable division of tasks has evolved in which the cooperatives concentrate more on grain and fodder, which can be produced most efficiently by large-scale operations, while private household farms focus on labour-intensive products where small-scale operations succeed better.

We do not want to paint an idealized picture: in fact, there are many problems in this area. There have been periodic capricious bureaucratic interventions into the household farming sector, confusing the farmers and weakening their confidence. There are gross distortions in prices offered to the private producers by the state trade organizations, who are the main buyers of many agricultural products. In spite of these problems, the household farms are relatively successful.

Auxiliary agricultural production. Hungary is a country with a strong agricultural tradition. People working in non-agricultural professions like to have a garden or a small plot, where they can grow fruit and vegetables, or raise poultry or pigs. The liberalization measures in agriculture gave new impetus to these activities. Auxiliary agricultural production turns out to be a non-negligible proportion of total output, covering not only a substantial portion of the participating households' own consumption, thereby decreasing demand for marketed products, but also contributing to the marketed supply. Some of these producing units developed into specialized, capital-intensive private farms producing commodities almost exclusively for the market.

State-owned farms. The share of state-owned farms in total agricultural output has not changed much, but their situation is now different. All the systemic changes discussed in Section III also apply to the state-owned area of agriculture. Here we also find dual dependence, but the relative strength of the market is stronger and that of bureaucratic coordination is weaker than in other branches of the state-owned sector. Prices are more reasonable, managers are more 'entrepreneurial', and the profit motive is more intense. The difference is explained mainly by the fact that in agriculture a small number of state-owned enterprises are surrounded by a very large number of more competitive, more market- and profit-oriented cooperatives and private household farms. The minority's behaviour adjusts to some extent to the behaviour of the dominant parts of the branch.

To sum up: Hungarian agriculture shows a particular blend of spectacular successes and unresolved problems. The main achievements are the significant improvement of domestic food supply, some good results in exports and the stronger motivation for work in all subsectors. But all these results were obtained at high cost: with the aid of a very large investment of capital and of the peasants' hard 'self-exploitation'.

The present size distribution is unsatisfactory; medium size units, smaller than the large-scale state-owned and cooperative units and larger than the 'mini'-scale units in household farming are almost non-existent. In other countries with highly developed agriculture the dominant form is a farm operating with a small number of people, but with high capital intensity. Such an efficient and highly productive form has not yet developed in Hungary either in the cooperative or in the private sector. Development in that direction has been hindered by the privileges of the existing large-scale units and by conservative bureaucratic restrictions.

2. Non-agricultural cooperatives

We now return to our main train of thought, discussing the various social sectors one by one. Our next topic is the cooperative sector and because we have discussed agricultural cooperatives in Section IV/1, we focus here on the non-agricultural cooperatives. Their significance has increased in the reform process in manufacturing, construction, commerce, and services. They are similar to the agricultural cooperatives in many respects; we will not repeat what has been said already.[48] One important distinction: there is less favourable treatment of non-agricultural than of agricultural cooperatives as far as credit, tax, subsidy, and import are concerned.

What are the main similarities and differences between state-owned firms and cooperative enterprises? Everything described in Sections III/1 and III/2, the abolition of mandatory plans and the dual dependence of the enterprise, applies to the cooperatives as well. There is, however, a difference in relative weights; in all issues (exit, entry, selection of managers, price, wage, tax, credit) there is somewhat less bureaucratic intervention and somewhat stronger influence of market forces than in the state sector. The budget constraint is somewhat harder; non-agricultural cooperatives (especially the smaller ones) cannot expect unconditional survival[49] and almost automatic bail-out by the bureaucracy. The cooperative is much more responsive to prices; its profit motivation is stronger.[50] The cooperatives receive less favourable treatment than state-owned firms in the allocation of investment credits and subsidies.

The average size of the cooperatives is much smaller than that of the state-owned firms, and this has been so especially in recent years, because more possibilities have opened up for establishing so-called small cooperatives that work under easier and more flexible legal and financial conditions than do the rest of the cooperatives.

The situation of cooperatives is important form the viewpoint of socialist ideology. The idea that cooperatives will be one of the basic forms of ownership in socialism, or even *the* basic form, has a long-standing intellectual tradition in the Hungarian Left. The advocates of the traditional cooperative idea have always stressed the principle of voluntary participation. Nowadays this principle is more or less consistently applied in the non-agricultural sector. (The same cannot be said about the formation of cooperatives in the past.) There is general shortage of labour in Hungary. The vast majority of present members therefore, have a genuine choice between entering and remaining in a cooperative or getting a job in other sectors. Those who stay seem to prefer this form because it combines the efficiency of a medium size firm with a certain degree of participation in managerial decisions. The linkage between individual and collective performance and individual earning is more direct than in the state-owned firm. Of course, a conclusive test can come only if the economic environment of the cooperative sector becomes more competitive and market oriented, and the cooperatives have to demonstrate efficiency and profitability against more vigorous competition.

3. The formal private sector

The most spectacular trend of the Hungarian reform process is the growth of the private sector. From the point of view of ideology, this is the boldest break with orthodoxy.

The term *private sector* has both narrower and wider definitions. In the present section we discuss only a well-defined part of it, the *formal* private sector; other parts and also some definitional problems will be the topics of the next section. What distinguishes the formal private sector from the other private ventures is that it is officially licensed by the bureaucracy.

Table 5 shows the size of the formal private sector. The majority of personnel are craftsmen, construction contractors, shopkeepers, and restaurant owners. They work alone or are assisted by family members or a few hired employees. The size of this sector has increased rapidly in the last few years when the authorities began to grant licenses more liberally. Also the regulations concerning employment became less restrictive: at present the maximum number of employees, apart from family members, is seven. This is, of course, a very small number for those accustomed to private market economies, but large in comparison with other socialist countries. It means the legalization of 'small capitalism'. We must add that medium- or large-scale capitalist business is prohibited in Hungary.

A new form has appeared recently: the so-called business work partnership, a small-scale enterprise based on the private ownership by the participants. It is a blend of a small cooperative and a small owner-operated capitalistic firm. This form also belongs to the formal private sector.

The formal private sector is still a minor segment of the economy (see Table 5). Nevertheless, its rate of growth is remarkable: mere permission to exist and perhaps also some encouragement in official speeches were enough to induce a sudden boom. Apparently thousands of people had a latent desire to enter private business, at the first opportunity, they ran to join the formal private sector. And this happened in the face of many difficulties. Private business is at a disadvantage in getting inputs from the state sector. It rarely gets credit from the state-owned banking sector and therefore must rely on raising money through private and frequently illegal channels. Private credit does not have satisfactory legal backing.

It is widely believed that tax evasion is quite common; in any case, enforcement of the tax law is rather lax. Tougher enforcement could easily scare away many people from private business. This leads to a wider issue, namely the problem of confidence.

Table 5: The size of the formal private sector (in thousand of persons)

	1953	1955	1966	1975	1980	1984
1. Private craftsmen	51.5	97.6	71.3	57.4	63.7	76.1
2. Employees and apprentices of private craftsmen	4.0	16.0	26.7	19.7	20.1	26.9
3. Private merchants	3.0	9.0	8.5	10.8	12.0	22.4
4. Employees of private merchants	-	1.0	1.5	3.4	8.2	28.5
5. People working full time in business work partnerships	-	-	-	-	-	11.0
6. Total number of people working full time in the formal private sector	58.5	123.6	108.0	91.3	104.0	164.9

Sources: Rows 1 and 2 in Columns 1, 2 and 3: CSO, 1972, pp. 12-13; Rows 3 and 4 in Columns 1 and 2: CSO, 1957, p. 61; Rows 1 and 2 in Columns 4, 5 and 6: CSO, 1985, p. 324; Rows 3 and 4 in Column 3: CSO, 1967, pp. 56, 199; Rows 3 and 4 in Columns 4 and 5: CSO, 1981, pp. 132-133, 325 and CSO, 1976, p. 93; Rows 3 and 4 in Column 6: CSO, 1985a, pp. 52-53, 210.
Note: Since 1968 individuals who have a regular full-time job in the state-owned or cooperative sector can get a license for a second part-time job in the formal private sector. Data for 1984: 47.2 thousand individuals work as part-time licensed private craftsmen, and 31.5 thousand individuals as part-time members of business work partnerships.

At present the majority of people working in the formal private sector are probably satisfied with their current income. Perhaps they are not all aware that their relative position in the income distribution is much better than that of small business people in a private market economy. There, craftsmen or small shopkeepers usually have very modest incomes. In Hungary, many of them are in the highest income group. Yet they cannot be sure how long that will last. These individuals or their parents lived through the era of confiscations in the forties. In spite of repeated official declarations that their activity is regarded as a permanent feature of Hungarian socialism, deep in their hearts they have doubts. That is why many of them are myopic profit maximizers, not much interested in building up lasting goodwill by offering good service, and quick and reliable delivery or by investing in long-lived fixed assets. Encouragement and discouragement alternate; quiet periods are interrupted by orchestrated media campaigns crying out against 'speculation' and 'profiteering'. A confidence-strengthening experience of many years is still needed to extend the restricted horizon.

4. The informal private sector, the second economy

We must start with conceptual clarification. Hungarian experts dealing with private activities and income earned outside the state-owned and cooperative sector do not agree on terminology and definitions.[51] The present paper applies the following notions.

To the *informal private* sector belong (a) all private activities pursued outside the formal private sector as defined in the earlier section and (b) all income that does not originate as payment for labour service rendered in government agencies, officially registered non-profit institutions, state-owned firms, cooperatives, and formal private business. The activity and income components (a) and (b) of the definition are not completely overlapping.

The *first economy* is composed of the governmental agencies, officially registered non-profit institutions, state-owned firms, and cooperatives. The *second economy* is the total of the formal and informal private sector.[52] A caveat: the decisive mark distinguishing 'first' and 'second' economy in this usage is not legality versus illegality, or payment of taxes versus tax evasion. (That is the common criterion in the Western literature on the 'shadow economy'.) Many activities in our second economy are legal; a part of second-economy income is taxed. We apply a system-specific classification. The first economy is the sphere that was regarded by the pre-reform orthodox interpretation as the genuine 'socialist' sector, the second economy was classified as 'non-socialist'. We discuss this manifold sphere from various angles.

Working time. Hungary, with some delay, follows the tendency of industrialized economies by reducing hours of work in the first economy. Simultaneously, activities in the second economy consume more time than ever before. Some people work in the second economy as their main activity. Some members of a family are active full time in the private household farm, while other members of the family are employed in the state-owned farm or in the cooperative. Many pensioners have a full- or half-time (illegal or 'half-legal') activity. But the majority work in the second economy as an activity supplementary to a first job in one of the formal sectors. They 'moonlight' in the evenings, weekends, during paid vacations. It happens, illegally, that people work while on sick leave, paid by the national health service, or during regular paid working hours at their first job.

Aggregate data are shown in *Table 6*. The incredibly high (one to two) ratio between total working time spent in the second and first economies demonstrates the high preference of a large part of the Hungarian population for more income and higher consumption over leisure. This is just one of the secrets of the 'Hungarian miracle': people are willing to work more if allowed; they will exert themselves for the sake of higher consumption. In a large percentage of families, members are working to the point of psychological and physical exhaustion.[53]

Of the 33 per cent of active time spent on second-economy activities, a smaller part is spent in the formal private sector, thus contributing to the officially recorded GDP. The larger part of the 33 per cent is spent in the informal private sector. Depending on how productivity is measured in the informal private sector, this subsector may add perhaps 20 per cent or more to the officially recorded GDP.

Table 6: The relative size of the second economy

	First economy (State-owned firms and cooperatives) (per cent)	Second economy (Formal and informal private sector) (per cent)
1. Distribution of total active time (excluding time spent on household work and transport) in 1984	67	33
2. Contribution of social sectors to residential construction measured by the number of new dwellings) in 1984	44.5	55.5
3. Contribution of social sectors to repair and maintenance services in 1983	13	87

Sources: Row 1: Tímár (1985b, p. 306); Row 2: CSO, 1985a, p. 139; Row 3: Belyó and Drexler (1985, p. 60). Both studies rely on micro-surveys (interviews and questionnaires).

Notes: The table covers both the officially recorded and unrecorded part of total activities. The figures concerning the latter are based on estimates elaborated by the researchers who compiled the data base of the table. Figures in row 1 are aggregates of all branches of production, including residential construction. The latter is also surveyed separately in row 2. The 'first economy' figures include the activities of so-called enterprise business work partnerships, which will be discussed in Section IV/5. The 'second economy' figures include household farming and 'auxiliary production of employees'. The 'second economy' figures in row 3 are the sum of three parts: formal private sector 14 per cent, informal private sector excluding 'do-it-yourself' activities 19 per cent, and 'do-it-yourself' activities within the household 54 per cent.

Production for own consumption: the role of the household. Before the reform there was a strong tendency to reduce the role of the family and the household as a producing and property-owning institution and to shift more and more activity and property into the domain of large and preferably state-owned organizations. The reform reversed this trend to some extent.

The reversal is not consistent and is accompanied by many frictions. A kind of vacuum is present in some areas: the old forms of socialized services are no longer fully responsible for meeting demands on them while the household and the family are not yet in a position to take over these responsibilities satisfactorily.[54]

We have already discussed an important form of production for own consumption: the extension of private household farming and auxiliary agricultural production. These activities serve partly the household's own needs. The other extremely important area is housing. The trend in the prereform system was towards public housing. All apartment houses were nationalized; tenancy was rationed by the bureaucracy. This trend has been reversed. In 1980, 71.4 per cent of the total housing stock was in private ownership and the rest was owned by the state. The trend continues: 85.7 per cent of the dwellings built in 1984 were private.[55] The new shift is associated with severe social and economic tensions.[56]

A further example is transport. Khrushchev advocated the complete abolition of private cars in favour of public transport as a desirable trend in socialism. Present-day Hungary is overcrowded with private cars. The number of privately owned cars increased 13.7 times from 1966 to 1984. But repair service and the building and maintenance of the road network cannot keep up with the increasing number of private cars.

There are many more examples of the reversal from 'socialization' toward self-sufficiency within the family and household: child care, sick care, cooking and other household work, and do-it-yourself repair and maintenance. How far the latter trend has gone is demonstrated in Table 6.

Contribution to consumer supply. Another approach to indicate the importance of the second economy is to look at the contribution to consumer supply. Table 6 presents a few characteristic data demonstrating the extremely large share of the second economy in this respect. And, of course, there are many more areas not shown in the table.

Yields of private property. The preceding paragraphs of Section IV/4 discussed activities where the participant in the second economy combined his own labour with his own equipment, say the toolkit of a repairman. It may happen, however, that he uses, illegally, the equipment of his first-economy employer. There is also another category of person: income earners whose source of second economy income is a return from some private property. The most common example is the subletting of privately owned housing or the renting out of second homes in recreation areas, either to long-term lessees or to short-term visitors and tourists.[57]

Legality. There is a wide continuum running from perfectly legal, 'white' and perfectly illegal, 'black' activities, the latter being only the caseswhere law is strictly enforced. An informal private sector or a second economy exists in all socialist countries. Quantitative comparison is not possible, but experts are convinced that the share of this sector in Hungary is much larger than in most other socialist economies. This is a direct consequence of the state's attitude. There is a deliberate effort to legalize formerly illegal activities, or to be tolerant of ambiguous cases, provided that these activities are regarded as socially useful or at least not harmful. This tolerance awakened tremendous energy in a large part of the population. It is certainly not a very satisfactory organization of human activity; it is full of conflicts and unfair actions, but still, without the tolerance, this energy would remain dormant. It must be added, however, that the spirit of tolerance and the trend toward legalization do not work consistently. What has been said about alternations of encouragement and discouragement of the formal private sector applies even more to the informal sector. As a consequence, the situation here is rather unstable.

5. Combined forms

A characteristic feature of the Hungarian reform is the experimentation with different mixed forms, combining state ownership with private activity or private ownership. We discuss briefly three forms.

Firms in mixed ownership. A few dozen firms are owned jointly by the Hungarian state and foreign private business. A sharing of business by the Hungarian ownership state and Hungarian private business does not exist.

Leasing. This form is widely applied in trade and in the restaurant sector. Fixed capital remains in state ownership, but the business is run by a private individual who pays a rent fixed by a contract and also taxes. He keeps the profit or covers the deficit at his own risk. The lessee is selected by auction; the person offering the highest rent gets the contract. In 1984 about 11 per cent of the shops and 37 per cent of the restaurants were leased this way.[58]

Enterprise business work partnership. In contrast to 'business work partnership', which is a form clearly belonging to the formal private sector as shown in Section IV/3, here we look at a group of people who are employed by a state-owned firm. They do some extra work under special contract for extra payment, but in some sense within the framework of the employer state-owned firm. In many cases the team is commissioned by its own firm. Or it gets the task from outside, but with the consent of the employer. In many instances the members are allowed to use the equipment of the firm. The 'enterprise business work partnership' can be established only with the permission of the managers of the firm; each member needs a permit from his superiors to join the team.[59]

The purpose of creating this new form is clear. It gives a legal framework for certain kinds of activities, formerly not legal, mentioned in Section IV/4 and at the same time allows the employing firm to keep some control over these activities. Many managers support this arrangement because they can get around central wage regulation in this way: the partnership undertakes work for extra payment that it would otherwise do (perhaps in regular overtime) within the framework of its regular job. The number of such units is increasing rapidly. It was 2,775 in 1982 and grew to 17,337 by the end of 1984.[60] Many observers are highly critical and question whether it is really efficient to have a first and a second job within the same organization. On the other hand, the arrangement may perhaps lead to some healthy intrafirm decentralization later on.

6. Summary: strong market orientation and bureaucratic constraints

As we have seen, the reform process has created or strengthened a large variety of non-state ownership forms and activities. It is a great merit of the reformers that they allowed or initiated such experimentation with courage and an open mind.

In the midst of the variety of forms, there are a few common features. The economic units in the non-state sector (perhaps with the exception of large cooperatives) have a hard budget constraint; they cannot rely on the paternalistic assistance of the state as far as survival and growth are concerned. They enter business in the hope of profits and they go out of business if they fail financially. All activities are more market oriented and price responsive than those carried out by the state-owned firms.

The non-state sector acts as a built-in stabilizer of the economy, which is less sensitive to the 'stop-go' fluctuations so strongly felt in the state sector. It is able to grow even when there are troubles with the balance of payments or restrictions on import and investment.

The non-state sector is, however, not free from bureaucratic control. There are permanent restrictions and regulations, and also unpredictable, improvised interventions and frequent changes of the rules. The same phenomenon we have just praised, namely, bold experimentation, can also be rather confusing. The lack of stability and the many bureaucratic restrictions do not give full scope to the initiative of the individuals engaged in the non-state sector.

Nevertheless, with all its shortcomings, the appearance of a vital non-state sector represents something brand new and important in the history of socialist countries.

V. OVERALL RESOURCE ALLOCATION
AND DISTRIBUTION

In Sections III and IV we surveyed various social sectors. In this section we shall be studying issues that cut across the economy, regardless of the breakdown by ownership forms. We shall also make a few remarks concerning the relationship between the social sectors.

1. Planning

In the usage of socialist countries 'planning' has a double meaning. First, it refers to an *ex ante* exploration of possibilities and comparison of alternative solutions. A plan sets targets and assigns instruments to fulfil the targets. The 'product' of the planners' work is the plan itself—a document accepted by the political and legislative bodies, which serves as a working program for the government. Second, the term *planning* is also used to denote what this paper calls direct bureaucratic control. The official ideology of the command economy deliberately wanted to convince people that these two concepts are inseparable.

We suggest a strict separation of the two concepts and reserve the term *planning* only for the first. The official documents of the Hungarian reform adopt this interpretation when they repeat that, although mandatory targets and quotas are abolished, planning must be maintained.

Nominally, these resolutions have been implemented. The planning apparatus is at work, and plans are elaborated in due course. Nevertheless, a closer examination shows that planning has not found its appropriate new role. One would expect that after being freed from the nuisances of 'dispatcher work' (that is, setting quotas, checking performance, urging deliveries, etc.), the planner's time and intellectual energy could finally be spared for his genuine tasks of exploration, calculation, comparison, and *ex ante* coordination. These possibilities have not been fully exploited. There are efforts to elaborate long-term plans, but the linkage between these plans and the actual regulation of economic affairs is rather weak. Planners have achieved impressive results in coordinating short-term macro-policy and the micro-regulation described in Section III/2 in a state of emergency (for example, when tensions developed in Hungary's international credit position). Yet the problem has not been solved. The old methodology suitable for imperative planning is no longer applicable and a consistent new methodology compatible with the systemic changes is not yet available.

2. Fiscal system

The fiscal system has remained extremely large.[61] Total central government expenditure was 52.8 per cent of GDP in 1970, grew to 62.7 per cent by 1980, and decreased slightly to 61.3 per cent by 1983.

In capitalist economies this ration is strongly correlated with the level of development (GDP/capita). For the sake of comparison we look at European capitalist countries that have reached about the same level of development as Hungary: in 1980 the government expenditure/GDP ratio was 37.7 per cent in Finland, 36.5 per cent in Greece, and 29.4 per cent in Spain.[62]

There are several reasons for the high degree of centralization of financial flows through the government budget. Most of them are associated with issues already discussed, the huge burden of subsidies, the deep fiscal involvement in financing investment, and the expenditures of the large bureaucratic apparatus. These properties of the fiscal system provide remarkable evidence that genuine decentralization of economic process through market coordination has not gone very far.

The next section will discuss the role of banks and the capital market. One remark can be made in advance. The fact that a very large proportion of the economy's net income flows through the central government budget allows less scope for the activity of banks, other financial intermediary institutions, enterprises and households in the reallocation of funds. This is eminently clear in the case of investment allocation. The larger the proportion of investment financed by the central budget, the less disposable capital is left to the discretion of other actors and the less possibility arises for the creation of a well-functioning capital market.

In that respect there is a trend toward decentralization. The share of investment financed by the central government budget was 40 per cent in 1968-70 and diminished to 21 per cent in 1981-84; the share of investment financed by bank credit and by the producers' own savings increased accordingly.[63]

3. Monetary system, capital market

In a fully monetized market economy money is a means of integrating the whole national economy. That is assured by the possibility that money is a universal medium of exchange, which can be used by each money holder for any purpose he chooses. The classical prereform system fragmented the economy in this respect. Certain types of money flows between different segments of the system were permitted while others were strictly prohibited. The state sector paid money wages to the households, but, except for minimal tightly restricted consumer credits granted by the monopoly savings bank, it could not give credit to customers. The household paid the price for goods and services marketed by the state sector, but could not invest its savings in real capital formation by the state sector. Even within the state sector money was 'ear-marked'. The firm had at least three kinds of money: 'wage money', 'money covering current costs other than wages', and 'investment money'. These categories of money could be used only for the assigned purpose.[64]

The reform has brought some relaxation in this respect; the economy has come closer to a system integrated by money. It is, however, still far from one with free flows on funds.

Banks. Until recently, Hungary has had a 'monobank system'. In that respect it has remained similar to the classical socialist economy. The Hungarian National Bank has combined two functions: it plays the usual role of a central bank and also acts as a commercial bank, practically as the monopoly commercial bank for most financial operations of the state-owned and cooperative sectors. There have also been a few specialized banks, for example, the foreign-trade bank and the bank for household savings, but these have enjoyed only a seeming autonomy.

There are now resolutions to establish a two-level banking sector in the near future. There will be a central bank at the top with the usual functions and a set of state-owned, but competing commercial banks on the lower level, regulated by the central bank. Even before this plan is realized, a few small financial intermediaries that can lend for specific purposes (certain kinds of investment, innovation, export promotion) have been established. In any case, we do not know yet how much genuine autonomy the units of the decentralized banking sector will enjoy and to what extent they will be subject to the pressure of the central and local bureaucracy.

Firms. Before the reform, the state-owned firm had almost no choice concerning financial decisions.[65] The portion of working capital that had to be deposited in the central bank was strictly regulated; there was a very small part of gross investment financed from retained profit and depreciation funds. Trade credit was prohibited. The bank had a strictly protected monopoly in granting credit to the firm.

Now the situation is different. Let us start with the asset side. A firm can deposit money in the bank and in the near future it will also be able to choose between banks. It can grant trade credit to other firms buying its output.[66] It can invest in its own plant or it can establish a small subsidiary, holding only a part of equity in the newly created firm. It can contribute to the capital of a newly founded company jointly with other firms or institutions. It can buy bonds issued by other firms or local authorities and traded on the bond market. *Table 7* provides information about the size of the bond market.

Table 7: The availability of bonds, May 1986

	Total nominal value (billion forints)[a]	Yield (per cent)	Relative size (per cent)
Available to private citizens	4.5	7-13	2.0[b]
Available to firms and institutions	2.0	7-15	9.7[c]

Sources: Data on nominal values, information given by the State Development Bank. Data on yield, *Heti Világgazdaság* (1986, p. 55).
[a] Covers all bonds issued prior to May 1986.
[b] Total nominal value/stock of household deposits in savings banks.
[c] Total nominal value/stock of outstanding bank investment credit.

On the liability side the situation is symmetrical; only a few additional remarks are needed. Interest rates have been raised several times since 1976. The average interest rate for medium- and long-term credits granted to state-owned firms was 13 per cent in 1985, that is, a real interest rate of about 5 per cent. There is no conclusive evidence concerning how firms responded to the increase in interest rates.[67] There is permanent excess demand for credit, though the ratio of rejected to accepted credit applications has declined a little. Most observers agree that the sudden decrease of investment activity was achieved mostly through direct bureaucratic intervention into the approval and execution of large projects, and by cutting credit supply—not by the influence of interest policy.

Formerly the only source of credit for the firm was the central bank. Now if the firm wants to raise capital, it can apply to one of the newly created intermediaries just mentioned. As for bonds, they can be bought by households, which opens a new source of fund raising.

The long list of options gives a more favourable impression than does a closer look at the real situation. There are still many formal and informal restrictions both on the asset and the liability side: blocked or temporarily frozen deposits, constraints on self-financed investment. Many of the options are promises for the near future and not yet facts. For example, it is remarkable that firms are not very enthusiastic about buying bonds; the total number of bonds is very small. Most firms prefer to use their savings for reinvestment in their own production even if the expected yield is lower than the return of bonds issued by other firms or local authorities.[68]

Households. The set of options open to households has also become wider. Before the reform households could deposit money in the savings bank.[69] They could also buy, under strong legal restrictions, precious metal or real estate. The reform extended the potential portfolio recently by permitting the purchase of bonds. The first steps were taken to establish a kind of institutionalized bond market. This is an important new possibility, but its true significance is hard to judge at this early stage.

As mentioned earlier, individuals can lend to other individuals or invest money in a 'silent partnership' of a private business. Without sufficient legal protection, however, this may involve high risks.

To sum up: the first vague contours of a credit and capital market are emerging, but the Hungarian economy is still far from overall 'monetization' and from the solidified institutions of a full-grown, well-operating, flexible credit and capital market.

4. Labour market

While steps toward an extended capital market are modest, movement towards a free labour market is substantial. At the peak of direct bureaucratic centralization, labour was rigorously tied to the workplace. There were various restrictions: administrative prohibition on changing jobs except on the explicit instructions of the authorities, prohibition against taking employment in cities without a special permit, and distribution of many goods and services through employers, the state-owned firms, of such items as housing, child care, recreation, food, and other consumption goods in kind.

In the course of reform the first two of these restrictions on individual choice have been abolished. Remnants of the third still exist in housing, recreation, health care, and child care. These are, however, less binding ties than before.

Not only has overall full employment been achieved, but hidden rural unemployment was also absorbed in the early seventies. This is an important success. The general chronic excess demand for labour, however, is accompanied by labour hoarding and does not exclude minor frictional unemployment in certain professions or regions.[70] Excess demand, together with the elimination of administrative ties, results in high quit rates: 15.7 per cent in 1982, as compared, for example, to 7 per cent in Czechoslovakia in the same year. Labour is sensitive to benefits and also to differentials between the wage offers of different firms and moves quickly in the direction of better terms.[71] This is true of the labour movement within the state-owned sector. It applies even more to the relationship between the state-owned and the private sectors. Income offered by the formal and informal private sector attracts labour away from state-owned firms, which pay much less. The formal private sector can offer full-time employment. Or employees of the first economy can engage in informal private activities, such as 'moonlighting' or even working illegally during regular working time. In any case, the extra activities exhaust the individual and use up much of his energy; hence he will work with less attention and diligence at his first job. Here lies a hidden cost of bureaucratic regulation. State-owned firms are restricted in raising wages, but the formal and even more so the informal private sector can get round the restrictions. This is a painful dilemma; simple deregulation of wages would not help if all other circumstances such as excess demand for labour, weak profit motive, soft budget constraint remain unchanged. It would only lead to more forceful wage-push inflationary pressures.[72]

5. Summary: coexistence and conflict of the social sectors

This completes our description of the systemic changes. The observations can be summarized as follows.

Hungary has a multi-sectoral economy; different forms of ownership coexist and compete with each other. But competition is on unequal terms. With some simplification we may speak about a preference ordering of the bureaucracy: 1. large state-owned firms, 2. small state-owned firms, 3. agricultural cooperatives, 4. non-agricultural cooperatives, 5. formal private sector, 6. informal private sector.[73] This ordering is followed in bail-outs (for 1, 2, and 3; with more certainty for 1), and in handing out credits (1, 2, 3, 4). The formal private sector only occasionally receives these favours; the informal private sector gets nothing. It does not mean, however, that the actual relative position of the various sectors follows the same ranking. Again with some simplification one may say, that the same ordering prevails regarding the following troubles and burdens: frequency and intensity of micro-interventions, inspections and auditing, especially interference with price and wage determination, and enforcement of tax laws. In these respects the informal private sector has the advantage of being farther away from the eyes of the bureaucracy. This is an important, although not the only reason why many people prefer, in spite of fewer formal favours, to work in sectors placed lower on the state's preference scale.

Bureaucratic and market coordination are thoroughly intertwined in all sectors. The lower we go on the state's preference scale, the more freedom for market coordination. That is not necessarily because the bureaucracy would deliberately grant this freedom, but at least partly because it is less able to apply the same methods to several thousands of business units or millions of individuals that it can to a few hundred large firms. But even the formal and informal private sectors do not work in a 'free' market; the bureaucracy regulates the scope of legality and has many other instruments of restriction and intervention.

There is a feeling of complementarity, but also a feeling of rivalry between the various sectors; and there are collisions between them. The sectors lower on the state's preference scale suffer because in many allocative processes regulated by the bureaucracy, they are 'crowded out' by sectors higher on the scale. At the same time, the same lower-preference sectors may be successful in 'crowding out' the favourites of the state in the competition on the market. The most important example, namely bidding for labour in short supply, has just been mentioned.

In short: the Hungarian economy is a symbiosis of a state sector under indirect bureaucratic control and a non-state sector, market oriented but operating under strong bureaucratic restrictions. Coexistence and conflict exist between the social sectors in many ways and all the time.

VI. TENSIONS AND IMBALANCES

The idea of market socialism is associated with the expectation that the 'marketization' of the socialist economy creates equilibrium of supply and demand. It is a crucial litmus test of reform to see whether such equilibrium has been established in Hungary or whether tensions and imbalances characteristic of the former bureaucratic command economy have remained or others appeared.

1. The classical shortage economy

The prereform classical system in Hungary suffered from chronic shortages, and shortages are characteristic of other socialist economies.[74] The shortage phenomenon and its causal explanation area analysed in more detail in the author's book *Economics of Shortage* (1980). There is wide-spread excess demand on many markets, associated with queuing, forced substitution of less desired but available goods for the goods desired, forced postponement of purchases, and forced saving. Shortage phenomena torment both the consumer and the producer, the latter in his capacity as buyer of inputs. There is also excess demand for investment resources, for foreign exchange, and, in the more industrialized socialist economies, shortage of labour as well. There are spill-over effects: short supply of inputs creates bottlenecks retarding production and generating shortage elsewhere. The unreliability of deliveries induces hoarding of inputs. Shortage breeds shortage.[75]

Chronic shortages do not exclude the appearance of underutilized resources, excess capacities, and excess inventories. On the contrary, shortages even contribute to the creation of unnecessary surpluses, because of hoarding and because of frequent bottlenecks that leave complementary factors of production underutilized.

Chronic shortages damage consumer welfare; the buyer feels frustrated because of unsatisfied demand and/or forced adjustment to available supply. It means the dominance of the seller over the buyer: the latter is treated rudely and is frequently humiliated. In production, the disturbances of supply and improvised forced substitutions in input-output combinations cause losses of efficiency. The seller has a safe market and the buyer is willing to accept unconditionally what he gets. This leads to the most detrimental consequence of shortage: the lack of stimulus for quality improvement and product innovation.

Chronic shortage is the joint result of several interactive causal factors.

In spite of restrictive efforts on the side of macro-policy, there are systemic tendencies for demand to run to excess. The strongest force is the so-called *investment hunger*, the insatiable demand for investment resources. The hunger appears at all levels of hierarchical control, starting with the top policy makers and planners who seek high growth rates and ending with firms' and shops' managers, who also have a drive to expand. This is closely linked to the 'soft budget constraint' syndrome discussed in Section III/3. Because potential investment failure does not threaten severe consequences, there is little voluntary restraint on the claimant's demand for investment resources, that is, for project permits, subsidies, or credits. If the budget of the decision-maker is not strictly constrained, his desire to expand remains unconstrained as well.

The rush to investment is more intensive in periods when central economic policy is pushing more aggressively for accelerated, forced, growth. Central policy pulsates in this respect; stop and go periods, decelerations, and accelerations alternate causing cyclical fluctuation.[76]

Demand for intermediate goods is amplified by the tendency to hoard mentioned before. The buyer does not insist on getting just what he deeds right now, but is willing to purchase everything that may be of some use at a later time.

Demand of producers for imported intermediate goods is very strong. As a counterbalance, central policy wants to push exports. Importers' demand in foreign economies is, of course, constrained.[77] Yet the foreign trade companies in the socialist country are willing to sell at lower prices just to increase the total amount of foreign exchange earned by export. If dumping leads to losses domestically, the loss will be covered by the manifold instruments of the soft budget constraint. In other words, the demand of the state-owned foreign trade sector vis-à-vis producers of exportable goods is almost unlimited, adding a further component to runaway total demand.

Households have a hard budget constraint; in the classical system their income is under tight central control. Therefore excess household demand may or may not appear, depending on macro-demand management exercised, in the first place, through wage and consumer price policy. In some countries in certain periods, however, excess household demand is one of the main sources of runaway total demand (for example in Poland in the last 5-10 years).

Relative prices are distorted. Many goods and services have absurdly low prices or are distributed free of charge, generating almost insatiable demand.

The adaptive properties of the system are poor for many reasons. That applies to short-term adjustment: quick modification of input-output combinations requires mobile reserves of all complementary factors at all points of production. If there are shortages of one or two factors, bottlenecks do not allow flexible adjustment. Long-term adaptation is also slow. Uncommitted slack capital should be available for entrepreneurs who want to make use of unforeseen opportunities. But the irresistible investment hunger ties up *ab ovo* all investment resources. The great concentration of net income in the central governmental budget, the bureaucratic procedures of project approval, and the lack of a capital market hinder a fast decentralized adjustment of investible resources.

Adaptation is also dependent on motivation. The producer-seller is in a contradictory position. On the one hand, he cannot be indifferent to the urging of the dissatisfied customer, who is supported by his own higher authorities in many cases. On the other hand, he is interested in preserving shortage, which makes his life easier on the output side, because he need not pay much attention to quality, delivery time, and costs.

The relative weight of the different shortage-causing factors is controversial.[78] There is, however, general agreement in that all these factors play an important role in explaining chronic shortage.

The issues described in Sections III/1, III/2 and III/3—direct bureaucratic control, soft budget constraint, weak price responsiveness—and the problems discussed above concerning the causes and consequences of chronic shortage are closely interrelated, or more precisely, they are interacting properties of the same system. Chronic shortage is the necessary consequence of a system that is dominated by bureaucratic coordination and that almost totally excludes market coordination. At the same time, shortage is indispensable for the command economy as a legitimation ('rationing, intervention, taut planning are needed because of shortage'), as a stimulant ('produce more because your output is urgently demanded by the buyer'), and as a lubricant of the creaking mechanism of adaptation (in spite of poor quality, unreliable delivery, and poor adjustment to demand, all output is accepted).

2. Preservation and elimination of shortages

Hungary has moved away from the classical shortage economy. In important spheres the change is apparent. All observers agree that the supply of food and of many industrial consumer goods is much better in Hungary than it is in other Eastern European economies. In the winter of 1985-86, when the this paper was written, Hungarian households are provided with electric energy and heating, while in Rumania and Bulgaria drastic measures were introduced to force people to cut energy consumption.

Highly visible signs of improvement notwithstanding, careful examination is needed, because the situation is complex and diverse. We focus on areas where shortages persist and start with a review of *consumer goods and services*.

Service supplied exclusively by non-business state organizations free of charge or at nominal prices.[79] The most important example is medical care. Almost insatiable excess demand prevails: long average waiting time for hospital admission (except for emergency), overcrowded hospitals and clinics, hurried examinations, and so on. There is legal private practice, but only for office visits to the physician. Shortage is accompanied by large gratuities to doctors and other medical staff.

Service supplied exclusively by state monopolies at effective prices. The most important example is the telephone service. Shortage is very severe in this field. The number of telephone lines increased at an annual rate of 4.5 per cent and the number of applications for a line at an annual rate of 7.6 per cent in the last 25 years. The average waiting time is getting longer and longer; at present it is about fifteen years *ceteris paribus*. The network is overutilized: customers have to wait a long time for a dial tone, lines are almost always busy, and wrong connections are frequent.

Goods and services supplied by a dual system. The most important example is housing. Most urban apartment houses are publicly owned and rented out at very low rates covering only a small fraction of construction and maintenance costs. Although the right to join the queue (different entitlements based on income, family size, etc.) has been subjected to more severe restrictions, the waiting time in the capital is still several years. The other subsector is composed of condominiums in private ownership, owner-occupied family houses, and sublets. In the private sector, prices and rents are very high. The market operates but with many frictions; real estate intermediaries are few.[80]

Another example of duality is the allocation of cars. The supply of new cars is monopolized by a state-owned company. The average waiting time is two to three years. Supply responses tending to preserve shortage can be observed. If the growth of demand is retarded by price increase, authorities and the car sellers monopoly retard supply as well.[81] About one-tenth of all new cars is sold to privileged customers jumping the queue. The other subsector is the private market for second-hand cars. Here, prices are determined by supply and demand.

Imported consumer goods. The bulk is both imported and distributed by state-owned firms. Supply is capricious. Equilibrium or excess supply occurs in some cases. Sometimes demand is created by introducing a new good imported from the West and then supply is cut, causing shortages. A small supplement is the private import of Hungarian tourists: imported (in many instances smuggled) goods are sold on the informal market.

Goods and services produced and sold simultaneously by various social sectors, including the formal and informal private sectors. A variety of situations exist. The most typical is equilibrium in the aggregate of a larger commodity group. For example, a sufficient quantity of 'shoes' or 'meat products' in the shops does not necessarily mean that demand is satisfied: frequently the consumer does not find the kind of shoe or meat product he is looking for, and must therefore resort to forced substitution. Excessive inventories and empty shelves may exist side by side. Concerning the attitude of the seller, in some markets one finds a healthy competition, where attention is paid to the demands of the customer. In some other markets, where shortage persists, the private seller exhibits all the well-known traits prevailing on a sellers' market: he can be rude, many try to cheat, and so on.[82]

As for intermediate goods, shortages are rather frequent. Firms do not suffer from brutal cuts of energy supply as in some other Eastern European countries or as in Hungary in the early fifties. It is rather the unreliability of deliveries that causes many losses. That is particularly true for imported intermediate goods, where short supply can cause great troubles in production.[83] There is an enlightening index, the composition of inventories. In a shortage economy firms hoard on the input side and output is easily sold: therefore, the ratio of input inventories to output inventories is relatively high. In an economy where selling difficulties are predominant, the reverse tends to be true.[84] *Table 8* shows that the Hungarian state-owned production sector is still closer to the characteristic situation of a sellers' than to that of a buyers' market.

Table 8: International comparison: composition of inventories in manufacturing industry

Country (Years of observation)	Ratio of input inventories to output inventories	
	Lowest	Highest
1. Austria (1975-76)	1.04	1.07
2. Canada (1960-75)	1.06	1.40
3. United Kingdom (1972-77)	1.20	1.56
4. Hungary (1974-77)	5.72	6.38
5. Hungary (1978-84)	4.90	5.25

Sources: Rows 1-4: Chikán (1981, p. 84). Row 5: CSO, 1979, p. 190; CSO, 1980, p. 194; CSO, 1981, p. 198; CSO, 1982, p. 134; CSO, 1983a, p. 127; CSO, 1984a, p. 130;CSO, 1985a, p. 128.
Note: 'Input inventory' covers stocks of purchased materials and semifinished goods; 'output inventory' covers goods ready for sale. For more detailed definitions see the sources.

As mentioned earlier, there is excess demand for credit in general, and for long-term investment credit in particular. Pressure for credit became stronger, because credit supply was cut in the late seventies. These cuts were parts of the general macroadjustment programme to improve Hungary's position on the international financial market. Following tough central intervention, investment activity and demand for investment goods fell off.

To sum up: Hungary today is less of a shortage economy than it was before the reform, and some segments have been able to rid themselves of tormenting shortages to some degree. The chance has been due more to changes in the proportionate weight of the various social sectors and less to the changes within the dominant state sector. The formal and informal private sectors play a substantial role in filling the gap left by the state sector. But even then, shortages have not been eliminated, because many of their causes have not disappeared.[85] A vicious circle exists: recentralization contributes to the generation of shortages and shortages contribute to the trend of recentralization.

3. Inflation

Table 9 shows that inflation has accelerated in the past decade.[86] According to a wide-spread view, the acceleration in Hungary was caused by the reform. This is an oversimplification, although it is not without some truth. Before the reform started, prices and wages had been tightly controlled and fixed for longer periods.

Firms were not particularly interested in profits; hence they had no strong reason to raise prices. Some creeping inflation, however, had been going on already long before the first reform measures (not sufficiently reflected in the official price indices). True, the reform relaxes price and wage control in many spheres and strengthened somewhat the firms' interest in higher profits. Yet these changes are not enough to constitute a full explanation of the acceleration; there are other explanatory factors at work as well.

Table 9: International comparison of inflation

	Rate of increase of average annual consumer price index (per cent)			
	1960-67	1967-73	1973-78	1978-84
Austria	4.8	4.9	6.8	5.2
Finland	4.8	6.6	13.8	9.2
Portugal	3.4	9.3	22.1	22.9
Spain	4.1	6.8	18.8	13.9
Hungary	1.0	1.6	3.9	7.5

Sources: United Nations (1970, pp. 524-29), (1979, pp. 690-96), 1983, pp. 200-206), and (1985b, pp. 220-24).

First of all, in the last few years, central macro-policy has been deliberately using inflationary measures as instruments of an austerity programme. Hungary has serious problems with foreign indebtedness and with the deterioration of the terms of Hungarian trade; policy-makers decided to shift the balance of trade from deficit to surplus by every means possible. As a precondition of such a shift, the growth of domestic consumption had to be stopped or cut back. Prices of many basic consumer goods and services were, therefore, raised again and again by government decrees accompanied by decisions to raise nominal wages as a partial compensation. The deliberate central price and wage increases have put in motion the whole price level, including prices and incomes in the formal and informal private sectors.[87] Using the terminology introduced in Section II/2, we can see that the change in *policy* and not the change in the system is the main causal factor. A similar policy was also applied in certain periods before the reform, for example, in the early fifties when the standard of living was deliberately kept down using the instrument of sudden price increases.

Central policy is ambivalent in this respect. While centrally decided price increases lead the inflationary process, there are official statements attacking managers of firms and the formal and informal private sectors for forcing prices up and for profiteering. Quite a few academic adherents of the reform show a similar ambivalence. They think that inflation, provided it is not too fast, may help the reform, because it makes the correction of distorted relative prices and wages easier. Actually, the same argument comes up also in the officialstatements justifying some of the price increases. Other economists, the author among them, feel that, with the protracted sequence of partial price increases, Hungary is walking a dangerous path. Each partial price rise has spillover effects in costs of production and/or in the cost of living. The interminable series of partial upward corrections puts in motion the well-known *dynamic process* of the price-cost-wage-price spiral.[88] That can do much harm to the core of decentralization: to financial discipline and rational calculation based on prices and profits. Inefficiencies can be comfortably covered up by passing over cost increases to the buyer.

One last remark on the interaction between shortage, inflation, and reform. Shortage, acceleration of inflation, deficits in the trade balance, the growing burden of indebtedness, liquidity troubles, or any other type of tension and unhealthy disequilibrium are good excuses for recentralization. They provide legitimation for suppressing market forces and reviving tight control, formal and informal interventions, and rationing of intermediate goods. This is a trap, because recentralization solidifies the deeper systemic causes that created most of the troubles. In some cases recentralization is accompanied by solemn promises that the measures are only provisional and will be applied only as long as the troubles prevail. The trouble is that the provisional bureaucratic measures tend to become permanent, because they restore the systemic roots of the difficulties.

4. External imbalances

Disequilibrium in the balance of trade and current accounts is not a system-specific phenomenon; many non-socialist economies are suffering form the same problem. What deserves special attention in this paper are some characteristic linkages in Hungary between external imbalances on the one hand and systemic changes and macro-policies on the other.

There is an ongoing dispute in and outside Hungary about the cause of the external imbalances. Did they occur mainly because of the deterioration of external conditions (worsening terms of foreign trade, intensified protectionism of Western importers, less access to foreign credit, increase of interest rates), or because of the delayed and inefficient response to the changing conditions? Nobody denies that both classes of factors played a certain role; the controversy is about their relative importance. The author joins those who put the emphasis on the latter group of explanatory factors, that is, on the deficiencies of Hungarian adjustment to the changes in the external world.

The dividing point in the time series shown in *Tables 10* and *11* is 1973-74, the first world-wide oil shock. Before this event Hungarian growth rates were rather similar to the rates achieved by European private market economies. (As in an earlier table, the small sample contains countries that are close to the level of development of Hungary.) There is, however, a striking difference in the response to the oil shock. While the capitalist economies sank into stagnation and recession following the oil shock, Hungary was progressing on the path of forced growth. The expansion drive continued without interruption; foreign credit was easily available. The accumulation of foreign debt was a consequence of two closely intertwined factors: macro-policy aiming at uninterrupted growth at any cost and the lack of genuine decentralization, that is, the inconsistencies in reforming the economy. It is difficult to separate 'policy' and 'system' in this respect. The incomplete change of the system produces (or at least intensifies) the expansionary policy at all levels of the hierarchy. Firms were sheltered from the losses due to the contraction of Western markets and the deterioration of the terms of foreign trade by softening the budget constraint and delaying appropriate changes of domestic relative prices.[89] This is striking evidence that the reform of the state-owned sector remained superficial: the national troubles were not 'decentralized' down to the firms, which consequently were not forced to adjust to the new world market situation. Instead of restraint in undertaking new investment and in carefully selecting projects well adapted to the new composition of external demand, an undiscriminating investment hunger continued and was even encouraged by the macro-policy of forced growth.

Table 10: Indicators of growth in Hungary, 1957-84

	Average annual growth rates (per cent)			
	1957-67	1967-73	1973-78	1978-84
		(in real terms)		
1. National income	5.7	6.1	5.2	1.3
2. Investment	12.9	7.0	7.8	-3.0
3. Real wage per wage earner	2.6	3.1	3.2	-1.4
4. Consumption per capita	4.2	4.6	3.6	1.4
5. Gross convertible currency debt		1971-73	1973-78	1978-84
in HUF		13.8	20.0	9.1
in USD		23.8	26.8	2.6

Sources: Row 1: CSO 1985a, p. 3; Row 2: CSO 1985a, p. 4; Rows 3-4; CSO 1985a, p. 17; Row 5: National Bank of Hungary.

Table 11: International comparison of growth rates
in construction activity

	Annual growth rates (per cent)		
	1968-73	1973-78	1978-81
Austria	5.5	1.0	0.0[a]
Finland	3.9	1.1	1.8
Portugal	8.9	0.9	-
Spain	5.9	-2.1	-1.9
Hungary	6.6	5.7	-0.6

Source: United Nations (1979, pp. 365-68; 1983, pp. 827-30; 1985a, pp. 828-29).

Note: We use construction activity as a proxy for investment activity.

[a] Last period for Austria: 1979-80.

Finally, after a long delay, macro-policy responded to the dangers emerging in the external position of the country. Suddenly brakes were applied: radical investment cuts followed by austerity measures and a decline of real wages as mentioned earlier. Again, this has been and has remained mostly a centralized policy. It is not the market response of decentralized agents to price and quantity signals (external prices and quantity signals converted into decentralized domestic signals). Or more accurately, such decentralized signaling plays only a relatively minor role. It is more a result of recentralization, a revival of administrative interventions in favour of important substitution and of a costly forced export drive that helped in solving the most burning troubles of trade imbalances and international liquidity. Hungary's balance of trade improved: its credit worthiness is rather exemplary compared to many other socialist and developing countries. But the deeper roots of external imbalances are alive. Bureaucratic control, both direct and indirect, is incapable of 'fine tuning'. A system cannot have two faces: rigidities, delays in deliveries, slow innovation and technical progress for domestic use and the opposite for the foreign customer. Efficient foreign trade can be assured only by a breakthrough in the reform process.[90]

5. Individual choice and distribution

We have now arrived at the end of the descriptive parts of the paper. There is one more problem to be raised before turning to the discussion of 'visions'. How do the systemic changes and the remaining or newly emerging tensions and imbalances affect the individual citizen? As shown in Table 10, real consumption was increasing impressively for a while, but was then followed by a slowdown. We pointed out in the previous section that the deceleration cannot be charged to the account of the reform. It is explained by an unfortunate coincidence of deteriorated external conditions, policy mistakes, and poor adjustment to the external changes due to the inconsistency of systemic change. Something more should be said, however, not about real consumption recorded in official statistics, but about a different aspect of the quality of life: the individual's right of choice.

We limit the discussion to economic aspects; choice in political, cultural, and moral dimensions is not the topic of the present paper. One more qualification: freedom of economic choice is not a simple question of 'yes' or 'no', but a matter of degree. We shall glance at the change in the degree of freedom in the different aspects of economic choice.

In the classical command economy the household could choose between marketed goods and services within its budget constraint. But the situation was very far from consumer sovereignty for many rasons.[91] A large part of total consumption was distributed through non-market channels by bureaucratic procedures as fringe benefits. As for the marketed part, chronic shortages created a situation in which the buyer bought not what he wanted but what he could get. Recurrent forced substitution is a violation of economic freedom.Prices did not reflect relative scarcities, and supply did not respond to prices. The consumer's choice had only a weak influence on the composition of supply. On the contrary, arbitrary relative consumer prices shaped demand.

A part of saving was forced by shortage; even after forced sub-stitution some money remained practically unspendable. There was no choice between alternative schemes of sick care or retirements. Savings could not be used for productive investment.

The individual's choice of work was limited. He was free from the great suffering of unemployment, but his choice of profession was, if not dictated, at least 'channelled' in the prescribed direc-tions. The working place was assigned in many instances and movement to another job was greatly restricted by administrative prohibitions.

The great achievement of the Hungarian reform is the signifi-cant extension of choices. And the great shortcoming of the reform is that it has not gone far enough in this extension.

Consumers' choice has become wider. Shortages are less intensive and less frequent, but they still exist. The domain of bureaucratically rationed goods and services has become narrower but has not been eliminated. There are goods and services where prices convey the consumers' signals to the producer, who responds to them with changes in supply. But this linkage is restricted to cer-tain spheres, mainly where the consumer is served by the non-state sector and even there the functioning of the market is distorted. In the rest of the economy the composition of supply is controlled by a peculiar combination of influences: in part by legitimate protec-tion furthered by well-considered plans that promote society's gen-eral long-term interests against myopic and individualistic deci-sions, but also by arbitrary paternalistic bureaucratic interference with the consumer's free choice,[92] and by the influence of the con-sumer's decision and, finally, also by merely random effects.

The choice set concerning saving and investment has become wider as well. The most important change is that individuals can invest in their own private housing instead of passively waiting for bureaucratic allotment. True, the purchase or building of a private house or condominium require tremendous sacrifices caused by bureaucratic obstacles, shortages, and scarcity of credit. There are new options in holding financial assets, although the number of alternatives is still small. There is still little choice between alternative schemes of medical insurance or retirement.

The individual now has much more choice in deciding on a profession and job. Administrative restrictions of labour movements have been eliminated. The most important new opportunity is the impetus given to the formal and informal private sector. Those who feel they have entrepreneurial abilities have some (rather modest) possibilities of using them. Those who are willing to work more for the sake of higher consumption can enter the second economy. The study by Róbert Tardos[93] showed that in response to the stagnation or decline of real wages, 47% of the families opted for working more in the first and second economy, because they wanted to maintain their standard of living. Again, the choice set is still rather restricted by frictions and administrative limits.

The problem of individual choice is strongly linked to income distribution. The prereform system associated the narrow limitations of individual choice with a certain type of egalitarian tendency. Income differentials of employees of the state-owned and cooperative sectors were moderate, although there was never a perfectly egalitarian distribution. Privileges existed for people higher up in the bureaucracy, not so much in the form of higher money wages as in perquisites: a service car, allotment of better housing, special shops with better supply, special hospitals and places of recreation and so on.

As mentioned earlier, the Hungarian economy achieved full employment and job security. The latter is a controversial issue; several economists point out negative side effects on working morale and on the artificial preservation of inefficient production lines. Income differential in the first economy exhibit a mild decreasing trend as demonstrated in *Table 12*. There are sugges-

Table 12: Income distribution

	Shares in total recorded money income (per cent)			
	1967	1972	1977	1982
1st decile	4.1	4.0	4.5	4.9
2nd decile	6.0	5.9	6.3	6.4
3rd decile	7.1	7.0	7.3	7.3
4th decile	8.0	7.9	8.1	8.1
5th decile	8.9	8.8	8.9	8.8
6th decile	9.9	9.8	9.8	9.6
7th decile	10.9	10.8	10.8	10.7
8th decile	12.2	12.1	12.0	11.9
9th decile	14.0	14.0	13.7	13.7
10th decile	18.9	19.7	18.6	18.6
Measure of inequality	1.92	1.96	1.84	1.82

Sources: Column 1: CSO, 1975, p. 65; Columns 2 and 4: CSO, 1985d, p. 13.

Note: The interpretation of the first 10 rows is as follows. The population is ranked in increasing order according to redorded per capita money income and divided into 10 classes. The first figure in the first column means: the poorest 10 % of the population received 4.1 % of the total recorded money income of the population in 1967.

The term *recorded money income* excludes recorded but non-money income (for example benefits in kind), and also unrecorded income, mostly earned in the second economy.

The last row shows a synthetic measure of inequality calculated by the Central Statistical Office in Hungary. Income earners are divided into two classes. Group 1: income earners above average; group2: income earners below average. 'Measure of inequality': ratio of average income of group 1 to average income of group 2.

tions that the rapid growth of the second economy counterbalanced this change or perhaps led to some increase of inequality, but there is no reliable evidence supporting these conjectures. Careful studies[94] show that Hungary now exhibits neither the characteristic inequalities prevailing in the prereform classical socialist system, nor the typical inequalities of a capitalist economy, but a peculiar combination of these. We still see differentials based on one's position in the hierarchy, but these appear less in the form of fringe benefits handed out in kind; they are more often reflected in money income differentials. (Although the shift is not complete, privileges in kind still exist.) At the same time, new inequalities have been created by the market, and in particular, by the appearance of the formal and informal private sector. While incomes at the upper end of distribution increased, social policy at the lower end did not develop sufficiently. For a long time, reformers had a one-sided technocratic orientation, concerned only with growth, efficient adaptivity, trade balance, and financial regulators and did not pay sufficient attention to the great moral objectives of social justice.[95]

In this respect as well, Hungary is a mixture of the distributional consequences of both bureaucracy and market.

VII. CONFRONTATION OF VISIONS WITH REALITY

Having described the reformed Hungarian economy we turn to alternative visions of market socialism,[96] discuss past ideas (Sections VII/1, 2) as well as contemporary Hungarian thinking (Sections VII/3, 4). Some visions took the form of pure theory as in the Lange model; others are blends of normative theory and practical proposals.

1. Oscar Lange's market socialism

The literature of the celebrated debate about socialism in the thirties, including the original writings and the later appraisals, fill up a library.[97] This paper does not survey the literature but concentrates on Lange's classical paper (1936-37) which is the central piece in the debate.

The first question is a positive one: is the reformed Hungarian system a 'Lange economy' or anything that comes close to a Lange economy? Based on information provided by Sections III and IV the reader has the answer already: a definite 'no'.

Caution is needed in formulating a fuller reply. Lange presents in a brief paper a *model*. Model building inevitably abstracts from complications of reality irrelevant to the main line of argument. It is a cheap and unfair criticism of a theoretical model to point out that reality is richer than the model. With certain simplification we focus on the most substantial assumptions and properties of the theory, both in a comparison with Hungarian reality and in considering the criticism of the theory that follows later.

Because a description of the Hungarian system has been presented already, very brief references will suffice. Lange thought of the possibility that socialism would be a dual economy consisting of a public and a private sector, but he formulated his disputed suggestions for the sector inpublic ownership. Therefore, it is legitimate to compare the Lange model with the Hungarian state-owned sector.

The Lange economy has a Walrasian information structure. Sufficient information is provided by the price system and by the observation of excess demand. A trial and error method generates Walrasian equilibrium prices or at least prices that converge toward them. Agents respond to prices. In contrast to that, the prices of the output produced by Hungarian firms even since the reform are not Walrasian prices and do not converge to such prices. Official declarations do not reveal even an intention to generate market-clearing prices everywhere in the economy.[98] The prices of products or services originating in the state-owned sector do not reflect relative scarcities. The prices of products and services originating in the non-state sector may come closer to Walrasian prices but only with severe distortions. The non-market-clearing prices of the state sector spill over to the rest of the price system. Apart from the question whether prices give the right signal, the main problem is that price responsiveness of the state-owned firms is weak. They give as much or, in many cases, more attention to other signals.

In the Lange economy the firm is essentially a profit maximizer. In contrast, the Hungarian firm has multiple objectives; the search for more profit is only one of its set of objectives and not necessarily the strongest one. The profit incentive is weakened by the soft budget constraint syndrome. The firm's vertical dependence on the superior bureaucracy dominates its horizontal dependence on the market.

In the Lange economy the central authorities restrict their activities to price determination. In the Hungarian economy the bureaucracy is busy intervening in all dimensions of economic life.

Intervention into price formation is only a small part of its hyper-activity.

The question is still open: is the establishment of a Lange economy viable and desirable? The first is the primary question, because in case of infeasibility, the second question loses relevance. Of course the experience of a single country cannot give a convincing answer, but can help in the reconsideration of speculative argumentation.

Lange's model is based on erroneous assumptions concerning the nature of the 'planners'.[99] The people at his Central Planning Board are reincarnations of Plato's philosophers, embodiments of unity, unselfishness, and wisdom. They are satisfied with doing nothing else but strictly enforcing the 'Rule', adjusting prices to excess demand. Such an unworldly bureaucracy never existed in the past and will never exist in the future. Political bureaucracies have inner conflicts reflecting the divisions of society and the diverse pressures of various social groups. They pursue their own individual and group interests, including the interests of the particular specialized agency to which they belong. Power creates and irresistible temptation to make use of it. A bureaucrat must be interventionist because that is his role in society; it is dictated by his situation. What is now happening in Hungary with respect to detailed micro-regulation is not an accident. It is rather the predictable, self-evident results of the mere existence of a huge and powerful bureaucracy. An inherent tendency to recentralization prevails.[100]

Lange's model is based on an equally erroneous assumption concerning the behaviour of the firm. He expects the firm to follow the Rule designed by the system engineer. But society is not a parlour game where the inventor of the game can arbitrarily invent rules. Organizations and leaders who identify themselves with their organizations have deeply ingrained drives: survival, growth, expansion of the organization, internal peace within the organization, power and prestige, the creation of circumstances that make the achievement of all these goals easier. An artificial incentive scheme, supported by rewards and penalties, can be superimposed. A scheme may support some of the unavowed motives just mentioned. But if it gets into conflict with them, vacillation and ambiguity may follow. The organization's leaders will try to influence those who imposed the incentive scheme or will try to evade the rules.

These remarks are well-known in the modern sociology, economics, and social psychology of bureaucracy, hierarchy and organizations. The Lange of the thirties, although a convinced socialist, lived in the sterile world of Walrasian pure theory and did not consider the socio-political underpinning of his basic assumptions.

Lange hoped that a market could be *simulated* by a bureaucratic procedure. This hope appears time and again in contemporary writings, for example in Hungary.[101] There is an inner contradiction in the logic of the idea. An army of bureaucrats is needed to adjust and readjust millions of prices almost continuously. The contemporary successor of Lange might say: determine with the aid of computers only price indices of large aggregates and give Rules to the actors prescribing calculation principles for breaking down the aggregates. This is happening, more or less, in Hungary. But as was said above, the firm can get around the calculation principles if these conflict with its interest. As a counter-measure, the authorities will add more detailed instructions, restrictions, and prohibitions. What emerges from this procedure is not a successfully simulated market, but the usual conflict between the regulator and the firms regulated by the bureaucracy.

The next objection concerns competition. Lavoie[102] rightly points out that in the neoclassical debate about socialism, the emphasis shifted one-sidedly to the issue of computing the correct price signals. What got lost was the crucial Mises-Hayek-Schumpeter idea regarding 'rivalry'. In a genuine market process actors participate who want to make use, and can make use, of their specific knowledge and opportunities. They are rivals. In that sense the market is always in a state of dynamic disequilibrium. The total potential of all rivals normally exceeds actual demand. Some win and some lose. Victory brings rewards: survival, growth, more profit, more income. Defeat brings penalties: losses, less income, and in the ultimate case, exit. Using the vocabulary of this paper, the Mises-Hayek-Schumpeter market implies a hard budget constraint and a buyers' market. As long as the system and the policy do not assure the prevalence of these two conditions, there is no genuine market. The great shortcoming of the Lange model is that it does not even contemplate these conditions and many of Lange's followers committed the same error.

This argument is related to our last remark. Lange had in mind a market using a Walrasian feedback mechanism that equilibrates supply and demand. There are, however, built-in tendencies in a centrally controlled system based on state ownership generating chronic excess demand in various spheres of the economy as described in Section VI.

2. The naïve reformers

This is a name given by the author to a group of economists who were the pioneers of the reform process. In Hungary, György Péter[103] must be mentioned first. Others are Sándor Balázsy,[104] Péter Erdős,[105] Tamás Nagy,[106] and István Varga.[107] The author, when writing his first book, *Overcentralization*, in 1955-56 (published in English in 1959), can be put in the same category.[108] Brus[109] in Poland, Yevsey G. Liberman[110] in the Soviet Union, and Ota Sik[111] in Czechoslovakia belong to the same group. This is an arbitrary and all too short list, just to illustrate the concept of naïve reformer. We refer here to early works of authors who, with the exception of Péter and Varga, are still alive; most have deviated more or less from their early theoretical position.

The group is heterogeneous; the members did not share identical opinions. We shall point out a few common characteristics. These seem to be all the more significant because it was exactly this set of common ideas that was so clearly reflected in the official resolutions and documents of the Hungarian reform in 1968.[112] What is more, rather similar ideas appear in Chinese official writings today. Most Hungarian economists have lost their naïveté through long and sometimes bitter experience. But many of their colleagues in other socialist countries, impatiently advocating the start of a reform, having no first-hand experiences as yet, show the same naïveté today and are irritated by the critical attitude of Hungarians.

Before turning to critical remarks, first a word of acknowledgement. The fact that the author's early work is included in the list above must not restrain us, out of false modesty, from recognizing the intellectual and political courage of the pioneering works. The descriptive part of these studies contains a deep and still valid critical analysis of the prereform system. The prescriptive part points in the direction of the later practical reforms in Hungary and China and to the reform attempts in Czechoslovakia and Poland: firms' autonomy, right price signals, profit incentive, use of market forces, shift toward a buyers' market, and so on. But the pioneers did not foresee many complications which, as it turned out, are the barriers to consistent applications of their proposals.

The naïve reformer does not recognize the conflicts between indirect bureaucratic control and the market. He thinks that abandoning the command system and turning from direct to indirect control is a sufficient condition for the vigorous operation of a market. His line of thought can be characterized as follows. Let us have a profit-maximizing, almost autonomous firm. It will respond with appropriate changes of supply and demand to the signals of relative prices, interest rates, taxes, credit rations. If so, there is no contradiction between central regulation and market. On the contrary, the market is an 'instrument' in the hands of the central policy-maker.

The officers in the central authorities pull all the strings of indirect control and the profit-maximizing agents respond like obedient puppets. As Hungarian experience demonstrates, this fundamental assumption is wrong.

The underlying philosophy is an optimistic belief that perfect harmony can be achieved or at least approached. A market is a rather good, but not perfect automation. Market imperfections should be corrected by central interventions, because the centre knows social interests *ex officio* better than do blind market forces. The naïve reformers admit that central planners are not infallible. But then, planners' imperfections can be eliminated with the aid of the market, which makes some corrections automatically. The faith placed in the harmonious, mutually correcting duality of 'plan' and 'market' (or, in the language of the present paper, bureaucracy and market) is the centrepiece of the pioneers' naïveté.

The coexistence of bureaucratic and market coordination does not guarantee that we get 'the best of both worlds'. It does not lead inevitably to the opposite case either,—the 'worst of both worlds'. These are extreme simplifications. Certain mutual corrections are possible. If market forces lead to income distribution that is judged to be unfair by society, or to undesirable externalities damaging to the environment and so on, the bureaucracy can and should apply corrective measures. (Even these corrections, however, are not made sufficiently in Hungary.) If state interventions have undesirable side effects, market disequilibria can give a signal and the planner can make adjustments provided that he listens to the signal. But such favourable complementarity cannot be relied on too much. As Section III/5 pointed out, the greater the bureaucratic intervention, the more one intervention weakens the effect of the other. Each string puller thinks that he can control the firm; the firm, confused by a hundred strings, starts to twitch. It does not respond clearly to bureaucratic regulation, but does not respond to market signals either. This what László Antal[113] aptly termed the 'illusion of regulation'.

The naïve reformers searched for a reasonable line of separation between the role of the bureaucracy and the role of the market. Many of them thought that such a separation line could be drawn like this: 'simple reproduction' (in Marxian terms) regulated by the market and 'extended reproduction' by the planners. In other words, current production controlled by the market and investment by the planner. It turned out that this separation is not viable. On the one hand, the bureaucracy is not ready to restrict its activity to the regulation of investment. On the other hand, the autonomy and profit motive of the firm become illusory, if growth and technical development are separated from the profitability and the financial position of the firm and are made dependent only on the will of higher authorities.

The pioneer reformers wanted to reassure all members of the bureaucracy that there would be ample scope for their activity. Their intention is understandable. The reform is a movement from 'above', a voluntary change of behaviour on the side of the controllers and not an uprising from 'below' on the side of those who are controlled. There is, therefore, a stubborn inner contradiction in the whole reform process: how to get the active participation of the very people who will lose a part of their power if the process is successful. The reassurance worked too well in the Hungarian case; the bureaucracy was not shattered. The number of people employed by the apparatus of economic administration changed hardly at all.[114] Small wonder that, instead of the harmonious coexistence of 'plan' and 'market' or the establishment of a 'regulated market', we got the phenomenon of dual dependence, described in Section III/2 which actually gives dominant influence to the bureaucracy. And as was explained earlier, once bureaucratic intervention exceeds a certain critical threshold, the market is more or less deprived of energy.

The naïve reformers were concerned with the problems of the state-owned sector and did not spend much hard thought on a reconsideration of the non-state sectors' role. It turned out,however, that up to the present time, it has been just the non-state sectors that have brought the most tangible changes into the life of the economy.

3. Galbraithian socialism

The present Hungarian economic community cannot be easily classified. In a certain sense, every economist and government official is an adherent of reform: reform is the officially declared policy of the political leadership and the government. What really matters is not general notions but the concrete appraisal of the present system and the practical proposals for the future. In these respects the views are heterogeneous; debates go on about dozens of issues. We economists who agree about one issue may disagree about a second. Each individual has his own personal collection of criticisms and proposals. Nevertheless, for the orientation of the foreign reader this section and the next will delineate two 'schools'. A warning is in order: there is some arbitrariness in my characterization. Those who undeniably belong to one or other school may still maintain some individual reservations or dissents. What we present are rather stylized 'prototypes' of two somewhat amorphous currents of thought.

We call the first school *Galbraithian socialism*. This is a name coined by the author; it may easily be that neither the members of the school nor Galbraith would be pleased. Anyway, Galbraith's work is a very characteristic reference in the writing of the school.[115] A dispute, marked sometimes by rather sharp polemics, goes on between them and the school of *radical reformers* whose thoughts will be reviewed in the next section. The ideas of the first school can be understood best in the framework of the dispute.

The Galbraithians contend that the radicals advocate an anachronistic system. The radicals, they say, want to introduce a mechanism into a socialist economy that would recall early 19th-century Manchester capitalism: a market free from any governmental intervention and the predominance of small economic units. They are socialistic Friedmanites—so the rebuke goes—although the true nature of contemporary capitalism is quite different. And here comes the emphatic reference to John Kenneth Galbraith[116] and to other authors describing modern private market economies. Contemporary capitalism is a dual economy. The first sector is a small group of huge and very powerful corporations, many of them in monopolistic or oligopolistic positions, intertwined with and sheltered by the government. It operates in an environment created by a large and powerful bureaucracy that intervenes in the economy continuously through Keynesian demand management, price and wage regulation, protectionist measures, and so on. The second sector is composed of small producers, small merchants, and the households, whose activities are coordinated by the market. Although both sectors do exist, the first is the really powerful and dominant one and the second is ancillary and subservient. If that is true in case of modern capitalism—so the argument of the Galbraithian school goes—there is no reason to require more decentralization in socialism. On the contrary: a socialist system has the possibility and the obligation to apply central planning and coordination more consistently and establish more thorough links between the central planners and the large enterprises. The crucial role of central planning must not be disguised bashfully, but should be openly and proudly declared and, of course, much better organized than before. The large monopolies, oligopolies, and the state associated with them must become 'entrepreneurial'; 'entrepreneurship' should not be a privilege of the small units.

The Galbraithian school is accused in some writings of desiring the restoration of the prereform command economy. As far as their published writings are concerned, these do not suggest a return to an all-embracing command economy. What they do suggest is the legitimation of the *status quo*. They justify the dualities of the present system: the coexistence of public and private sectors, bureaucracy and market, large and small firms, provided that the first component in all these pairs has the undisputed upper hand. Some of their writings suggest that they do not have much confidence either in the market or in the private sector and would rather see their roles diminished. They would legitimate the actual state of affairs, suggesting minor changes for improvement, but reject any further radical change that would go much beyond the present situation. For that purpose the school proposes to utilize all theoretical results and practical experience of contemporary capitalism: Kaleckian and Keynesian macro-economics, the textbooks of Western business schools, the lessons drawn from study tours to ministries, large banks and corporations in industrialized countries. Every bit of experience that points in the directions outlined above is welcome.

It is, of course, a paradoxical 'ideological' support for present Hungarian practice to say: 'Look, the system is in many respects not so very different from the practice of modern capitalism.' The trouble is that the similarity is exaggerated. True, modern capitalism is a system very different from a perfectly competitive atomistic Walrasian world. Admitting that, there are decisive differences between today's Hungarian economic mechanism and the system of highly developed capitalist economies (the 'West' for short in what follows). Without seeking completeness we underline only a few attributes relevant in the present context.

There is a state- and a non-state sector in the agriculture, industry, and commerce of both systems, but the proportions are radically different. The state sector is dominant in Hungary, while it is an important but minor sector in the West.

There are powerful large firms in both systems, but the size distribution is very different. The concentration in Hungary is much higher than in the West, as shown in Table 3.

The 'soft budget constraint' syndrome appears in both systems. In Hungary it is the normal way of life; in the West similar phenomena are more nearly an exception. Related to this is the issue of price responsiveness, which is rather weak in the Hungarian state-owned sector and strong in Western business life, including large corporations.

There are bureaucratic interventions in both systems. In Hungary it is all-encompassing; millions of micro-interventions make the state-owned firm highly dependent on the authorities. In the West the influence of the governmental bureaucracy is not negligible, but the frequency and intensity of intervention are much smaller. By and large it does not exceed the critical threshold where the vigour of the market would be diminished.

Shortage and surplus coexist in both systems. In Hungary shortages are wide-spread; strong competition of the sellers for the favour of the buyer is rather exceptional. In the West, the reverse is true. Shortages appear sporadically, but the typical situation is rivalry between competitors for the buyers' attention. That applies not only to small business but to the large corporations as well. They too feel the threat of actual or potential competition, of newcomers, large or small, of new products brought to the market by firms in the same sector or in other sectors, and also the competition of foreign sellers.

In the dialectics of the debate, however, the proponents of the 'Galbraithian' school deserve full attention, because they put their fingers on some weak points in the argumentation of the other school, the radical reformers.

4. The radical reformers

This is not a group with a commonly accepted consistent reform programme. We are talking about economists working in different research institutes or in the apparatus of some higher authorities who share more or less similar opinions about the reform. The most characteristic writings are those of Nyers and Tardos,[117] Tardos,[118] Bauer,[119] Antal,[120] but there is a much larger set of articles written in a similar spirit.[121]

Radical reformers elaborate profound critical analyses of the present situation; this paper has made extensive use of these studies. We focus here on their normative proposals. Out of the fragments a blueprint of market socialism takes shape. These are more circumspect suggestions than those of the naïve reformers of 20-30 years ago. The main ideas may be summarized as follows.

A system of market-clearing prices is needed; this and only this price determination principle is acceptable. Price determination must be left to the market. Deviation from these principles can be allowed only exceptionally. Profit incentives should be strengthened to make them sufficiently responsive to prices. Beyond that, new incentive schemes must be introduced; firms should be stimulated to try to increase their net worth as their primary goal.[122]

The distortion of the size distribution should be corrected. It would be good to encourage the appearance of medium- and small-size economic units by a variety of policies to support the free entry of new units and the breakup of monopolies or overconcentrated, excessively large units. Large firms are needed only when they generate economies of scale and are able to operate successfully in world-wide competition.

Barriers to competition must be eliminated. Various forms of competition should be promoted: rivalry between units belonging to different social sectors between large, medium, and small units between domestic production and import.

A reform of the system dedicated consistently to these objectives, together with appropriate macropolicy, should greatly extend the scope of the buyers' market.

Barriers to a free labour market must be eliminated. The state sector must not be at a disadvantage relative to the rest of the economy in acquiring labour. More flexibility of wage determination is needed.

Tough financial discipline, the hardening of the budget constraint, must be assured. This effort must be combined with more decentralization in the allocation of funds and with the creation of a flexible capital market. The possibility of bankruptcy must be an ultimate threat. At the same time, prosperous firms must have the opportunity to expand quickly by self-financing, by loans or by raising capital on the capital market. As a precondition for such changes the share of the government budget in the total flow of income must be diminished.

A commercial banking system must be fully developed and must operate according to business principles.

More competition must be allowed in export and import activities. Realistic exchange rates must become more influential. Conditions of import liberalization and full convertibility must be created.

Laws are needed that protect private business and clarify unambiguously the legal possibilities and limitations of private activities.

Political conditions of systemic economic changes must be created; the various social and economic groups must get appropriate political representation. At the same time, the state must continue to play an active role in the economy. Its main obligations are the macro-management of demand, the regulation of monopolies, the development of the infrastructure, the protection of society against harmful externalities, the redistribution of personal income for the sake of social justice.

The changes listed above and perhaps a few more important measures must be introduced in a consistent manner, as a 'package'. Any one of these changes, implemented separately without the appropriate conditions created by the other necessary changes can be risky or harmful.

The author is convinced that the implementation of these proposals is highly desirable. Yet quite a few substantial question are left open. The problem of ownership and property rights is not clearly elaborated in the writings of the radical reformers. This large issue can be divided into two subproblems.

First, what should be the future of non-state ownership and, in particular, private ownership in the blueprint of a reformed socialist system? Can its share be enlarged? Is a small unit with seven employees the upper limit of a private enterprise acceptable in a socialist country?

Second, is the traditional form of state ownership compatible with the proposed changes listed above, including strong profit motivation, free entry, hard budget constraint, flexible wage determination, workable capital market?[123] Different authors offer various solutions for separating the firms' management from the governmental bureaucracy. Some economists suggest labour-management, because that might assure independence from the bureaucracy.[124] There are counterarguments: the history of Yugoslav labour-management and also the first experiences with the participation of employees in the selection and appointment of managers are not sufficiently reassuring. Others, for example Tardos,[125] suggest the separation of management from a special institution that would be the declared representative of 'ownership interests'. The latter, like a board of directors in a capitalist joint stock corporation would appoint and supervise the managers. Critics are sceptical: can ownership interest be simulated by an artificially created body, which is commissioned (by whom? by the bureaucracy?) to represent society as the 'owner'?

Many arguments put forward in earlier sections of this paper come to mind. Is genuine autonomy of the public firm under the conditions of the Hungarian political structure feasible? Will the bureaucracy observe a voluntary restraint of its own activity without exceeding the limits assigned by the proposals surveyed above?

Such questions lead to the ultimate problem: can a reform process in a socialist country go much beyond what has been accomplished in Hungary? Or does contemporary Hungary exhibit more or less the ultimate limits of reform?[126] Other minor systemic changes, whatever their desirability, are irrelevant when considering the essence of this question.

The author must frankly confess his own ambivalence. As a Hungarian citizen he sincerely hopes that the answers to the series of questions raised above will be positive. As an occasional adviser he may try to help the process go in the direction outlined. As a researcher he reserves the right to doubt.

One lesson that can be safely drawn from study of the socialist economies is the large degree of unpredictability as far as deep system-wide changes are concerned. The questions raised above cannot be answered by speculation, only by historical experience. Up to now, Hungary does not provide a conclusive answer. We must wait and see what may be revealed by Hungarian or Yugoslav or Chinese experience or by the history of any other socialist country that may take the route of reform.

Notes

1. Reprinted from the *Journal of Economic Literature*, Vol. XXIV (December 1986), pp. 1687-1737. The paper was also published in János Kornai, *Vision and Reality, Market and State. Contradictions and Dilemmas Revisited*, Budapest: Corvina, 1985, pp. 99-182.
2. First of all, I am greatly indebted to Moses Abramovitz, for his encouragement and constructive help. I am grateful to many colleagues, especially to Tamás Bauer, Abram Bergson, Zsuzsa Dániel, Katalin Farkas, Károly Fazekas, János Gács, Gregory Grossman, Edward A. Hewett, Pál Juhász, János Köllő, Mária Lackó, Mihály Laki, Paul Marer, Ágnes Matits, Tamás Nagy, Richard Porters, András Simonovits, Aladár Sipos, Márton Tardos, and Laura D'Andrea Tyson for helpful suggestions and criticism of the first outline and the drafts. I should like to express my thanks for the support of the Institute for Advanced Study (Princeton), the Institute of Economics of the Hungarian Academy of sciences, and the Department of Economics at Harvard University. The devoted assistance of Mária Kovács is gratefully acknowledged. Naturally, responsibility for the views expressed and any remaining errors are exclusively mine.
3. Lange (1936-37).
4. Gregory and Stuart (1981).
5. *Ibid*, p. 299.
6. This paper has made use of many of those pieces of writing; see References.
7. A brief sample of summary reviews and appraisals of the Hungarian reform can be found in: Portes (1977), Balassa (1978, 1983), Nyers and Tardos (1979), Hewett (1981), Hare et al. (1981), Bognár (1984), Antal (1985a) and Marer (1986a, b). My intellectual debt to these works is gratefully acknowledged.
8. The history of the reform, including its intellectual history is surveyed in Berend (1983) and Pető and Szakács (1985). Szamuely (1982, 1984) and Kovács (1984) discuss mainly intellectual history.
9. Péter (1954a, b).
10. The literature of comparative economics offers various, mostly overlapping interpretations of the notion *economic system*. See for exam-

ple Neuberger and Duffy (1976) and Montias (1976).

11. For further elaboration see Kornai (1984). The influence of Weber [1922] (1947), Polányi (1944), Lindblom (1977), Williamson (1975) and Konrád and Szelényi (1979) is acknowledged.

12. The term *bureaucratic* is frequently used pejoratively in the Eastern European literature. The present paper does not follow this usage: according to the Weberian tradition, the term is a value-free denomination of a particular form of coordination.

13. Other basic 'pure' forms exist also. As important as these might be, for our topics the consideration of forms *a* and *b* will be sufficient.

14. The size of the officially unrecorded output will be discussed later.

15. More detailed description can be found in Granick (1954), Berliner (1957), Balassa (1959), Brus [1961] (1972), Nove (1983a, b), Bornstein (1981), and Gregory and Stuart (1981).

16. Here and throughout the paper we do not discuss the role of the Party separately. The Party is not simply a political movement as in a nonsocialist country, but also an apparatus in charge of running all affairs. Although from a legalistic point of view the Party and the government are separate entities, in practice they are intertwined and they work jointly in all relevant control processes. The Party has the leading role in the joint operation. Hence the term *bureaucracy* or *bureaucratic control* in this paper refers to the role played by the Party apparatus.

17. Hunter (1961).

18. The problem has been discussed in Eastern Europe since the fifties. There the phenomenon is called 'base-year approach'. The Western literature introduced the apt name 'ratchet principle' (Berliner 1957, Keren 1972, Keren et al. 1983).

19. This observation and a few more to which we refer in the paper are based on a large-scale project examining the balance sheets of all Hungarian state-owned firms during 1975-82. This project is directed by the author and Ágnes Matits; results are discussed in Kornai and Matits (1983, 1984), Matits (1984a, b, c), and Várhegyi (1986). See also Laki (1982, 1984), Lamberger et al. (1986), and Papanek et al. (1986).

20. Gács (1982).

21. Critical comments can be found in Hoch (1980) and Zelkó (1981).

22. Csikós-Nagy (1985).

23. Halpern and Molnár (1985).

24. *Ibid*, p. 824.
25. Fazekas and Köllő (1985b).
26. Tallós (1976).
27. Falubíró (1983).
28. Várhegyi (1986).
29. Kornai and Matits (1983, 1984).
30. Matits and Temesi (1985).
31. Várhegyi (1986).
32. Two remarks. First, a manager's bonus is linked to post-tax profitability, giving the manager an extra stimulus to fight for less tax and more subsidy. Second, profit sharing is levelled off; in contrast to the high variance of profitability, the ratio of profit sharing and wage per worker has a very small variance (Kornai and Matits 1983, 1984).
33. Kornai (1979, 1980, 1986).
34. Granick (1984).
35. Soós (1984).
36. Szabó and Tarafás (1985).
37. Molnár (1985).
38. Antal (1985a).
39. Kornai and Matits (1984).
40. Schweitzer (1982), Révész (1979), Ehrlich (1985a, b)
41. Román (1985). The 637 product aggregates cover about 75 per cent of total manufacturing.
42. Csanádi (1979, 1980, 1983), Szalai (1982), Matits (1984c).
43. Bauer (1976, 1985b).
44. Portes (1972, p. 657) made the same general point much earlier, writing that 'there is a threshold beyond which decentralization must go to take firm roots'. He was, however, rather confident that Hungarian 'strategy and tactics has brought the reform across this border'. These views were shared by many outside observers. The opinion expressed in the present paper is different: the Hungarian reform did not cross the critical threshold that separates a genuine market economy (associated with a certain degree of bureaucratic intervention) from an economy basically controlled by the bureaucracy (with certain elements of market coordination).
45. Donáth (1980), Swain (1981), Csáki (1983), Marrese (1983), Sipos (1983).
46. Rupp (1983).

47. The cooperative members are entitled to a household plot not larger than 0.57 hectares.
48. See Agonács et al. (1984) and Tellér (1984) for important studies about the indirect bureaucratic control of cooperatives.
49. Agricultural cooperatives are much more sheltered. Small wonder that this segment of the economy stubbornly opposes the introduction of bankruptcy laws and other measures of hardening the budget constraint.
50. All these differences are smaller and the similarities greater between *large* cooperatives and state-owned enterprises.
51. The most important Hungarian writings are by Gábor (1979, 1985), Gábor and Galasi (1981), Kolosi (1979), Belyó and Drexler (1985), Timár (1985a, b), and Falus-Szikra (1986). In the foreign literature pioneering work was done by Grossman (1977) concerning the Soviet second economy; a detailed bibliography is presented in Grossman (1985).
52. Here we follow more or less the definition of the second economy used by Gábor, the leading Hungarian expert in the field.
53. As mentioned in the note to Table 5, many individuals have a first job in the state or cooperative sector and a second job in the formal private sector. Although we count this activity as part of the formal private sector, the comments above concerning the extension of working time apply also to this group.
54. Bauer (1985b).
55. CSO (1984, p. 470), (1985b, p. 10).
56. Szelényi (1983), Dániel (1985).
57. Tenants in a public apartment have in practice a 'quasi ownership' under the conditions of chronic shortage. Tenancy can be inherited, sold for money illegally to a new tenant or legally to the state. Therefore it is not out of place to put the arrangement of subletting in a public apartment in the same category as using the equipment of a first-economy employer.
58. CSO (1985a, p. 210).
59. More detailed descriptions and analysis can be found in Laky (1985) and Stark (1985).
60. CSO (1985a, p. 326).
61. Kupa (1980), Muraközy (1985).
62. The Hungarian ratio in 1980 was somewhat higher even than the ratio of Sweden, Denmark, and the Netherlands, although all three

countries are at much higher level of development and spend relatively much more on welfare purposes. The ratio of governmental expenditure on production (mainly investment and subsidies) in industry, agriculture, transport, commerce, and service as a percentage of GDP was 25 in Hungary and less than 9 in the average of a sample of 14 industrialized capitalist countries. The figures are calculated on the basis of definitions assuring comparability. They refer to the same set of expenditures (including central and local government expenditures). GDP is calculated according to Western definitions for Hungary.

Source of all data is Muraközy (1985, pp. 746-47) and an unpublished paper of Muraközy.

63. Dudás (1985).
64. Brus [1961] (1972), Grossman (1966), Kornai (1980), Tardos (1980).
65. Because space is limited, we cannot discuss the same issue as far as other social sectors are concerned.
66. This is only partly a sign of healthy 'commercialization' of trade relationships. A large fraction of trade credit is involuntary; the buyer simply does not pay the bill in the agreed time, in this way forcing the seller to grant credit. Actually this arrangement is becoming a common method of 'softening the budget constraint'. Involuntary trade credit was, of course, known before the reform.
67. Breitner (1985), Grósz (1986).
68. This phenomenon indirectly supports the observation that state-owned firms are not highly profit motivated. They are more interested in the expansion of their own capacity.
69. The interest rate paid for a one-year deposit to households by the savings bank is 5 per cent, while the inflation rate in the last few years has been about 6-9 per cent according to the official statistics.
70. Galasi and Sziráczky (1985), Fazekas and Köllő (1985a).
71. Fazekas and Köllő (1985b).
72. Gábor and Kővári (1985), Falus-Szikra (1986).
73. In some instances large agricultural cooperatives get more favourable treatment than small state-owned firms.
74. The first studies were Kornai [1957] (1959), Holzman (1960) and Levine (1966).
75. There is an important school of thought (frequently called, rightly or wrongly, the 'disequilibrium school') dealing with centrally planned

economies which denies that shortage is chronic in the classical pre-reform socialist system or at least on the consumer market of this economy. The intellectual leader of this school is Richard Portes (Portes and Winter 1977, 1978, 1980; Portes 1984; Portes et al. 1986). Many remarkable and valuable studies have been produced using the theoretical ideas and econometric methods of this school. An extended bibliography can be found in Portes 1986. The author has an ongoing debate with the disequilibrium school (Kornai 1980, 1982). The controversy concerns questions of aggregation, measurement and interpretation of the notion of aggregate excess demand, the insulation of the consumer market from the rest of the economy, independence versus co-determination of demand and supply, the existence of forced saving, the relationship between shortage and labour supply, etc. This is not the place to go into these controversial issues. We shall come back to some empirical results of the disequilibrium school in the next section.

76. Bauer (1978, 1981), Soós (1975-76), Lackó (1980, 1984).

77. Except for the import hunger of other shortage economies for certain goods.

78. Soós (1984), Szabó (1985), Gomulka (1985), Kornai (1985a, b).

79. Each price has a critical value. Under this value the own-price elasticity of demand is zero; that is, the price is nominal. Above the critical value the own-price elasticity of demand is non-zero; that is, the price is effective. Many goods and services have nominal prices in socialist economies.

80. Dániel (1985).

81. Kapitány et al. (1984), Tibor (1984).

82. The attitude of the seller vis-à-vis the buyer is determined by the seller's membership in a certain social sector (state-owned firm versus private business) and by the state of disequilibrium in the market (seller's versus buyers' market). Hungarian experience shows that the second factor is the more important.

83. Gács (1982).

84. Fábri (1982), Chikán (1981, 1984).

85. The most important Hungarian representative of the disequilibrium school mentioned in endnote 75 is Katalin Hulyák (1983, 1985). Based, at least partly, on a different theoretical foundation and the estimation methods applied by Portes and his associates, her empirical results are in conformity with the observations presented above.

She demonstrates chronic excess demand for housing, automobiles, and investment resources. As for aggregate consumption, she shows fluctuations in the intensity of general shortage. The chronology and the signs of the fluctuations are closely correlated with fluctuations revealed by other studies, for example Kornai (1982).

86. We compare Hungary with a small sample of capitalist countries that are close to the Hungarian level of development (measured by GDP/capita). We do not make comparisons with other socialist countries concerning inflation rates, because adequate information about the statistical methodology of constructing price indices in these countries is not available. Many analysts agree that some hidden inflation exists in all socialist countries all the time. Certain kinds of price increases are not sufficiently reflected in the official price indices because of systematic bias in measurement methods (Kornai 1980, section 15.4, and Nuti 1985).

87. Unfortunately, the observation of prices and incomes in the formal and informal private sectors is not organized in a satisfactory manner. Petschnig (1985a, b) provides many examples of the fact that price increases in these sectors are much faster than in the rest of the economy.

88. Csoór and Mohácsi (1985).

89. The effect of the oil shock was also dampened by the fact that Hungary could obtain Soviet energy at prices below world market level.

90. Marer (1981), Balassa and Tyson (1983), Köves and Obláth (1983).

91. The problem is discussed in a wider context by Fehér et al. (1983).

92. The arbitrariness of intervention in consumer choice is demonstrated by the high dispersion of turnover tax rates on consumer goods. No reasonable social preference imposed on individual preferences can explain a turnover tax of +11 per cent on household chemicals, +5 per cent on shoes, of –11 per cent on sugar and of –26 per cent on fish (Csikós-Nagy 1985, p. 58).

93. Róbert Tardos (1983).

94. Kolosi (1980), Szelényi (1983).

95. Ferge (1984).

96. The alternative visions of *market* socialism are only a small subset of the much larger variety of visions concerning alternative forms of socialism.

97. The most outstanding works in the Great Debate were Barone [1908]

(1935), Mises [1920] (1935), Taylor [1929] (1964), Hayek (1935), and, of course, Lange (1936, 1937). The classical summary is Bergson's (1948) review. Important new points have been added by Bergson (1967), Nove (1983a, b), and Lavoie (1985).

98. Csikós-Nagy (1985).
99. What Lange had in mind concerning the role of the Central Planning Board and the market when he wrote his paper is controversial. In a private letter addressed to Hayek he stressed the importance of market forces directly determining prices in sectors where genuine competition prevails (Kowalik 1984). This paper does not discuss Lange's thinking in the thirties, but the so-called Lange model as perceived by the profession (in textbooks and papers referring to Lange) from the time of publication up to now.
100. Laky (1980).
101. Csikós-Nagy (1985).
102. Lavoie (1985).
103. Péter (1954a, b, 1956, 1967).
104. Balázsy (1954).
105. Erdős (1956).
106. Nagy (1956).
107. Varga (1957).
108. References to surveys are listed in endnote 7.
109. Brus [1961] (1972).
110. Liberman [1962] (1972).
111. Sik (1967).
112. The most significant documents can be found in the collection by Henrik Vass (1968). See also the book of Nyers et al. (1969). Nyers was the secretary of the party in charge of economic affairs at the time of the 1968 measures and can be regarded as the chief architect of the 1968 blueprint.
113. Antal (1979).
114. Kornai (1984).
115. Horváth (1976), Kozma (1983a, b), Sugár (1984), Szegő (1983).
116. Galbraith (1967a, b).
117. Nyers and Tardos (1978, 1979, 1984).
118. Tardos (1986).
119. Bauer (1984, 1985a).
120. Antal (1985a, 1985b).
121. A pioneer of radical reform was Tibor Liska (1963, 1969). Later he

elaborated a blueprint of socialism based on leasing state-owned capital to individuals. His ideas are clearly distinguishable from the proposals of other radical reformers listed above. Space does not permit
me to take up his suggestions and their criticism. Liska's programme
is discussed in Bársony (1982), Macrae (1983), and Siklaky (1985).

122. This is a reasonable desideratum. Unfortunately the doubts raised in
earlier sections against the viability of artificial 'rules', 'incentive
schemes' imposed on living organizations with inherent endogenous
motivations, apply to this proposal too.

123. This is an objection raised repeatedly by the opponents of these proposed changes. Szegő (1983).

124. Bauer (1984), Csillag (1983). A comprehensive survey is presented
in Sárközy (1982).

125. Tardos (1982).

126. Those few sentences require additional explanation. The socialist
system referred to in this study has certain specific distinguishing
marks: 1. the communist party exercises undivided political power.
2. Marxism-Leninism serves as the official ideology, and 3. state
ownership is predominant. These attributes are assumed in the lines
above when the limits to the reform process are discussed. If any
essential change should occur in any of these three fundamental
attributes, that counts not as a reform of the prevailing system any
longer but as a *revolutionary* transformation, i.e. a transition from
one system into another, even if it takes place gradually and without
any violence. In this sense the events that were taking place in
Hungary and Poland in 1988 and 1989 went beyond the limits of
what this paper refers to as a 'reform process'. (An additional note
appended by the author in August 1989 while the volume *Vision and
Reality, Market and State*, see note 1, was being prepared.)

REFERENCES

Agonács, Gábor, Bak, József, Domokos, József, Juhász, Pál, Szénay, László and Tellér, Gyula (1984) 'A szövetkezeti mozgalom a gazdasági folyamatban' (The Cooperative Movement in the Process of the Economic Reform). *Valóság,* 27 (2), pp. 17-27.

Antal, László (1979) 'Development with Some Digression. The Hungarian Economic Mechanism in the Seventies', *Acta Oeconomica,* 23 (3-4), pp. 257-273.

Antal, László (1985a) *Gazdaságirányítás és pénzügyi rendszerünk a reform útján* (The Hungarian System of Economic Control and Finance on the Way of Reform). Budapest: Közgazdasági és Jogi Könyvkiadó.

Antal, László (1985b) 'About the Property Incentive', *Acta Oeconomica,* 34 (3-4), pp. 275-86.

Balassa, Béla (1959) *The Hungarian Experience in Economic Planning.* New Haven: Yale University Press.

Balassa, Béla (1978) 'The Economic Reform in Hungary. Ten Years After', *European Economic Review, 11* (3), pp. 245-268.

Balassa, Béla (1983) 'Reforming the New Economic Mechanism in Hungary', *Journal of Comparative Economics,* 7 (3), pp. 253-276.

Balassa, Béla and Tyson, Laura (1983) *Adjustment to External Shocks in Socialist and Private Market Economics.* Mimeo. Washington, DC: World Bank Development Research Department.

Balázsy, Sándor (1954) 'Javítsuk meg tervezési módszereinket' (Let Us Improve Our Planning Methods). *Többtermelés, 8* (11), pp. 2-12.

Barone, Enrico [1908] (1935) 'The Ministry of Production in the Collectivist State', in *Collectivist Economic Planning,* Ed.:

Friedrich A. Hayek. London: Routledge & Kegan Paul, pp. 245-290.

Bársony Jenő (1982) 'Tibor Liska's Concept of Socialist Entrepreneurship', *Acta Oeconomica, 28* (3-4), pp. 422-455.

Bauer, Tamás (1976) 'The Contradictory Position of the Enterprise Under the New Hungarian Economic Mechanism', *Eastern European Economics, 15* (1), pp. 3-23.

Bauer, Tamás (1978) 'Investment Cycles in Planned Economics', *Acta Oeconomica, 21* (3-4), pp. 243-260.

Bauer, Tamás (1981) *Tervgazdaság, beruházás, ciklusok* (Planned Economy, Investment, Cycles). Budapest: Közgazdasági és Jogi Könyvkiadó.

Bauer, Tamás (1984) 'The Second Economic Reform and Ownership Relations: Some Considerations for the Further Development of the New Economic Mechanism', *Eastern European Economics, 22* (3-4), pp. 33-87.

Bauer, Tamás (1985a) 'Reform Policy in the Complexity of Economic Policy', *Acta Oeconomica, 34* (3-4), pp. 263-274.

Bauer, Tamás (1985b) *The Unclearing Market.* Mimeo. Budapest: Institute of Economics.

Belyó, Pál and Drexler Béla (1985) *Nem szervezett (elsősorban illegális) keretek között végzett szolgáltatások* (Services Supplied Within Nonorganized, Mainly Illegal,Framework). Mimeo. Budapest: Szolgáltatási Kutatóintézet-KSH.

Berend, T. Iván (1983) *Gazdasági útkeresés (1956-65). A szocialista gazdaság magyarországi modelljének története* (Searching for New Ways in the Economy). Budapest: Magvető.

Bergson, Abram (1948) 'Socialist Economics', in A *Survey of Contemporary Economics*. Ed.: Howard S. Ellis, Homewood, IL: Irvin, pp. 1412-1448.

Bergson, Adam (1967) 'Market Socialism Revisited', *Journal of Political Economy 75* (5), pp. 655-673.

Berliner, Joseph S. (1957) *Factory and Manager in the USSR.* Cambridge, MA: Harvard University Press.

Bognár, József (1984) 'Further Devolopment in Economic Reforms', *The New Hungarian Quarterly*, Autumn, *25* (95), pp. 45-54.

Bornstein, Morris, ed. (1981) *The Soviet Economy: Continuity and Change*. Boulder, CO, & London: Westview Press.

Breitner, Miklós (1985) 'Milliárdok egy százalékpontból' (Billions out of One Percentage Point). *Figyelő, 29* (34) p. 5.

Brus, Wlodzimierz [1961] (1972) *The Market in a Socialist Economy*. London: Routledge & Kegan Paul.

Central Statistical Office (1957) *Statisztikai Évkönyv 1956* (Statistical Yearbook 1956). Budapest: Központi Statisztikai Hivatal.

Central Statistical Office (1967) *Statisztikai Évkönyv 1966* (Statistical Yearbook 1966). Budapest: Központi Statisztikai Hivatal.

Central Statistical Office (1972) *Magánkisipari adattár 1938-1971* (Reference Book of Private Small-scale Industry (1938-1971). Budapest: Központi Statisztikai Hivatal.

Central Statistical Office (1975) *A családi jövedelmek színvonala és szóródása 1972-ben* (Level and Dispersion of Family Incomes in 1972). Budapest: Központi Statisztikai Hivatal.

Central Statistical Office (1976) *Statisztikai Évkönyv 1975* (Statistical Yearbook 1975). Budapest: Központi Statisztikai Hivatal.

Central Statistical Office (1979) *Statisztikai Évkönyv 1978* (Statistical Yearbook 1978). Budapest: Központi Statisztikai Hivatal.

Central Statistical Office (1980) *Statisztikai Évkönyv 1979* (Statistical Yearbook 1979). Budapest: Központi Statisztikai Hivatal.

Central Statistical Office (1981) *Statisztikai Évkönyv 1980* (Statistical Yearbook 1980). Budapest: Központi Statisztikai Hivatal.

Central Statistical Office (1982) *Statisztikai Évkönyv 1981* (Statistical Yearbook 1981). Budapest: Központi Statisztikai Hivatal.

Central Statistical Office (1983a) *Statisztikai Évkönyv 1982* (Statistical Yearbook 1982). Budapest: Központi Statisztikai Hivatal.

Central Statistical Office (1983b) *Mezőgazdasági adattár V.* (Reference Book of Agriculture Vol. 5). Budapest: Központi Statisztikai Hivatal.

Central Statistical Office (1984) *Statisztikai Évkönyv 1983* (Statistical Yearbook 1983). Budapest: Központi Statisztikai Hivatal.

Central Statistical Office (1985a) *Statisztikai Évkönyv 1984* (Statistical Yearbook 1984). Budapest: Központi Statisztikai Hivatal.

Central Statistical Office (1985b) *Lakásstatisztikai Évkönyv 1984* (Yearbook of Housing Statistics 1984). Budapest: Központi Statisztikai Hivatal.

Central Statistical Office (1985c) *Mezőgazdasági Évkönyv 1984* (Agricultural Statistical Yearbook 1984). Budapest: Központi Statisztikai Hivatal.

Central Statistical Office (1985d) *A családi jövedelmek színvonala és szóródása* (Level and Dispersion of Family Incomes). Budapest: Központi Statisztikai Hivatal.

Chikán, Attila (1981) 'Market Disequilibrium and the Volume of Stocks', in *The Economics and Management of Inventories*. Ed.: Attila Chikán. Amsterdam: Elsevier, pp. 73-85.

Chikán, Attila (1984) *A vállalati készletezési politika* (Firms' Inventory Policy). Budapest: Közgazdasági és Jogi Könyvkiadó.

Csáki, Csaba (1983) 'Economic Management and Organization of Hungarian Agriculture', *Journal of Comparative Economics*, 7 (3), pp. 318-328.

Csanádi, Mária (1979) 'A vállalatnagyság, a jövedelmezőség és a preferenciák néhány összefüggése' (A Few Aspects of the Size, and Profitability of Firms and Preferences). *Pénzügyi Szemle*, 23 (2), pp. 105-120.

Csanádi, Mária (1980) *A differenciált erőforráselosztás és támogatások újratermelődésének néhány összefüggése* (A Few Aspects of the Differentiated Resource Allocation and the Reproduction of Subsidies). Mimeo. Budapest. Pénzügykutatási Intézet.

Csanádi, Mária (1983) *Beavatkozás, szelekció, kölcsönös alkalmazkodás* (Invention, Selection, Mutual Adjustment). Mimeo. Budapest: Pénzügykutatási Intézet.

Csikós-Nagy, Béla (1985) *Árpolitikánk időszerű kérdései* (The Topical Questions of the Hungarian Price Policy). Budapest: Közgazdasági és Jogi Könyvkiadó.

Csillag, István (1983) 'Az új vállalati szervezet alapvonásai' (The Main Features of the Firms' New Organization). *Valóság*, 26 (7), pp. 45-59.

Csoór, Klára and Mohácsi, Piroska (1985) 'Az infláció fő tényezői, 1980-84' (The Main Factors of Inflation (1980-84). *Gazdaság*, 19 (2), pp. 21-39.

Dániel, Zsuzsa (1985) 'The Effect of Housing Allocation on Social Inequality in Hungary', *Journal of Comparative Economics*, 9 (4), pp. 391-409.

Donáth, Ferenc (1980) *Reform and Revolution: Transformation of Hungary's Agriculture 1945-1975*. Budapest: Corvina.

Dudás, János (1985) 'A beruházások alakulása, 1945-1984' (Changes in Investments 1945-1984). *Statisztikai Szemle*, 63 (4-5), pp. 389-411.

Ehrlich, Éva (1985a) 'The Size Structure of Manufacturing Establishments and Enterprises: An International Comparison', *Journal of Comparative Economics*, 9 (4), pp. 267-295.

Ehrlich, Éva (1985b) 'A termelőegységek méretstruktúrája 18 ország feldolgozóiparában' (Production Units' Size Structure in the Manufacturing Industries of 18 Countries). *Gazdaság*, 19 (3), pp. 81-114.

Erdős, Péter (1956) 'A tervgazdálkodás néhány elméleti kérdéséről' (On a Few Theoretical Problems of Planned Economy). *Közgazdasági Szemle*, 3 (6), pp. 676-694.

Fábri, Ervin (1982) 'Superficial changes and Deep Tendencies in Inventory Process in Hungary', *Acta Oeconomica, 28* (1-2), pp. 133-146.

Falubíró, Vilmos (1983) 'Szabályozás és vállalati magatartás 1968-tól napjainkig' (Regulation and Firms' Behaviour from 1968 up to Now). *Gazdaság, 18* (4), pp. 31-49.

Falus-Szikra, Katalin (1986) 'Wage and Income Disparities Between the First and Second Economies in Hungary', *Acta Oeconomica, 36* (1-2), pp. 99-103.

Fazekas, Károly and Köllő, János (1985a) 'Fluctuations of Labour Shortage and State Intervention after 1968', in Péter Galasi and György Sziráczky, eds., 1985, pp. 42-69.

Fazekas, Károly and Köllő, János (1985b) *Munkaerőpiac és munkaerőpolitika a hetvenes években* (Labour Market and Labour Policy in the Seventies). Mimeo. Budapest: Institute of Economics.

Fehér, Ferenc, Heller, Ágnes and Márkus György, (1983) Dictatorship over Needs. Oxford: Blackwell.

Ferge, Zsuzsa (1984) 'Szociálpolitika a gazdaságban és társadalomban' (Social Policy in Economy and in Society). *Társadalomkutatás, 2* (2), pp. 54-70.

Gábor, R. István (1979) 'The Second (Secondary) Economy. Earning Activity and Regrouping of Income Outside the Socially Organized Production and Distribution', *Acta Oeconomica, 22* (-34), pp. 291-311.

Gábor, R. István (1985) 'The Major Domains of the Second Economy', in Péter Galasi and György Sziráczky, 1985, pp. 133-178.

Gábor, R. István and Galasi, Péter (1981) *A "második" gazdaság. Tények és hipotézisek* (The "Second" Economy. Facts and Hypotheses). Budapest: Közgazdasági és Jogi Könyvkiadó.

Gábor, R. István and Kővári, György (1985) 'Keresetszabályozás és munkahelyi ösztönzés. Kísérlet egy tévhit eloszlatására' (Income Regulation and Incentive: An Attempt to Dispel a Fallacy). *Közgazdasági Szemle, 32* (6), pp. 724-742.

Gács, János (1982) 'Passive Purchasing Behaviour and Possibilities of Adjustment in the Hungarian Industry, *Acta Oeconomica, 28* (3-4), pp. 337-349.

Galasi, Péter and Sziráczky, György (1985) *Labour Market and Second Economy in Hungary.* Frankfurt & New York: Campus.

Galbraith, John Kenneth (1967a) *The New Industrial State.* Boston: Houghton-Mifflin.

Galbraith, John Kenneth [1952] (1967b) *American Capitalism.* Boston: Houghton-Mifflin.

Gomulka, Stanislaw (1985) 'Kornai's Soft Budget Constraint and the Shortage, Phenomenon: A Criticism and Restatement', *Economics of Planning, 19* (1), pp. 1-11.

Granick, David (1954) *Management of the Industrial Firm in the USSR.* New York: Columbia University Press.

Granick, David (1984) 'Central Physical Planning, Incentives and Job Rights', in *Comparative Economic Systems: Present Views.* Ed.: Andrew Zimbalist. Boston, The Hague: Kluwer-Nijhoff.

Gregory, Paul R. and Stuart, Robert C. (1980) *Comparative Economic System.* Boston: Houghton-Mifflin.

Gregory, Paul R. and Stuart, Robert C. (1981) *Soviet Economic Structure and Performance.* New York: Harper and Row.

Grossman, Gregory (1966) 'Gold and the Sword: Money in the Soviet Command Economy', in *Industrialization in Two Systems.* Ed.: Henry Rosovsky, New York: John Wiley, pp. 204-36.

Grossman, Gregory (1977) 'The Second Economy of the USSR', *Problems of Communism, 26* (5), pp. 25-40.

Grossman, Gregory (1985) *The Second Economy in the USSR and Eastern Europe: A Bibliography.* Mimeo. Berkeley & Durham: University of California and Duke University.

Grósz, Tivadar (1986) 'A kamat közgazdasági funkcióinak érvényesülése' (The Economic Impact of the Interest Rate). *Bankszemle, 30* (2), pp. 26-30.

Halpern, László and Molnár, György (1985) 'Income Formation, Accumulation and Price Trends in Hungary in the 1970s', *Acta Oeconomica, 35* (1-2), pp. 105-131.

Hare, Paul, Radice, Hugo K. and Swain, Nigel, eds. (1981) *Hungary: A Decade of Economic Reform.* London & Boston: Allen & Unwin.

Hayek, Friedrich A., ed: (1935) *Collectivist Economic Planning.* London: Routledge & Kegan Paul.

Heti Világgazdaság (1986) May 17, p. 55.

Hewett, Edward A. (1981) 'Lessons of the 1970's and Prospects for the 1980's', in *East European Economic Assessment. Part I, Country Studies.* A Compendium of Papers Submitted to the U. S. Congress: Joint Economic Committee, Washington, DC: U. S. GPO.

Hoch, Róbert (1980) 'A világpiaci árak és az árcentrum' (World Market Prices and the Price Centre). *Közgazdasági Szemle, 27* (10), pp. 1153-1158.

Holzman, Franklyn D (1986) 'Soviet Inflationary Pressures 1928-1957: Causes and Cures', *Quarterly Journal of Economics, 74* (2), pp. 167-88.

Horváth, László (1976) 'Az ágazati irányítás elvei és gyakorlati problémái' (Principles and Practical Problems of Sectoral Control). *Gazdaság, 10* (4), pp. 7-26.

Hulyák, Katalin (1983) 'Egyensúlyhiányok a lakossági fogyasztásban I-II.' (Imbalance in Household Consumption I-II). *Statisztikai Szemle, 61* (3), pp. 229-243. and April, *61* (4), pp. 369-380.

Hulyák, Katalin (1985) 'A külső és belső egyensúly ökonometriai elemzése (1965-1981)' (Econometric Analysis of External and Internal Equilibrium 1965-1981). *Tervgazdasági Fórum, 1* (2), pp. 41-52.

Hunter, Holland (1961) 'Optimal Tautness in Developmental Planning', *Economic Development and Cultural Change, 9* (2), pp. 561-572.

International Currency Review (1981) May, *13* (2), p. 31.

Kapitány, Zsuzsa, Kornai, János and Szabó, Judit (1984) 'Reproduction of Shortage on the Hungarian Car Market', *Soviet Studies, 36* (2), pp. 236-256.

Keren, Michael (1972) 'On the Tautness of Plans', *Review of Economic Studies, 39* (4), pp. 469-486.

Keren, Michael, Miller, Jeffrey and Thornton, James R. (1983) 'The Ratchet: A Dynamic Managerial Incentive Model of the Soviet Enterprise', *Journal of Comparative Economics, 7* (4), pp. 347-367.

Kolosi, Tamás (1979) *Második gazdaság és társadalomszerkezet* (Second Economy and Social Structure). Mimeo. Budapest: Országos Tervhivatal.

Kolosi, Tamás (1980) 'A társadalmi egyenlőtlenségről' (On Social Inequelities). *Társadalmi Szemle, 35* (6), pp. 45-58.

Konrád, György and Szelényi, Iván (1979) *The Intellectuals on the Road to Class Power.* New York: Harcourt Brace Jovanovich.

Kornai, János (1959) *Overcentralization in Economic Administration.* London: Oxford U. Press.

Kornai, János (1979) 'Resource-Constrained Versus Demand-Constrained Systems', *Econometrica, 47* (4), pp. 801-19.

Kornai, János (1980) *Economics of Shortage.* Amsterdam: North-Holland.

Kornai, János (1982) *Growth, Shortage and Efficiency.* Oxford: Blackwell.

Kornai, János (1984) 'Bureaucratic and Market Coordination', *Osteuropa Wirtschaft, 29* (4), pp. 306-319.

Kornai, János (1985a) 'On the Explanatory Theory of Shortage. Comments on Two Articles by K. A. Soós', *Acta Oeconomica, 34* (1-2), pp. 145-164.

Kornai, János (1985b) 'Gomulka on the Soft Budget Constraint: A Reply', *Economics of Planning, 19* (2), pp. 49-55.

Kornai, János (1986) 'The Soft Budget Constraint', *Kyklos, 39* (1), pp. 3-30.

Kornai, János and Matits, Ágnes (1983) *Az állami vállalatok jövedelmének redisztribúciója* (Redistribution of the Income of State-Owned Firms). Mimeo. Budapest: Ipari Minisztérium.

Kornai, János and Matits, Ágnes (1984) 'Softness of the Budget Constraint—An Analysis Relying on Data of Firms', *Acta Oeconomica, 32* (3-4), pp. 223-249.

Kovács, János Mátyás (1984) 'A reformalku sűrűjében' (In the Depths of the Reform Bargain). *Valóság, 27* (3), pp. 30-55.

Köves, András and Obláth, Gábor (1983) 'Hungarian Foreign Trade in the 1970s', *Acta Oeconomica, 30* (1), pp. 89-109.

Kowalik, Tadeusz (1984) 'Review on the Economics of Feasible Socialism Written by Alec Nove 1983', *Contribution to Political Economy, 3* (1), pp. 91-97.

Kozma, Ferenc (1983a) 'A vállalkozó szocialista állam' (The Enterprising Socialist State). *Gazdaság, 17* (2), pp. 56-75.

Kozma, Ferenc (1983b) 'Gazdaságirányítási rendszerünk tovább-fejlesztése a szocialista építés szolgálatában' (The Further Development of the Economic Control and Management System of Hungary with a View to the Building of Socialism). *Társadalmi Szemle, 38* (11), pp. 11-29.

Kupa, Mihály (1980) *Jövedelemelosztás—költségvetés—gazdasági folyamatok* (Income Distribution—Budget—Economic Process). Budapest: Közgazdasági és Jogi Könyvkiadó.

Lackó, Mária (1980) 'Cumulating and Easing of Tensions', *Acta Oeconomica, 24* (3), pp. 357-77.

Lackó, Mária (1984) 'Behavioural Rules in the Distribution of Sectorial Investments in Hungary, 1951-1980', *Journal of Comparative Economics*, 8 (3), pp. 290-300.

Laki, Mihály (1982) 'Liquidation and Merger in the Hungarian Industry', *Acta Oeconomica*, 28 (1-2), pp. 87-108.

Laki, Mihály (1984) 'The Enterprise Crisis', *Acta Oeconomica*, 32, pp. 113-124.

Laky, Teréz (1980) 'The Hidden Mechanism of Recentralization in Hungary', *Acta Oeconomica*, 24 (1-2), pp. 95-109.

Laky, Teréz (1985) 'Enterprise Business Work Partnership and Enterprise Interests', *Acta Oeconomica*, 34 (1-2), pp. 27-49.

Lamberger, Galina, Matolcsy, György, Szalai, Erzsébet and Voszka, Éva (1986) *Vállalatmegszűnés. Hét eset a nyolcvanas évekből: tapasztalatok és következtetések* (Exit of Enterprises. Seven Cases from the Eighties: Experiences and Conclusions). Mimeo. Budapest: MTA Ipargazdaságtani Kutatócsoport.

Lange, Oscar (1936, 1937) 'On the Economic Theory of Socialism', *Review of Economic Studies* October 1936 & February 1937, 4 (1-2), pp. 53-71, 123-142.

Lavoie, Don (1985) *Rivalry and Central Planning. The Socialist Calculation Debate Reconsidered*. Cambridge: Cambridge University Press.

Levine, Herbert (1966) 'Pressure and Planning in the Soviet Economy', in *Industrialization in Two Systems*. Ed.: Henry Rosovsky. New York: John Wiley, pp. 266-85.

Liberman, Yevsey G. [1962] (1972) 'The Plan, Profits and Bonuses', in *Socialist Economics: Selected Readings*. Eds.: Alec Nove and Domenico M. Nuti. Middlesex: Penguin Books, pp. 309-318.

Lindblom, Charles (1977) *Politics and Markets. The World's Political Economic Systems*. New York: Basic Books.

Liska, Tibor (1963) 'Kritika és koncepció. Tézisek a gazdasági mechanizmus reformjához' (Criticism and Conception. Theses for the Reform of the Economic Mechanism). *Közgazdasági Szemle, 10* (9), pp. 1058-1076.

Liska, Tibor (1969) 'A bérlakás kereskedelmi koncepciója' (The Concept of the Trade of State-Owned Flats). *Valóság, 12* (1), pp. 22-35.

Macrae, Norman (1983) 'Into Entrepreneurial Socialism', *The Economist*, 19-25. March, pp. 23-29.

Marer, Paul (1981) 'The Mechanism and Performance of Hungary's Foreign Trade, 1968-79', in Paul Hare et al., pp. 161-204.

Marer, Paul (1986a) *East-West Technology Transfer. Study of Hungary 1968-1984.* Paris: OECD.

Marer, Paul (1986b) 'Economic Reform in Hungary: From Central Planning to Regulated Market', *East European Economics: Slow Growth in the 1980's.* Country studies on Eastern Europe and Yugoslavia. Vol. 3, Joint Economic Committee, Congress of the United States, Washington, DC: U. S. GPO.

Matits, Ágnes (1984a) *A redisztribúció szerepe az állami vállalatok jövedelmezőségének alakulásában: 1981-1982* (The Role of Redistribution in Determining the Profitability of State-Owned Firms: 1981-1982). Mimeo. Budapest: Economix.

Matits, Ágnes (1984b) *Az egyéni jövedelmek és a vállalati jövedelmezőség* (Personal Incomes and the Firms' Profitability). Mimeo. Budapest: Economix.

Matits, Ágnes (1984c) *A vállalatnagyság szerepe a redisztribúcióban megnyilvánuló részrehajlásban* (The Role of Firms' Size in the Bias of Redistribution). Mimeo. Budapest: Economix.

Matits, Ágnes and Temesi, József (1985) A vállalati jövedelmezőség és a beruházási tevékenység kapcsolata (Firms' Profitability and Investment Activity). Mimeo. Budapest: Economix.

Marrese, Michael (1983) 'Agricultural Policy and Performance in Hungary', *Journal of Comparative Economics, 7* (3), pp. 329-45.

Mises, Ludwig von [1920] (1935) 'Economic Calculation in the Socialist Commonwealth' in *Collectivist Economic Planning*. Ed.: Friedrich A. Hayek. London: Routledge & Kegan Paul, pp. 87-130.

Montias, John M. (1976) *The Structure of Economic System*. London & New Haven, CT: Yale University Press.

Muraközy, László (1985) 'Hazánk költségvetéséről—nemzetközi összehasonlításban' (The Hungarian Budget—An International Comparison). *Pénzügyi Szemle, 29* (10), pp. 745-754.

Nagy, Tamás (1956) 'A politikai gazdaságtan néhány kérdéséről' (A Few Problems of Political Economy). *Közgazdasági Szemle, 3* (6), pp. 657-675.

Neuberger, Egon and Duffy, William (1976) *Comparative Economic Systems: A Decision-Making Approach*. Boston & London: Allen & Bacon.

Nove, Alec (1983a) *The Economics of Feasible Socialism*. London: Allen & Unwin.

Nove, Alec (1983b) *The Soviet Economic System*. London: Allen & Unwin.

Nuti, Domenico Mario (1985) 'Hidden and Represented Inflation in Soviet-Type Economics: Definitions, Measurement and Stabilisation', *EUI Working Paper*, No. 85/200, October.

Nyers, Rezső, Bagota, Béla and Garam, József (1969) *Economic Reform in Hungary. Twenty-five Questions and Twenty-five Answers. An Interview with Rezső Nyers*. Budapest: Pannónia.

Nyers, Rezső and Tardos, Márton (1978) 'Enterprises in Hungary Before and After the Economic Reform' *Acta Oeconomica, 20* (1-2), pp. 21-44.

Nyers, Rezső and Tardos, Márton (1979) 'What Economic Development Policy Should We Adopt?' *Acta Oeconomica, 22* (1-2), pp. 11-31.

Nyers, Rezső and Tardos, Márton (1984) 'The Necessity for Consolidation of The Economy and the Possibility of

Development in Hungary', *Acta Oeconomica, 32* (1-2), pp. 1-19.

Papanek, Gábor, Sárkány, Péter and Viszt, Erzsébet (1986) *A nehéz pénzügyi helyzet rendezése iparvállalatainknál* (Settling Financial Difficulties of Hungarian Industrial Enterprises). Mimeo. Budapest: MTA Ipargazdaságtani Kutatócsoport.

Péter, György (1954a) 'A gazdaságosság jelentőségéről és szerepéről a népgazdaság tervszerű irányításában' (On the Importance and Role of Economic Efficiency in the Planned Control of the National Economy). *Közgazdasági Szemle, 1* (3), pp. 300-324.

Péter, György (1954b) 'Az egyszemélyi felelős vezetésről' (On Management Based on One-Man Responsibility). *Társadalmi Szemle,* August/September *9* (8-9), pp. 109-124.

Péter, György (1956) 'A gazdaságosság és a jövedelmezőség jelentősége a tervgazdálkodásban I-II.' (The Importance of Economic Efficiency and Profitability in a Planned Economy I-II). *Közgazdasági Szemle, 3* (6), pp. 695-711 and *3* (7-8), pp. 851-869.

Péter, György (1967) 'On the Planned Central Control and Management of the Economy', *Acta Oeconomica, 2*, pp. 23-45.

Pető, Iván and Szakács, Sándor (1985) *A hazai gazdaság négy évtizedének története 1945-1985. I.* (Forty-years' History of the Hungarian Economy 1945-1985. I) Budapest: Közgazdasági és Jogi Könyvkiadó.

Petschnig, Mária (1985a) *Fogyasztói árindexünk—A kritika tükrében* (The Hungarian Consumer Price Index—In the Mirror of Criticism). Mimeo. Pécs-Budapest: Institute of Economics.

Petschnig, Mária (1985b) 'Mennyi az annyi?' (How Much is so Much?) *Heti Világgazdaság,* 1 June, *6* (22), p. 7.

Polányi, Karl (1944) *The Great Transformation.* New York: Farrar & Rinehart.

Portes, Richard (1970) 'Economic Reforms in Hungary', *American Economic Review, 60* (2), pp. 307-313.

Portes, Richard (1972) 'The Tactics and Strategy of Economic Decentralization', *Soviet Studies, 23* (4), pp. 629-658.

Portes, Richard (1977) 'Hungary: Economic Performance, Policy and Prospects', in *East European Economics post Helsinki*. Joint Economic Committee, Congress of the United States, Washington, DC: U. S. GPO.

Portes, Richard (1984) *The Theory and Measurement of Macroeconomic Disequilibrium in Centrally Planned Economies*, MS. University of London: Birkbeck College.

Portes, Richard, Quandt, Richard, Winter, David and Yeo, S. (1986) *Macro-Economic Planning and Disequilibrium: Estimates for Poland'*, London: Centre for Economic Policy Research Discussion Paper No. 91.

Portes, Richard and Winter, David (1977) 'The Supply of Consumption Goods in Centrally Planned Economies', *Journal of Comparative Economics, 1* (4), pp. 351-365.

Portes, Richard and Winter, David (1978) 'The Demand for Money and for Consumption Goods in Centrally Planned Economies', *Review of Economic Statistics, 60* (1), pp. 8-18.

Portes, Richard and Winter, David (1980) 'Disequilibrium Estimates for Consumption Goods Markets in Centrally Planned Economies', *Review of Economic Statistics, 47* (1), pp. 137-159.

Révész, Gábor (1979) 'Enterprise and Plant Size: Structure of the Hungarian Economy', *Acta Oeconomica, 22* (1-2), pp. 47-68.

Román, Zoltán (1985) 'The Conditions of Market Competition in Hungarian Industry', *Acta Oeconomica, 34* (1-2), pp. 79-97.

Rupp, Kálmán (1983) *Entrepreneurs in Red*. Albany: State University of New York Press.

Sárközy, Tamás (1982) 'Problems of Social Ownership and of the Proprietory Organization', *Acta Oeconomica, 29 (3-4),* pp. 225-258.

Schweitzer, Iván (1982) *Vállalatméret* (The Firm's Size). Budapest: Közgazdasági és Jogi Könyvkiadó.

Sik, Ota (1967) 'Socialist Market Relations and Planning', in *Socialism, Capitalism and Economic Growth. Essays Presented to Maurice Dobb.* Ed.: C. H. Feinstein. Cambridge: Cambridge University Press, pp. 133-157.

Siklaky, István (1985) *Koncepció és kritika: vita Liska Tibor 'szocialista vállalkozási szektor' javaslatáról* (Conception and Criticism: Discussion of Tibor Liska's Proposal of a'Socialist Enterprising Sector'). Budapest: Magvető.

Sipos, Aladár (1983) 'Relations Between Enterprises in the Agro-Industrial Sphere in Hungary', *Acta Oeconomica, 31* (1-2), pp. 53-69.

Soós, Károly Attila (1975-76) 'Causes of Investment Fluctuations in the Hungarian Economy', *Eastern European Economics, 14* (2), pp. 25-36.

Soós, Károly Attila (1984) 'A Propos the Explanation of Shortage Phenomena: Volume of Demand and Structural Inelasticity', *Acta Oeconomica, 33* (3-4), pp. 305-320.

Stark, David (1985) 'The Micropolitics of the Firm and the Macropolitics of Reform: New Forms of Workplace Bargaining Hungarian Enterprises', in *State Versus Markets in the World-System.* Eds.: Peter Evans, Dietrich Rueschmeyer and Evelyne Humber Stephens. Beverly Hills, CA: Sage, pp. 247-269.

Sugár, Tamás (1984) 'A piac és a látható kéz' (The Market and the Visible Hand). *Társadalmi Szemle, 29* (3), pp. 89-99.

Swain, Nigel (1981) 'The Evolution of Hungary's Agricultural System Since 1967', in Paul Hare et al., pp. 225-251.

Szabó, Judit (1985) 'Kínálati rugalmasság, elszaladó kereslet, készletek és hiány' (Inelasticity of Supply, Runaway Demand, Stocks and Shortage). *Közgazdasági Szemle, 32* (7-8), pp. 951-960.

Szabó, Judit and Tarafás, Imre (1985). 'Hungary's Exchange Rate Policy in the 1980's' *Acta Oeconomica, 35* (1-2), pp. 53-79.

Szabó, Kálmán (1967) 'A szocialista gazdaságirányítási rendszer' (The Socialist System of Economic Control and Management), in *A szocializmus politikai gazdaságtana*. (The Political Economiy of Socialism). Eds.: Berei, Andor et. al. Budapest: Kossuth Könyvkiadó, pp. 248-294.

Szalai, Erzsébet (1982) 'The New Stage of the Reform Process in Hungary and the Large Enterprise', *Acta Oeconomica, 29* (1-2), pp. 25-46.

Szamuely, László (1982) 'The First Wave of the Mechanism Debate in Hungary 1954-57', *Acta Oeconomica, 29* (1-2), pp. 1-24.

Szamuely, László (1984) 'The Second Wave of the Economic Mechanism Debate and the 1968 Reform in Hungary', *Acta Oeconomica, 33* (1-2), pp. 43-67.

Szegő, Andrea (1983) 'Gazdaság és politika—Érdek és struktúra' (Economy and Politics—Interest and Structure). *Medvetánc, 3* (2-3), pp. 49-92.

Szelényi, Iván (1983) *Urban Inequalities under State Socialism*. Oxford: Oxford University Press.

Tallós, György (1976) *A bankhitel szerepe gazdaságirányítási rendszerünkben* (The Role of Bank Credit in the Hungarian System of Economic Control and Management). Budapest: Kossuth.

Tardos, Márton (1980) 'The Role of Money: Economic Relations Between the State and the Enterprises in Hungary', *Acta Oeconomica, 25* (1-2), pp. 19-35.

Tardos, Márton (1982) 'Development Program for Economic Control and Organization in Hungary', *Acta Oeconomica, 28* (3-4), pp. 295-315.

Tardos, Márton (1986) 'The Conditions of Developing a Regulated Market', *Acta Oeconomica, 36* (1-2), pp. 67-89.

Tardos, Róbert (1983) 'Magatartástípusok a családi gazdálkodásban' (Behavioural Types in Family Economy). *Közgazdasági Szemle, 30* (1), pp. 63-76.

Taylor, Fred M. (1929) 'The Guidance of Production in a Socialist State', *American Economic Review, 19* (1), pp. 1-80. Reprinted in Ed.: *On the Economic Theory of Socialism.* Benjamin E. Lippincott. New York: McGraw-Hill, [1938] (1964).

Tellér, Gyula (1984) 'Ómechanizmus, újmechanizmus, ipari szövetkezetek' (Old Mechanism, New Mechanism, Industrial Cooperatives). *Medvetánc, 4-5,* (4-1), pp. 143-165.

Tibor, Ágnes (1984) 'Statikus automobilizmus' (Static Automobilism). *Heti Világgazdaság,* April 28, *6* (18), pp. 53-55.

Tímár, János (1985a) *A társadalmi újratermelés időalapja* (The Total of Manhours Available for Social Reproduction). Mimeo. Budapest: Karl Marx University of Economics.

Tímár, János (1985b) 'Idő és munkaidő. A munkaidő és a társadalmi újratermelés időalapjának néhány problémája Magyarországon' (Time and Working Time. Some Problems of Working Time and of the Total of Man-Hours Available for Social Reproduction). *Közgazdasági Szemle, 32* (12), pp. 1299-1313.

United Nations (1970) *Statistical Yearbook 1969.* New York.

United Nations (1979) *Statistical Yearbook 1981.* New York.

United Nations (1983) *Monthly Bulletin of Statistics,* January, (37) 1.

United Nations (1985a) *Statistical Yearbook 1982.* New York.

United Nations (1985b) *Monthly Bulletin of Statistics,* October, (39) 10.

Varga, István (1957) 'A Közgazdasági Szakértő Bizottság elgondolásai' (Concept of the Economic Expert Committee). *Közgazdasági Szemle, 4* (10), pp. 997-1008 and *4* (12), pp. 1231-1248.

Várhegyi, Éva (1986) *A hitelrendszer hatása a vállalati költségvetési korlátra* (Impact of the Credit System on the Firm's Budget Constraint). Mimeo. Budapest: Economix.

Vass, Henrik ed. (1968) *A Magyar Szocialista Munkáspárt határozatai és dokumentumai 1963-1966* (Decrees and

Documents of the Hungarian Socialist Workers' Party 1963-1966). Budapest: Kossuth.

Weber, Max [1922] (1947) The *Theory of Social and Economic Organization*. Oxford: Oxford University Press.

Williamson, Oliver (1975) *Markets and Hierarchies: Analysis and Antitrust Implications*. New York: The Free Press.

Zelkó, Lajos (1981) 'A versenyárrendszer elméleti és gyakorlati problémáihoz' (On the Theoretical and Practical Problems of the Competitive Price System). *Közgazdasági Szemle, 27* (7-8), pp. 927-940.

Chapter II

**Paying the Bill for Goulash Communism:
Hungarian Development and Macro Stabilization
in a Political Economy Perspective**[1]

I. INTRODUCTION: FOUR CHARACTERISTICS[2]

The Hungarian economy's road from a centralized, planned economy to a market economy displays a number of features that distinguish it from other post-socialist countries, despite the underlying similarities. Without aiming to provide a complete picture, I shall pick out four important features. One or other of these may occur singly in other countries in the region as well, or more precisely in a few countries in particular periods. The specific feature of Hungarian development is the lasting coexistence of these four characteristics.

First, Hungary, in its economic-policy priorities, placed great weight on raising present day material welfare, and in the subsequent period of mounting economic problems and stagnating or declining production, on curbing the fall in living standards. Conditions in Hungary had earlier been christened 'goulash communism'. The policy for several years after the change of political system continued the previous one in this respect, and can aptly be called 'goulash post-communism'.

Second, a paternalist 'welfare state' covering the entire population was developed over several decades. Hungary can vie with the most developed Scandinavian countries in the range of codified entitlements to benefits and in the proportion of GDP devoted to social spending, whereas *per capita* production is only a small fraction of theirs. Although similar tendencies arose at the time in all Eastern European countries, Hungary went furthest by far, and in this respect stands alone in the region.

Third, the process of transformation in Hungary has extended over several decades; the initial steps were taken back in the 1960s. Though a few milestones can be mentioned, the process as a whole

123

has been notable for its gradualism. Similar gradual development in this respect has only occurred in Slovenia.[3] In the eyes of those who distinguish 'shock therapy' or 'big-bang' strategy from 'gradualist' strategy, Hungary represents an extreme and special case of the latter: 'gradualism Hungarian style'.

Finally, Hungary has been marked for decades by a relative political calm. While the transformation in some countries has been accompanied by civil warfare, here not a shot has been fired. While the change of political system in some countries took place at lightning speed amidst spectacular circumstances (collapse of the Berlin Wall, mass demonstrations in the streets of Prague, execution of the Romanian dictator), Hungary continued restrained negotiations over an extended period, with the ruling politicians of the old order and the hitherto repressed opposition reaching agreement on free elections and a new constitution. For decades there were hardly any strikes or street demonstrations. Though the economic problems have worsened, successive governments have preferred to muddle through rather than resolve on measures that would arouse strong opposition and entail a risk of political destabilization.

These four characteristics together form the specific difference of the Hungarian transformation. This study sets out to contribute to an understanding of why these four characteristics came about, how they have affected each other, and what favorable and detrimental effects they have exerted.

I employ the approach of political economy to examine the economic phenomena. The thinking of politicians and mentality of the public are shaped by history, in which politics and the economy are embedded. This context and the interaction between politics and the economy are often ignored in economic-policy analysis and recommendations characterized by technocratic approaches. I would like to contribute to offsetting this biased approach.[4]

In some places I draw comparisons with other countries. These, however, are designed solely to shed light on some feature of Hungarian development. I also refrain from judging which country is following the better road, and which country's politicians have been making wiser decisions.

II. A SURVEY OF POLITICAL HISTORY

From the point of view of my subject the last four decades of Hungarian history can be divided into periods, as shown in *Figure 1*.

1. The revolution of 1956 and the years of reprisals

Singled out in Figure 1 from the socialist period, as a date of great import, is 23 October 1956, the day the Hungarian revolution broke out. Hungary was the only country in the history of the socialist world which experienced an armed rebellion against the prevailing political order and Soviet occupation.[5] The revolutionary forces took power, if only for a brief period. Those few days of freedom sufficed for parties to organize. A multi-party government that revived the coalition before the communist assumption of power was formed under the leadership of a reform communist, Imre Nagy.

Though sporadic, there were cases of anti-communist lynching during the revolution. Harassment or replacement of the heads of many factories and public offices began. The fear engendered by all this left indelible memories in the minds of the party-state's leading stratum.

Hardly two weeks later, the revolution was crushed by the Soviet army. A one-party system with the communist party holding a monopoly of power was reimposed under the leadership of János Kádár. Armed resistance to the Soviet tanks lasted a short while and a general strike went on for some weeks before that was abandoned as well. Then came the reprisals. Imre Nagy and his associates and many other active participants in the revolution were executed; altogether 229 death sentences were carried out.[6] Thousands were

Figure 1 The last four decades of Hungarian history, divided into periods

Events	Periods in the political sphere	Periods in the economic sphere		
		Economic-policy priorities	Transformation of property relations and institutions	
23 October 1956 Outbreak of revolution	Revolution			
4 November 1956 Beginning of Soviet intervention	Reprisals			
22 March 1963 Political amnesty	Softening of dictatorship	Priority given to current welfare, security and calm		
1 January 1968 Beginning of 'new economic mechanism'			Gradualist transformation	Reform-socialist phase
13 June 1989 Beginning of negotiations between communist party and opposition	Change to multi-party system			
23 May 1990 First sitting of democratically elected parliament	Parliamentary democracy			Post-socialist phase
12 March 1995 Announcement of stabilization program		Measures to restore macro equilibrium		

imprisoned or detained in internment camps, and tens of thousands sacked from their jobs. The intimidation extended to a large part of the population. Hundreds of thousands had expressed their sincere opinions and begun to organize into non-communist and anti-communist movements and parties during the days of revolutionary freedom. Now they could all feel that reprisals might strike at any minute.

Memories of 1956 and the ensuing period have to be recalled, for as we shall see later, they explain much about the characteristics of Hungary's process of reform.

2. 'Softening' of dictatorship and the political turning point

Let us jump forward a few years, to the period when the numb fear gradually relaxed and the brutality and mercilessness of the repression eased. In 1963, some years after the mass executions, a general amnesty was declared; those who had been imprisoned for the part they had played in the revolution were released. A 'softening' of the dictatorship began. The name of János Kádár, the man who had directed the reprisals, is also linked to this policy of gradually easing the political repression.

But as this curious, inconsistent, hesitant 'liberalization' continued, so did the erosion of the communist system, founded on repression. The process speeded up in 1989, when even those in power felt that the political monopoly of the communist party could no longer be sustained. Negotiations began with the opposition forces, which were now organizing themselves openly. In a few months, if not a few days, enormous strides were taken in the political sphere. The one-party system was replaced by a multi-party system; a new constitution came into force; in the spring of 1990 free elections with the participation of rival parties were held for the first time in 43 years; a government chosen by the new parliament was formed; the governing parties and the parliamentary opposition stated their intention of protecting and developing private ownership, freedom of contract and a market economy.

The beginning of parliamentary democracy is dated in Figure 1 from the day of the first sitting on 23 May 1990 of the democratically elected parliament. In the political sphere, this point in time (or to be more accurate, the 1989–90 period of the talks on changing the political regime, the drafting of the constitution and the holding of the first free elections) marked a real turning point. But the initial and terminal dates of the characteristic periods in the economic sphere fell at different points of calendar time from those in the political sphere.

III. PRIORITY FOR TODAY'S WELFARE, SECURITY AND CALM

One of the main propositions of this study (as seen in the macroeconomic column of Figure 1) is that a curious continuity prevailed in the priorities motivating Hungarian economic policy, extending beyond the political turning point of 1989–90 (Figure 1). So the same orientation persisted for 25–30 years. Only the announcement of the stabilization program on 12 March 1995 broke this continuity. Sections III/1–III/3 of this chapter analyze the period 1963–95, Section III/4 deals with the stabilization program.

1. Avoidance of upheavals and conflicts

From the outset, those directing and playing an active part in Hungary's economic transformation, both before and after the political turning-point of 1989–90, have been guided by a resolve to avoid upheavals and conflicts.

The roots of this stance go back, in my view, to 1956. The days of revolution and subsequent years of reprisals caused a grave trauma. The ruling elite of the time, the communist 'cadres', looked back in terror on the revolution, the mass demonstrations before 23 October, the street fighting and the popular fury vented against the secret police and party functionaries. They felt they had to be on much better terms with the masses in future, lest they rebel again. The multitude of average people, if not the heroes who had worked actively for the revolution and stood by its ideals, had also been scared by the upheaval—by both the revolution and its subsequent suppression. They were intimidated by the harassment and persecution of relatives, friends and colleagues. So there was an intense desire for peace and calm, among the leading stratum and the millions of ordinary people alike. This climate of public opinion explains the psychological motivation behind Hungarian economic policy. Euphemistically this could be called moderation and ability to compromise, the pursuit of consensus. A pejorative description would be appeasement and cowardice. Both verdicts contain elements of truth.

Such was the motivation at the beginning of the process, when those who had been through 1956 were still present and active. But this climate of opinion, routine of behavior and system of moral norms caused by the grave national trauma became ingrained, persisting even after 1956 had become a remote historical event in the minds of younger people.

So what is the prime factor here? Is it a mass concern to avoid upheaval, to which politicians react? Or is it the other way round: politicians fearful of possible mass protest and open confrontation with their opponents seeking to forestall them? Do cringing, bargaining politicians bring society up to behave the same way? Presumably there are effects in both directions.

Poland in 1956 did not go as far as an armed uprising and bloody street fighting, but 20–25 years later, millions were prepared to strike and Solidarity was formed, with a militancy that not even military intervention could stifle for good. The struggle began with the customary trade-union demands in defense of real wages and jobs. Confrontation between those in power and the masses heightened. Concurrently in Hungary, 20–25 years after a defeated revolution, the attention of the leading stratum and the millions of ordinary people turned not towards strikes and political struggles, but calmly towards the economy. Ordinary people chased around after extra earnings, built houses and grew vegetables.

There was an almost logical continuation of this after 1990. Poland underwent another great flare-up under a Solidarity-led government prepared to implement a radical package of stabilization and liberalization demanding great sacrifice. Hungary's governing coalition was not so prepared. Indeed the victorious party in the first free elections, the Hungarian Democratic Forum, had declared in its campaign that it would follow the policies of a 'calm force', which had been one of its electoral attractions.

In October 1990, early in the new government's term, a peculiar mass demonstration broke out. Taxi-drivers protesting at a petrol-price rise planned by the government blockaded Budapest's main intersections and brought traffic to a halt. Bargaining between the representatives of the taxi-drivers and the government took place before the television cameras. The opposition of the day, instead of supporting the legitimate government intent on maintaining law and order and imposing an unpopular but necessary price increase, backed the organizers of the blockade instead. Eventually the government retreated and a compromise was reached.[7] The episode acted as a precedent. The Antall and Boross governments of 1990–94 never again ventured an action that would elicit mass opposition, and the Horn government that took power in 1994 behaved the same way for several months.

Looking back on a period of three decades since the mid-1960s, it can be seen that whenever an economic conflict threatened, whether it was a strike or a mass demonstration, the tension would practically always be defused by bargaining and compromise. Confrontation was avoided, more successfully, in fact, than in many established market economies.

The successive governments were imbued with very different ideologies. In the final years before 1990, the reform wing of the communist party was in power. In 1990–94 there was a coalition with a national and Christian democratic orientation. Since 1994 there has been a coalition of socialists and liberals. Yet there was almost complete continuity until March 1995 in maintaining the tradition of compromise and conflict evasion, based on making concessions to the dissatisfied.

2. The now-or-later problem

Hungarian economic policy from the early 1960s onwards was pro-consumption. This marked a sharp break from the Stalinist, classical socialist priorities of economic policy, in which investment, a forced pace of growth and the fastest possible acquisition of strong industrial and military might were the top priorities. In Hungary, for instance, this entailed a relegation of consumption.

It is not my province to analyze the psychology of individual politicians. What induced them to be consumption oriented? Sincere concern for people's material welfare, or political Machiavellianism? It is clear from what has been said so far that the prominence given to material welfare could again be related to the trauma of 1956. If the communist powers wanted to be on good terms with the masses they ruled, they had to pay much more heed to their material standard of living; they had to content them. That would smooth over the conflicts; that was the best way to prevent protests, demonstrations and uprisings. Ultimately the degree to which the two posited mentalities applied to politicians is immaterial to the economic effect.

This new economic-policy orientation had a golden age between 1966 and 1975, with household consumption rising year after year without recession or stagnation, by an annual average of 5.3 per cent (*Table 1*). This was the time in many families' lives when they bought their first refrigerator, their first Trabant car, and later on took their first trip to the West. This was when most of the Hungarian public came to associate reform with growing welfare. This was when the West began to develop a partly true, partly distorted picture of the Kádár regime as 'the happiest barrack in the camp'. This was the offensive phase of consumption-oriented economic policy.

Table 1: Absorption of GDP in Hungary, 1960–93 (annual average rates of growth, %)

Period	GDP	Final consumption		Gross investment	
		Total	of which: total household consumption	Total	of which: accumulation of fixed assets
1961–95	4.4	3.7	3.4	5.2	5.1
1966–75	6.3	5.3	5.3	8.5	9.1
1976–87	2.7	2.3	2.2	0.1	0.8
1981–91	-4.0	-2.5	-2.9	-7.3	-5.1
1988–93[a]	-3.3	-0.7	-1.7	-4.1	-3.7

Source: Central Statistical Office (1995b), p. 2.
Note: [a] The 1993 figure for total final consumption includes arms imports from Russia received as debt repayment.

Production at that time was still growing fast—faster than consumption. However, under a Stalinist economic policy the gap between the growth rates of production and consumption would have been much higher. The leadership would have used the surge of growth to achieve a higher investment rate, and thus a much higher growth rate of GDP. Meanwhile it would have been contented with a far more modest improvement in consumption. One more point to make (and this will be discussed later in the study) is that the growth in production, and consumption, began in the 1970s to be gained partly at the price of accumulating foreign debt.

The proportions of the domestic utilization of GDP began to change in the late 1970s, with consumption's share rising and investment's falling. The growth in production steadily slowed down, remaining near to stagnation for a long time, and then starting to fall sharply in 1991. This is just the sort of situation that tests what weight consumption has in the priorities of economic policy. The consumption-oriented economic policy continued persistently against a stagnating and even shrinking economy. This it did before, during and after the change of political system, by then in a defensive manner. 'If a fall in consumption is inevitable, let it fall as slowly and as little as possible,' was the attitude (*Table 2*). This aim was plainly apparent in the period 1988–93, when GDP fell by an average of 3.3 per cent a year, while the fall in total household consumption averaged only 1.7 per cent a year (Table 1). Investment, not consumption, acted as the residual variable under the 'pro-consumption' policy of the late Kádár period and in the first five years of parliamentary democracy. This can be seen clearly in Table 1, where the accumulation of fixed assets first slows down and then declines faster than GDP.

Table 2: Trends in GDP, consumption, real income and real wages in Hungary (1987=100)

Year	GDP[a]	Per capita real consumption	Per capita real income	Real wages per earner[b]
1988	100	100	99	95
1989	101	106	102	96
1990	97	100	101	92
1991	85	91	99	86
1992	83	91	95	85
1993	82	93	91	81
1994	85	—	95	87

Source: Central Statistical Office (1995b), pp. 2 and 11.
Notes: [a] The GDP figure does not show GDP *per capita*.
[b] Up to 1990, the figures cover only the category of workers and emploees, excluding workers on agricultural cooperatives. The latter are included from 1991 onwards.

This presents a special case of the well-known time-preference problem of 'now or later'. The main aim of Hungarian economic policy for at least two decades could be described as seeking at any time to maximize consumption in the present and immediate future, at the expense of debt that would devolve on later periods. Initially this ensured a rapid growth of consumption, but it was already beginning to backfire to some extent after a decade: the rise in production, and with it consumption, began to slow down. Later a decline in production and consumption set in, partly because of the policy inprevious years resulting in debt accumulation. Yet the objective function, maximization of short-term consumption, was still unchanged. It continued, of course, with its sign changed, as minimization of the fall in consumption, and the price of this aim was still accepted: further accumulation of debt.

Here I use the concept of debt in its broadest sense. This comprehensive interpretation has already been employed by several authors.[8] Let us look at its main components.

First, debt is what the country owes abroad. With this kind of debt, the connection is obvious: consumption today is being financed abroad, but this will have to be repaid tomorrow at the expense of tomorrow's consumption.[9] This kind of debt is oppressively large in Hungary's case (*Table 3*). The defensive policy of

Table 3: Indeces of Hungary's convertible currency foreign debt and debt servicing

Year	Gross debt (US$ bn)	Per capita gross debt (US$)	Debt servicing/goods exports (%)
1975	3.9	369	25.3
1980	9.1	850	41.4
1985	14.0	1326	85.6
1990	21.3	2057	62.7
1993	24.6	2393	44.5
1994	28.5	2782	—

Sources: Gross debt, 1975-81: United Nations Economic Commission for Europe (1993), p. 130; 1982-93: National Bank of Hungary (1994), p. 137; per capita gross debt: Central Statistical Office (1994b), p. 1 and (1995a), p. 9; debt servicing/goods exports: National Bank of Hungary (1994), p. 269 and (1995), p. 108.

curbing the reduction of consumption has been implemented primarily at the expense of foreign debt.

Among other factors contributing to the build-up of foreign debt is the fact that the exchange-rate policy pursued has tended to overvalue the currency, which has weakened the incentive to export and allowed excessive import demand to develop. It was apparent in several periods, most recently from 1993 up to 12 March 1995, that the financial authorities were postponing an increasingly inevitable devaluation.[10] This fitted in well with the economic policy of always postponing unpopular measures to the last minute. Devaluation, especially when coupled with a tighter wage policy, is known for cutting deep into living standards.

Second, let us start by assuming it is possible to determine what proportion of GDP must be invested to ensure the maintenance and a modest but acceptable expansion of national wealth on the one hand, and a modest but acceptable expansion of production on the other.[11] If the proportion is lower, some tasks that should be done now will be omitted and left for later. The arrears formed by the postponed acts of investment are a form of debt, which a later generation will have to pay instead of the present one. So they can be considered as part of the debt in the broader sense.

Since no exact calculation has been made of the size and trend of the investment proportion required for lasting growth and technical development, I can give no estimates of the size of the investment arrears. All I can do is convey the gravity of them indirectly.

Table 4 compares the trend of persistently high investment proportions in some moderately developed, fast-growing countries with the declining trend over time in Hungary's investment proportion. I am not saying Hungary should necessarily have maintained its earlier high proportion of investment,[12] but the very great extent of the decrease demonstrates the line of thinking above: an accumulation of investment arrears.

Table 4: Trends in gross domestic investment in fast-growing developing countries and in Hungary, 1980–93 (as percentage of GDP)

Year	Hungary	Indonesia	South Korea	China	Malaysia	Thailand
1980	30.7	24.3	32.0	30.1	30.4	29.1
1985	25.0	28.0	29.6	38.6	27.6	28.2
1990	25.4	30.1	36.9	33.2	31.5	41.4
1991	20.4	29.4	38.9	32.7	37.0	42.2
1992	15.2	28.7	36.6	34.4	33.8	39.6
1993	19.7	28.3	34.3	41.2	33.2	40.0

Source: World Bank (1995c), pp. 58-61.

Expenditure in Hungary on maintenance and renovation of housing and infrastructural facilities (roads, railways, bridges, and so on) has fallen sharply. Let me take housing construction as an example. This has been declining for two decades, and in recent years the volume of housing constructed has positively plunged. This is offset in part by the fact that far fewer dwellings than before are being removed from the housing stock: dwellings ready for demolition are being retained.[13]

Especially menacing is the drop in certain slow-return investment projects which have a long gestation period. Infrastructural investment and the development of scientific research fall into this group.[14]

Third, another component of debt in the broader sense is formed by legislative commitments to future consumption. These include promises of legally guaranteed pensions, family allowances, maternity benefits, sick pay and all other welfare payments. These are promissory notes from the present generation, which the next generation will have to redeem. When they are eventually redeemed, they too will compete for resources with the investment required for economic development, and so it is justified to consider them a component of debt.[15]

In what follows I shall call these three kinds of debt social debt.[16]

At the beginning of the section I mentioned pro-consumption economic policy. The points made subsequently have helped to show that a short-sighted pro-consumption stance and a very high social discount rate prevails. By pushing a snowball of social debt before us, we prevent a higher standard of consumption later.

All this sounds familiar to older generations of Hungarians. Once upon a time, Mátyás Rákosi, the leading figure in Hungarian Stalinism, argued in these terms for the very high proportion of investment in the economic plan: let us be sure not to kill the goose that will lay the golden eggs. The Kádár regime gained popularity by laying this 'Rákosi-ite' doctrine aside and setting about consuming the goose. Much of the public still greets any call for sacrifice with suspicion and rejection.

Table 5 cites an opinion poll that reflects very well the despondency, the mood of 'no thought for the morrow' and the mounting tendency towards hedonism. Even when the bitter outcome of the short-sighted, short-term preferences applied earlier have become clear, with slower growth and then a decline in consumption, attitudes do not change. They even undergo a self-destructive enhancement: people become yet more impatient and still less willing to make sacrifices.[17]

What is the relationship between the main characteristics of Hungarian development? How do the gradual nature of the transformation, the marked preference for 'now' and the desire for political calm fit together? The compromises and conflict avoidance required for gradualism require the pursuit of an *attractive* policy. Politicians are not prepared to put forward unpopular 'belt-tightening' programs. The Ceauşescu regime used brutal repression. This allowed it to repay its previous debts, even at the cost of grave public deprivation. The soft dictatorship of the Kádár regime, on the other hand, eschewed brutal means of oppression for its last decade or two, which partly explains why it had to pursue an economic policy which courted popularity.

Table 5: Opinion on more distant goals in life and on ideals and values (%)

Statement	Year	Respondents			Total
		disagree	partly agree	wholly agree	
		with statement			
Everything is changing so fast that people do not know what to believe in.	1978	46	33	21	100
	1990	17	35	48	100
	1994	13	38	49	100
People live from one day to the next; there is no sense in making plans in advance.	1978	69	17	14	100
	1990	17	35	48	100
	1994	20	34	46	100

Source: Andorka (1994), Table 4.

The same macroeconomic dilemma faced the new, democratically elected parliaments and governments. The politicians who came to power in Poland and Czechoslovakia judged this historic moment of euphoria to be a time when the public would be willing to make great sacrifices. The opportunity had to be seized to adjust the macroeconomic proportions.[18] The Hungarian government, on the other hand, was not prepared to do the same. Why not? Perhaps it was guided by political realism, finding that the Hungarian public was now accustomed to an easing of repression and thought extensions of its rights and freedoms only natural, so that it displayed no marked euphoria over the change of political system, simply noting it with calm satisfaction. Perhaps it was also because the new government's behavior was obeying the old reflex—by no means alien to experienced politicians in parliamentary democracies either—in not undertaking anything that was going to be unpopular, or even elicit mass protest. Whatever the case, the Hungarian government rejected all versions of shock therapy, radical stabilization surgery or belt-tightening programs of cuts, in favor of continued maximization of consumption (or more precisely, minimization of the fall in consumption). *Table 6* shows the trend in real wages, signifying the degree to which Czechoslovakia, and later the Czech Republic and Slovakia, accompanied by Poland and Slovenia, differed in this from Hungary, where gradualism applied. To this day I cannot reconcile myself to the idea that the first democratic Hungarian government missed a historic, unrepeatable opportunity in 1990.[19]

Table 6: Real wages: an international comparison, 1990–93

Country	Real wages (% change over previous year)				1993 as a percentage
	1990	1991	1992	1993	of 1989
Czech Republic	-5.4	-23.7	10.1	4.1	82.7
Hungary[a]	-3.5	-6.8	-1.5	-4.0	85.0
Poland	-24.4	-0.3	-2.7	-1.8	72.0
Slovakia	-5.9	-25.6	8.9	-3.9	73.3
Slovenia	-26.5	-15.1	-2.8	16.0	70.4

Sources: 1990-93: United Nations Economic Commission for Europe (1994a), p. 79 and (1994b), p. 41; Hungary, 1990-93: Central Statistical Office (1994b), p. 11; Czech Republic and Slovakia 1990-91: World Economy Research Institute (1994), p. 37.
Note: [a] The figure for 1990 covers only the category of workers and employees, excluding workers on agricultural cooperatives. The latter are included from 1991 onwards.

Since then there has been another great historical occasion: the sweeping electoral victory of the Socialist Party in 1994; the Socialist Party, along with its liberal coalition partner, which was prepared to support radical measures, won a 72 per cent majority in parliament. The 'now-or-later' dilemma posed itself more sharply than ever when the new government came to power. There is a well-known rule of thumb in parliamentary democracies, that a government with unpopular measures to take should take them at the start of the parliamentary cycle. By the next elections the voters will have forgotten them, and it may even be possible by then to discern the benefits of the rigorous measures taken several years before. Of course this was not such a dramatically historic opportunity as 1990, when democracy arrived. This was just a normal chance offered by the beginning of a new parliamentary cycle. None the less, the new government let the opportunity slip again, hesitating for another nine months. All that he leading party of the coalition, the Socialist Party that had grown out of the reform wing of the old communist party, did in this case was to obey the established reflexes of its predecessor. For months there was a tug-of-war between the trade-union and party opponents of further sacrifices on one side and the more radical economist reformers, prepared for a tougher economic policy, on the other. In the end, it was always the latter who made the concessions, and the economic policy of muddling through continued as before.

Analogies with populism inevitably spring to mind.[20] The economic policy described—subordination of the long-term interests of economic development to the requirements of political popularity and the unilateral concern for living standards—bears a clear resemblance to it. Still, I do not think it would be right to see this simply as an Eastern European version of populism. Latin American populism (and earlier populist trends in Europe) employed aggressive demagogy and pursued economic policies of unbridled irresponsibility. The economic policy I have described as typical of Hungarian development for decades was less reckless. It was cautious rather than tub-thumping, attempting repeatedly to strike a compromise between the public's living-standard expectations and the legitimate long-term macroeconomic requirements. Yet it can be said that the economic policy steadily incorporated features resembling populism,[21] and a leaning towards populism has always haunted and strongly influenced political decision-makers.

3. Redistribution and paternalism

The previous section examined economic-policy priorities as aggregate categories, focusing on the question of 'consumption versus social debt'. Now let us examine what redistribution processes govern consumption.

Table 7 shows that if household income in Hungary is taken as a whole, the proportion of income earned from work is steadily falling. Meanwhile the proportion of income received through state and social-security redistribution is tending to rise.

Table 8 presents another cross-section. Attention was drawn in a study by Assar Lindbeck (1990) to a dangerous trend in the Swedish economy: the proportion of employed whose income derives from the market is falling fast, while the proportion of those whose income derives from the state budget is rising. Hungarian figures for 1993 were compiled for a comparison, with astonishing results: the Hungarian ratio of 1:1.65 far exceeds the Swedish ratio of 1:1.32 that Lindbeck found alarming. Not even the country to go furthest of any mature market economy in state and social-security redistribution attains Hungary's ratio of those 'living off the state budget' to those 'living off the market'.

Section III/2 contained a mention of the defensive period of economic policy, when the aim was to slow down the fall in living standards. This attempt was not directed at real wages, which fell to roughly the same extent as production (Table 2). On the other hand, while the country's economic situation steadily deteriorated, the system of transfers tended to expand. Family allowances grew

Table 7: Household income by main sources of income in Hungary, 1960–92 (% of total income)

Year	Income from work	Social benefits		Together	Income from other sources
		in cash	in kind		
1960	80.4	7.0	11.4	18.4	1.2
1970	76.1	11.3	11.3	22.6	1.3
1975	71.5	15.5	11.7	27.2	1.3
1980	68.0	18.9	13.1	32.0	0.1
1985	65.6	19.9	14.1	34.0	0.4
1990	58.1	22.6	16.6	39.2	2.7
1992	52.8	25.0	16.4	41.4	5.8

Sources: 1960: Central Statistical Office (1971), p. 387; 1970 and 1975: Central Statistical Office (1981), p. 356; 1980 and 1985: Central Statistical Office (1986), p. 240; 1990 and 1992: Central Statistical Office (1994a), p. 30.

Note: 'Income from work' means the sum, within the net income of households, of the income in money and in kind directly connected with the performance of work. It covers income from employment, cooperative membership, and household, auxiliary and private farming, including personal income from entrepreneurial activity, and the value of work done by households in their own homes. 'Social benefits in cash' denotes the part of the net money income of households received under social insurance and other social-policy measures, and financed out of social insurance, central and local-government budgets, and to a lesser extent by business organizations. 'Social benefits in kind' are the part of consumption by households for which they do not pay, these benefits being financed out of the budget, social insurance, or business organizations. See Central Statistical Office (1994a), p. 232.

more ubiquitous; maternity allowances became generous, at least in the length of entitlement. The system of unemployment benefits in Hungary provided a wider range of entitlement than in many developed market economies. Hungary's proportion of welfare spending to GDP far exceeds the OECD average.[22]

Table 8: Number of participants in the market and non-market sectors in Sweden and in Hungary

	Activity	Number of participants (thousands)		
		Sweden		Hungary
		1970	1989	1993
1.	Public administration and services	806	1427	875
2.	Pensioners	1135	1899	2647
3.	Unemployed	59	62	694
4.	Employed in labour-market programmes	69	144	54
5.	On sick leave	264	317	150
6.	On parenthood leave	28	126	262
7.	Total of 1–6	2361	3975	4682
8.	Employed in market sector	3106	3020	2842
9.	*Ratio of 7 to 8*	*0.76*	*1.32*	*1.65*

Sources: Sweden: Lindbeck (1990), p. 23; Hungary, Rows 1 and 2: Central Statistical Office (1994b), pp. 14 and 54; Rows 3 and 4, Labour Research Institute (1994), p. 45; Row 5: Central Statistical Office (1994b), p. 54, and (1994d), p. 22; Rows 6 and 8: CentralStatistical Office (1994b), p. 54. *Notes*: *Row 1*: For Hungary, the figure refers to employment in budget-financed institutions. *Row 2*: Figures include old-age pensioners and early retirees; for Hungary the figure omits employed pensioners (223 000 in 1993), who are not included in any of the other market or non-market categories either. *Row 3*: For Hungary, registered unemployed only. *Row 4*: For Hungary, the figure is the sum of those undergoing retraining and in public-works employment. *Row 5*: For Hungary, the proportion of employees and industrial-cooperative members on sick leave (5.1 per cent) was projected on to active earners in the market sphere. Workers in the budget-financed sector on sick leave do not feature in the figure for those on sick leave, to prevent double counting. The figure for active earners in the market sphere does not include those on sick leave. *Row 8*: This includes state-owned firms and public utilities.

To use an expression I coined in an earlier piece of writing, Hungary became a premature welfare state.[23] The countries with very high proportions of welfare spending surpass Hungary in economic development many times over.[24] So why did Hungary undertake to finance state welfare transfers beyond its capabilities? It is most important to the government at any time to reassure people. The paternalist redistribution certainly has a soothing effect, compensating to a large extent for the reduction in, and uncertainty about, real wages earned legally in the market sector.

I would like to emphasize in particular the problem of uncertainty. The characteristic feature of Hungary in the last two or three decades has not simply been that more weight was given to the economic-policy priority of consumption. Similar weight was attached to the requirement of socio-economic security. The market economy, which increases uncertainty, and the paternalist redistribution system, which decreases it, developed in parallel.[25] Increasing redistribution fitted in better with the prevailing socialist ideology and the power aspirations of the leading group than putting higher income at the disposal of households would have done. It was left to the central authorities to decide who should share in the redistribution transfers, when and to what extent.

The shift in proportions just described did not derive from a forward-looking, long-term government program. It arose out of improvisation, through rivalry between distributive claims. First one group, stratum or trade, then another, would demand more, or at least struggle against curtailment of its existing rights. This was done by every ministry and every office in the bureaucracy, every trade union and other special-interest group, and, on behalf of their district, by members of parliament and party officials. A great many dissatisfied groups could be silenced if the state undertook a new legal obligation that would always apply in the future, not just in the following year. In many cases the discontented could be pacified by a recurrent softening of the budget constraint: a firm, bank or local government would be saved from bankruptcy by a fiscal grant or a soft bank loan.

This distributive appeasement of dissatisfaction is one of the main factors explaining the financial disequilibria and tensions in the economy.[26] The budget deficit is augmented by pushing welfare spending up to levels that tax revenues cannot cover, and by using state subsidies to bail out firms, banks and local authorities in distress, so as to save jobs. Weakening of wage controls and softening of the budget constraint with soft loans fuel inflation, and so, of course, does monetization of the budget deficit, that is financing of it by the central bank. The growing cost of servicing the external debt contributes to the deficit on the current account. The connection between this and the one-sided consumption orientation of economic policy was discussed in the previous section.

There is a connection in the opposite direction as well. Once the financial disequilibria have emerged, it becomes impossible for a government whose policy is hallmarked by 'consumption-protection', paternalist state care and distributive appeasement to bring itself to take the drastic restrictive measures required.[27] Here again there was continuity after the 1990 change of system,[28] right up to 12 March 1995.

The steady spread of redistribution, with a steady stream of successive little concessions, also led to 'gradualism Hungarian style'. The changes were made in tiny fragmented, concurrent and consecutive stages, step by step. All this also saved the political sphere from traumatic upheavals and contributed to the relatively calm political atmosphere.

4. A departure: The stabilization program of spring 1995

The Hungarian government announced a stabilization program on 12 March 1995.

I do not attempt in this study to analyze this program from the economic point of view. I examine the question using exclusively an approach based on political economy, analyzing, in other words, the mutual effects of politics and economic policy. As a reminder, let me sum up the main components of the programme.[29]

1. There was an immediate, substantial devaluation of 9 per cent, followed by introduction of the system of a pre-announced crawling peg. A substantial surcharge of 8 per cent was placed on imports.
2. Restrictions on budgetary spending were introduced, including cuts in certain items of welfare spending.
3. The government sought to achieve a sharp reduction in real wages. It therefore placed strict limits on the incomes paid in the public sector and on wages in state-owned firms. It was assumed that this would curb wage rises in the private sector as well.

The implementation of the stabilization program has been going on for more than a year at the time of writing. However, it is too early to make a full assessment of the program from the point of view of political economy.[30] Since the rest of the study analyses the general features spanning 20–30 years; it would be out of proportion and hasty to examine the experiences of a short period in the same depth. The mere announcement of the program was a significant development and the government has been following its declared policy quite consistently. The program marks a clean break with the four main features that have typified the Hungarian road of reform and systemic change hitherto.

First, consumption is replaced as the top priority by the aim of restoring the seriously upset macroeconomic balance, so as to establish the conditions for lasting growth and, at a later stage for growing consumption. The defensive action to ward off the decline in consumption has been suspended. A sudden change has been made in the time preference of economic policy. Up to now the future has been sacrificed to the present. Now sacrifices are being demanded of the present for the sake of the future. Up to now the accumulation of social debt has been accepted for the sake of present consumption (slowing of the fall in consumption, or possibly stagnation or a slight rise in consumption). Now a reduction in present consumption has been undertaken to prevent a further build-up of social debt.[31]

Second, the paternalist welfare transfers by the state and the welfare entitlements of the public were taboo until 12 March 1995. There was no political force ready to recommend a well-specified reduction in them. Now a change has occurred. It has been shown to be possible not only to grant entitlements, but to revoke them as well. Since the announcement of the stabilization program the issue of reforming the welfare state has come to the fore in political debate and intellectual discussions. Furthermore, the first steps to reduce welfare entitlements have been taken. For instance, tuition fees were introduced for higher education; the principle of need became a guiding principle in distributing certain welfare benefits, and so on.

Third, in sharp contrast to the gradualism, hesitancy and piecemeal policies characteristic of recent decades, a package of measures with traumatic effects has been introduced with dramatic suddenness. True, this is a far less comprehensive program than the earlier shock therapy in Poland, the Czech Republic or Russia, but that is partly justified by the difference in Hungary's situation in 1995. Yet a degree of similarity remains: the break with continuity, the sudden reversal, and the trauma.

Finally, the stabilization package has brought the political calm to an immediate end. No one could imagine that the 12 March measures had a consensus in support of them. On the contrary, they have been greeted by the widest variety of interest groups and political forces at best with doubts and criticism, and at worst with vehement protest.

Why did the government that took office in July 1994 hesitate for nine months?[32] To answer this means going back to the results of Hungary's last general election in May 1994, and asking the following question: Who voted for the winning Socialist Party and why?[33] Why did the coalition that had won a large parliamentary majority four years before suffer a grave electoral defeat? Let me suggest a couple of answers. One of the motives of the electorate was undoubtedly negative in character: many simply wanted to vote against the ruling coalition, because of the bad economic situation. Contributing to this was the arrogant tone adopted by many government members and leading politicians. The socialists were expected to display more modest, rather plebeian behavior. Many politicians in power were amateurs at governing. The socialists with experience in administering the state and the economy were expected to show more expertise.

The Socialist Party's constituency was very varied. The party gained backing from many employees, mainly (though not exclusively) blue-collar workers. Large numbers of pensioners voted for them. So did many members of the intelligentsia, either from a social democratic conviction or because they were repelled by the nationalist, anti-Semitic, pro-Horthy manifestations under the previous government.[34] Also among the socialist supporters were many entrepreneurs and managers, whose transfer from the party nomenclature into the business world of the market economy had taken place not long before, so that they had retained their connections with their old associates. This list, which is far from complete, shows that the party's constituency included groups not only in agreement with each other, but also with strong conflicts of interest between them.

The Socialist Party's campaign was ambivalent. Its professional technocrats tried to point out frankly to voters that the country was in a difficult position and miracles could not be expected. But certain statements by party speakers left room for the assumption that the Socialist Party could promise a swift improvement in living conditions. What is more important, whether such an improvement was promised to the voters or not, is that many people voted for the Socialist Party hoping that it stood for socialist ideas. The party would be 'left-wing'. It would take sides with the poor, not the rich. It would soon set about improving the living conditions of the workers, the needy and the pensioners. Voters hoped the party would defend the state system of paternalist care, and perhaps even restore full employment and job security. Similar expectations in several other post-socialist countries have also given electoral success to socialist and social democratic parties derived from communist parties. It is all the more understandable that this should have been expected in Hungary, since Hungarian reform socialism went furthest in serving the interests of material welfare and social security.

After the elections, the Socialist Party entered a coalition with the Alliance of Free Democrats, whose history goes back to the dissident movement before the change of system. It is a quirk of history that the opposition and their successors, and those who harassed them and their successors should now be in the same cabinet, voting together. The Free Democrats had been calling for a radical restoration of macroeconomic equilibrium in the previous two years, and they said the same during the elections. They did not disguise the fact that the country has grave economic difficulties and that restrictive measures demanding sacrifices will be required. Their ideas mainly cover European liberal thinking, but some of the party's supporters are not averse to social democratic principles either.[35]

The coalition of the two parties has 72 per cent of the seats in parliament. This is enough to vote through the government's proposals even on legislation requiring a qualified, two-thirds majority. Looking just at the proportions of seats, it might be thought that the coalition parties could immediately push through anything they set their minds on. But it was just this—the need for governmental resolve, agreement between the two parties, and above all unity within the Socialist Party—that caused problems in the nine months after the election. This returns us to the question of stabilization.

It is clear from what has been said that the Socialist Party did not have a mandate from its voters to introduce a stabilization program of severe restrictions and austerity. Most of the socialist politicians tried to avoid the task through the kind of routine behavior imprinted on them in the past. They dared not face their voters. Not only was division apparent at discussions within the Socialist Party and negotiations with the trade unions, but the opponents of a radical program of stabilization appeared to be stronger than the supporters. For months the government was dogged by hesitation, equivocation and almost total incapacity on fundamental questions of economic policy.

The government finally decided it could hesitate no longer. It had to begin paying the bill for the overconsumption of previous generations. One might ask why this had to wait until March 1995 to happen and why precisely in March 1995? Why did the present leadership not try to continue with the policy of muddling through? I do not know what went on behind the scenes of the political process, and so I can only outline some hypotheses. Perhaps the disquieting economic statistics had a sobering effect. To mention just one of them, Hungary's deficit on the current account in 1993 was equal to 9 per cent of GDP; despite hopes of improvement, it increased to 9.5 per cent in 1994. Perhaps the events in Mexico caused the alarm. The Hungarian situation is certainly more favorable in many respects, for example the debt is consisting mainly of long-term credits. Yet the sight of a financial crash in a country that was seemingly developing well may have spread fears among Hungary's leaders. Finally there was another factor: the foreign assessment of Hungary was becoming increasingly negative. As long as the leaders of the Hungarian economy were only in dispute with the IMF, it was possible to think of this as just the usual kind of dispute between the IMF, insisting on rigor, and a small country in difficulties. But condemnations began to multiply in the international financial press, in analyses by prestigious credit-rating institutions and large foreign private banks, and in conversations with leading politicians of other countries. Hungary, the model pupil of Eastern Europe, more and more frequently received a bad report. All these, and perhaps some other factors as well, led the Hungarian political leadership to take a sudden decision to announce a strict and very unpopular program. After decades of conflict avoidance, it undertook to face the inevitable mass indignation.

Having chosen its course of action, the government went about it almost like a coup. It did not submit the 12 March announcement beforehand to wider forums in the Socialist Party. It did not request prior agreement from the socialist faction in parliament or the unions sympathetic to the party. It did not consult with social-policy experts in the state bureaucracy. Deterred by the example of earlier barren negotiations, the government tried to present its supporters with a *fait accompli*.

So what kind of rearguard political defense can the program expect? To an extent it can rely on groups of technocratic experts, and some sections of the liberal intelligentsia with influence over public opinion. The entrepreneurs more or less agree with the program, with many reservations and criticisms, and can be expected to support it so long as it opens up the road to growth, from which they expect greater and safer earnings. It can hope for tolerance, if not support, from employees in expanding branches and firms, and at work places where surplus labor has already been shed, in other words from employees who do not feel their direct interests are infringed. Will this level of support or passive endurance suffice?

A dispassionate observer cannot give any other answer to this vital question than to say it is uncertain. The first year brought encouraging initial results in the most important macroeconomic indices: the monthly budget deficit fell, inflation slowed down again after the initial spurt of price rises, and the monthly deficit on the current account decreased considerably. These, however, are all the kinds of sign that only economists respect. The public do not feel them in their daily lives, whereas the fall in real wages is already hurting, and they are bitter about the reduction in some redistributive benefits. The political and social reaction to the program by broad sections of society is rejection. The various professional groups and representative bodies are protesting one after the other. The program is being attacked strongly by the opposition, inside and outside parliament, while there is much dissension and criticism from within the ranks of the main governing party. The Constitutional Court has annulled several essential components of the stabilization act.

The criticism and protest came in a great variety of forms. There were those people who only objected to the details of the program's implementation and above all the way it had been announced. They were not convinced that the package had been compiled with sufficient care. Many people thought that the decisions on the trade-offs were mistaken: the amount of the reduction in the fiscal deficit did not compensate for the mass protest it had provoked. Many were angry because the government failed to explain patiently and convincingly why the measures were necessary. The restrictive measures were announced in an unfeeling style, devoid of compassion for those who would lose by them. There was indignation in the leading ranks of the Socialist Party and among the trade-union bureaucracy, which is tied to them by many strands, because these weighty measures were taken almost in the form of a coup, without the prior consultation to which they claimed an entitlement.

The question remains: Would the rejection have been so intense if the mistakes of detail and of communication with the public had been avoided, but the essence, the restriction and the start made on whittling down paternalist welfare expenditure had remained? The answer to this is all the more important because the country is still only at the beginning of the program. Releasing macroeconomic tensions that have built up over 20 or 30 years is not achieved by a single, energetic action over a few months. Correcting the deeper disproportions behind the constant reproduction of current-account and budget deficits, reducing the debt, permanently and substantially curbing inflation, and undertaking a comprehensive reform of the welfare sector—these are tasks that will take years, and will often demand sacrifices from many people.

The atmosphere is calming down now and people are becoming used to the new situation. Could a large part of society come to see the economic need for the measures, or at least put up with them without strong protest? Or will the mass protest grow stronger again, leading to comprehensive, long-lasting strikes and large street demonstrations that undermine the economic results of the stabilization? These questions conclude my initial comments on the political background to the stabilization program. I return to these questions in the final section of the study.

IV. GRADUAL TRANSFORMATION OF PROPERTY RELATIONS AND INSTITUTIONS

Reform of the Hungarian economy's property relations and institutions began in the second half of the 1960s, after the relaxation in the political and ideological spheres. Let us look again at Figure 1. Preparations for the first measures of reform took several years. On 1 January 1968 a milestone was reached when the classical command economy suddenly ended, and a curious hybrid form took over.[36]

This was the only sudden leap in the history of Hungarian economic reform. Ever since, the transformation of property relations and institutions has taken place gradually, in a series of small steps. The slow economic reform had been progressing for 22 years when the tempestuous political change of 1989–90 occurred. This, however, did not end the gradualism of the transformation taking place in the field of property relations and institutions, although the changes speeded up considerably.

Bearing in mind this political turning point, the course of institutional change in the economy can be divided into two phases: a slow and less radical, 'reform-socialist' phase (1968–89), and a faster, more radical 'post-socialist' phase that still persists.[37] The border between the political periods, however, did not bring a sudden, dramatic change to the institutional structure of the Hungarian economy.

1. The historical conditions and political background

At the beginning of the post-socialist transition, a debate began over the desirable speed of transformation.[38] Two extreme positions emerged. One was represented earliest and most consistently by Jeffrey Sachs,[39] who believed that most of the transformation should be implemented over a very short period. He himself borrowed the expression 'shock therapy' from psychiatry for the program he recommended, but the term 'big bang', known from cosmology, became widespread as well.[40] In the early stage of the debate, the most prominent representative of the opposing position was Peter Murrell, who argued that the transformation would take place gradually, by an evolutionary path, and this was as it should be.[41] This program is usually called 'gradualism' in the literature on the subject.

The debate at the time covered both the speed at which to overcome the inherited macroeconomic disequilibria and the speed at which to transform property relations and institutions. Since the first of these has been covered in Section III, discussion here will be confined to the second.

Some participants in the debate of the time declared allegiance to one of the two 'pure' programs. Others took up intermediate positions. Different speeds were recommended for the various dimensions of the transformation,[42] or the choice of the time schedule was made dependent on various specific conditions.[43]

Five or six years have gone by since the post-socialist transition began. Experience already shows that the transformation of property relations and institutions has been taking place at different speeds in the region's various countries.[44] Hungary's road to transforming property relations and building up the institutions of a market economy can be described in various ways: organic development, cautious, moderate or considered progress, or hobbling towards a market economy hampered by frequent hesitation and protest. It is debatable which description fits best (all of them do to some extent), but no one could ever say Hungary had taken a *leap* towards a market economy.

It is tempting to put the differences between countries down to different philosophies among leading figures or perhaps leading groups of a few people, or even to the schools to which the advisers whose recommendations were adopted belonged. These certainly had a part to play. I think, however, that the decisive influences were the dissimilar historical antecedents, and the political power relations, structure of society and public mentality, in other words factors that limited and affected the choice of political leaders between alternative courses of action. Before entering into more detail about Hungary's transformation, let me say something about these historical and political factors. Once again, the intention is not to offer a complete analysis, but simply to pick out a few examples.

The 'reform of the economic mechanism', the gradual process of transforming Hungary's property relations and economic institutions that began in the 1960s, was part of a reaction to the trauma of 1956 by the leading political stratum and the whole of society. Perhaps only the blindest of party cadres could believe that people had been brought to rebellion in 1956 solely by the incitement of counter-revolutionaries. Very many members of the governing élite at the time were shaken in their faith as they set about restoring the socialist system. This was the intellectual soil that the idea of market-socialist reform managed to fertilize. Right up until the system collapsed in 1990, this kind of thinking led to a search for some acceptable hybrid. The élite wanted to take market coordination (or some of it) over from capitalism, and perhaps something of property relations (as long as it was on a small scale), but without giving up their power. This meant maintaining the political and military alliance with the Soviet Union, sole rule by the communist party, dominance by the state in controlling the economy, and state ownership of enterprises. There remained in the leading political and economic stratum an extremist type of diehard Stalinist, but this became rare after 1956. The vast majority of the elite showed ambivalence, or one might say political schizophrenia. On the one hand they wanted to save the communist system, to which they were bound by conviction and self-interest. On the other they realized the system had to be changed. So erosion of the system's political base took place first of all inside the minds of these people, as more and more of them abandoned the original, classical communist view on more and more issues, in favor of reform.

A contribution to formulating this idea of reform was made by a semi-deliberate, semi-unwitting change of world political orientation. Though the party cadres knew they had been restored to power by the armed might of the Soviet Union, anti-Soviet feelings arose in many of them. They looked down on the primitive nature of the Soviet system and felt embarrassed by its barbarity. Concurrently with the domestic reform, the country opened up progressively to Western influence. The public and the nomenclature alike began to travel. They would have liked somehow to marry the efficiency and wealth they saw in the West with the Eastern system on which their power rested.

This curious erosion of old faith is the main reason why the change began early and took place gradually, in many small steps. The most enlightened reformers would put forward specific proposals. Initially these had to be made less radical. Later the opposition weakened, and they could apply more radical proposals as well. Many changes took place spontaneously, rather than by government order.

There is one further dimension in which the reform ties in with the response to 1956. The revolution had broken out as a political, not an economic protest. The post-1956 political leadership welcomed developments that distracted the attention of the public from politics, particularly the intelligentsia. One good substitute for pursuing politics was for economists, lawyers, engineers, state officials

and managers to rack their brains about reforms and push fervent-
ly for their introduction. It was better still if the intelligentsia and
the other strata in society concerned themselves with how to earn
more money by extra work in the first economy and by various
kinds of semi-legal, but tolerated activity in the second economy.
This was probably the main mechanism for defusing the tensions,
as it harnessed the energies of society's most active members.

Amidst all these changes, many people also changed their personal course. Within the old socialist society another, capitalist
society began to take shape. Many individuals began to shift, partly or wholly, to a position consistent with the new society. The
impetus may have come from a change in personal thinking, or
from the attractions of an entrepreneurial life style. There was a
wide distribution in terms of who began to change careers and
when, and in when the change was complete, which meant that for
the whole set of the élite there was a continual, gradual transfer.

By the time the political liberation came in 1990, many things
were already half-prepared for the development of a market economy. *Table 9* shows changes had taken place in Hungary before
1990, of a kind that most countries in the region had to make after
1990. Perhaps more important still, far more people in Hungary had
gained experience of how a market operates, in the 'market-socialist' state-owned enterprises, in the private sector or gray economy,
or possibly by studying or working abroad.

The transformation speeded up considerably after the political
renewal. The ideological barriers came down, and there was no
more need for euphemism in discussing private property or capitalism, or concealment of private ownership of production assets.
People were positively encouraged to become entrepreneurs and
owners, and the passage of legislation to conform with a market
economy speeded up greatly in the new democratic parliament. Yet
this acceleration still did not produce a leap, most of all because
leaps cannot be made in this field. Constraints on the mass produc-

Table 9: Chronology of reform measures

Reform measures introduced in Hungary before 1990	Hungary	Poland	Czechoslovakia[a]
Abolition of compulsory delivery system in agriculture	1956	1971	1960
Abolition of mandatory plans	1968	1982	1990
Abolition of central quotas	1968	1991	1990
First steps in price liberalization	1968[b]	1957, 1975[c]	1991
Uniform exchange rates	1981	1990	1991
Entry into IMF and World Bank	1982	1986	1990
Considerable freedom for entrepreneurship and to found private companies	1982	no restrictions	1991
Bankruptcy legislation	1986[d]	1983[e]	1991, 1992
Two-tier banking system	1987	1988	1990
Personal income-tax system	1988	1992	1993
Value-added tax system	1988	1993	1991
Legislation on incorporated companies	1989	1990	1991
Liberalization of trade	1989	1990	1991
System of unemployment allowances	1989	1990	1991

Notes: [a] The reform measures taken during the 'Prague Spring' of 1968, but withdrawn during the Husák restoration are not indicated in this table.
[b] For example, 58 per cent of industrial producer prices became market prices, and market prices applied to 2 per cent of consumer goods in 1968.
[c] Gradual liberalization after 1957, with a surge in 1975, when 40–50 per cent of prices were liberalized.
[d] The first Bankruptcy Act was not enforced. A new act was passed in October 1991.
[e] This act was not enforced. Although it was tightened up in 1988, very few firms went bankrupt.

tion of legislation are imposed in a constitutional state by the capacity of the drafting and legislative organizations. It takes time to
abolish old organizations and institute new ones. Even the far more
violent communist change of system had taken years to accom-
plish. Moreover, the abolition of each organization and position of
power provokes opposition of those with a vested interest in it,
which again slows the process down.

In this respect the Hungarian transformation backs up the
gradualist principle that a coherent system of institutions and customs cannot be transformed all at once. If the 'half-ready' market
economy of Hungary has taken years to mature and is still not fully
developed, the same must be even more true of other countries,
which had not gone so far as the Hungarian one initially. There is
no country whose experience can refute this hypothesis.

'Gradualism Hungarian style' in transforming property relations and institutions was not a result of a grand master-plan. But
neither would it be correct to accept the pace of Hungary's transformation uncritically as inevitable and determined just by blind
fate. Very many aspects of it should have been started and completed earlier. The blame for every case of hesitation and protrac-
tion rests with those running the process and, ultimately, with the
government of the day. But the retarding factors, like vacillation
among the leadership, professional incompetence, inexperience,
pliancy in the face of opposition, and of course the opposition itself,
born of vested interests of various kinds, are all parts of historical
reality.

2. Privatization of state-owned enterprises[45]

By the abolition in 1968 of compulsory plan directives, part of
one of the fundamental property rights, that of control, passed to the
management of the state-owned enterprise. Yet the central authorities continued to intervene in enterprises in many indirect ways.

Most importantly, selection, appointment, promotion and dismissal of managers remained in the party-state's hands.[46] But the managers became a much more influential force, and they became capable of asserting their own ownership interests, in the later, post-socialist period as well.

When privatization came onto the agenda after 1990 and new private firms arose on a mass scale, more and more strands tended to combine and merge the sociological groups of managers of state-owned and private firms and owners of independent firms and joint-stock or limited companies. A passage opened up between the roles of managers and owners. Ultimately these people together form the 'business class'. The former army of submissive party stalwarts carrying out plan directives gradually yields candidates for the business and manager stratum of today, which new people also join, of course. This transformation of the leading stratum takes place without bigger interruptions over a period of decades, and speeds up in the 1990s. The process is demonstrated in *Table 10*. Sociologist Iván Szelényi and his fellow researchers have shown the extent of the continuity in Hungary's economic élite,[47] despite the strongly anti-communist rhetoric of the coalition that took office in 1990 and its attempts to implant its party supporters in many business positions. Most of its own business people also came from the old economic élite.

Table 10: The origins of Hungary's new élites and new economic élite (%, 1993)

Position held in 1988	All new élites	New economic élite
Nomenklatura	32.7	34.8
Other high officials	47.5	54.7
Non-elite	19.8	10.5

Source: Szelényi (1994), p. 39.
Note: Based on life-history interviews with members of the economic, political and cultural élites in 1993. Samples: 783 (all) and 489 (economic).

Hungary in 1988 was the first socialist country to pass a so-called Company Act, whereby state-owned enterprises could commercialize and convert themselves into a modern company form. The first privatizations took place before 1990, but only after 1990 did privatization become one of the prominent features of government policy. Both the governing and the opposition parties agreed that the privatization should fundamentally take place by sale on the market, not free distribution,[48] and this is what happened.[49] So the Hungarian road to privatization differs sharply, in its prior announcements and programs and in the actual course of events, from that in other countries, above all the Czech Republic and Russia, where much state property was handed free of charge to citizens or to managers and employees of firms.[50]

Let me pick out some characteristics of the Hungarian privatization process.[51]

Many commentators on events in Eastern Europe—politicians, journalists and sometimes even representatives of international financial organizations—have dwelt on a single index: the percentage of the original state sector that has been 'privatized', that is, no longer counts as state-owned enterprise. Taking this figure alone, roughly half the state-enterprise sector in Hungary had been privatized by July 1994 (see *Table 11*). For about a year under the new government no further substantial progress had been made that would change this aggregate index.[52] At the end of 1995, however, the process accelerated spectacularly when large parts of the electricity, gas and oil sector and telecommunication had been privatized, mostly to foreign investors, and the privatization of the banking sector gained momentum as well. The present government has promised to complete privatization by 1998.[53]

This single index in itself says little, however, for it may distort the true property relations, and poses many problems of measurement. A private owner with a mere 20–25 per cent of the shares may play a dominant role in a joint stock company, if he or she sets the tone on the board and the representative of the state's stake

Table 11: Degree of privatization in Hungary on June 30, 1994

Method of privatization or reducing state assets	Percentage of the total book value of state assets in 1990[a]
1. Total assets of companies 100% sold	11.5
2. Total assets of companies in majority private ownership	10.1
3. Privately held shares in companies in majority state ownership	4.5
4. Assets sold by enterprises or companies managed by the State Property Agency (ÁVÜ) or State Asset-Management PLC (ÁV Rt.), and assets these invested in new companies	4.4
5. Small-scale 'pre-privatization' sales[b]	0.9
6. Assets of firms in liquidation[c]	15.8
1–6. Degree of privatization; assets of the ÁVÜ and AV Rt. affected by privatization	*47.2*

Source: Hungarian Government (1994), p. 20.

Notes: [a] The book value of the state's assets was established in 1990 by methods agreed with the World Bank. The total was put at HFt 2000 billion at the time.

[b] State assets sold under the Pre-privatization Act of 1990 (some 10 000 establishments, mainly commercial and catering premises).

[c] Assets of firms that underwent liquidation proceedings. There has been practically no privatization revenue from these.

remains passive. On the other hand there may be cross-ownership, the state as such is no longer the owner of the company, but there is a big stake and influence held by a state-owned bank.[54]

The main issue is not the proportion of assets privatized, but the results (permanent, not temporary) that some privatization strategy generates. Sections IV/2 b–IV/2 f attempt to clarify this by describing the experiences in Hungary.

a) Diverse property constellations

Privatization in Hungary is often linked with reorganization and restructuring. Many enterprises break down into smaller firms. Some of these pass into private ownership and some into mixed ownership. The remainder continue to be owned by the state, perhaps indirectly, with the reorganized firm becoming the property of other state-owned firms or banks (cross-ownership). There is a real proliferation of the most diverse property constellations, to use Stark's apt expression,[55] a recombination of property.

Privatization takes place in various legal and organizational forms, through a variety of techniques. The largest and most valuable enterprises are sold by the central agencies by competitive bidding or auction. For smaller and medium-sized firms there are several simplified procedures for transferring the property rights. Where possible, shares are sold for cash, but there are various credit schemes as well, some of which charge market interest rates. There are also credit schemes with preferential interest and repayment terms designed to promote purchases by domestic entrepreneurs. With some firms, all or the majority of shares are sold at once, while with others they are offered gradually, in stages. There are special procedures to facilitate management or employees' buyouts. Although it has rarely happened so far, there are plans for investment companies to take over the shares of several state-owned firms, so that buyers will be able to purchase mixed portfolios. All these forms have arisen by trial and error, not out of any preconceived, uniform plan or central directive. Sometimes consideration for the government's political popularity has caused some form or other to be promoted or relegated.

Hungarian privatization can certainly not be accused of proceeding in a 'constructivist' manner (to borrow Hayek's phrase). On the contrary, it is full of improvisation. Previously determined concepts may be withdrawn, and a campaign launched to speed events up, only for the delays to begin again, and so on. The experimentation on the one hand creates legal uncertainties and delay, protracting the process, which dampens the enthusiasm of buyers and investors. On the other hand it allows lessons to be learnt from mistakes and new methods to be tried, which many people consider one of the main advantages of evolutionary development.[56]

Unfortunately, several months passed after the formation of the new government in mid-1994 before it had assembled its privatization ideas and submitted a new privatization bill, which parliament then enacted.

The privatization process is a curious mixture of centralized and decentralized, bureaucratic and market actions. Gigantic central bureaucracies have been created, and they are seeking to seize the control for themselves in repeated campaigns, or at least obtain strict supervision over them. Yet time and again, events slip from their grasp.

b) 'Crumbling away'

In fact some former state-owned enterprises in their original form have a negative market value, because they can only be run at a loss. This state property worth a minus sum has been crumbling away along the Hungarian road to privatization. The enterprise is wound up by judicial proceedings, and only its material assets are sold. Alternatively, part of the true commercial value, particularly the intangible parts of it (commercial goodwill, expertise or the routine of production, buying and selling), is siphoned off into private firms in legal or illegal ways. Both these processes form important components of the formal and informal privatization of the state's wealth. In evaluating the crumbling-away process, two closely connected aspects of it must be distinguished. One is the decline in real wealth. Some physical productive capital is lost irrevocably in the process of liquidation and change of ownership, while some intellectual capital becomes unusable as well. There are no reliable estimates for this, but expert observers are unanimous in stating that the loss of real wealth is very significant. It is far more common and on a greater scale than the structural change in the economy renders inevitable. The other, completely separable aspect, is the loss of wealth by the state, as owner. The wealth may remain, but the new, private owner has not given adequate compensation to the old owner, the state. To put it plainly, the state has had its pocket picked, even though the new owners may make good use of the appropriated wealth for their own benefit. I shall return to this phenomenon, confining myself here to emphasizing that the process of crumbling away provides clear opportunities for squandering the state's property on the seller's side, and for legalized theft of it on the buyer's.[57]

c) Revenue from privatization

Privatization has yielded substantial fiscal revenue, which has amounted to US$ 7427 million by the end of 1995[58] (see *Table 12*). This is a major advantage of the sales strategy over free distribution, although the proceeds have been less than hoped for, with much being deducted by the high costs of privatization and the central agencies. None the less, the revenue makes no small contribution to a state with serious fiscal problems. Some of the most important acts, including the privatization of electricity and gas production and distribution and the sale of oil and oil products, generated significant revenue.

Table 12: Privatization revenue, 1990–95 (USD million)

Sources and forms of revenue	Direct privatization revenue from sales of existing assets			
	1990–93	1994	1995	Total, 1990–95
From foreign clients	1528	123	3122	4773
From domestic clients (cash)	609	228	195	1031
From domestic clients (credit)	354	279	30	663
Compensation vouchers	209	611	140	960
Total	*2700*	*1241*	*3486*	*7427*

Sources: State Property Agency (ÁVÜ), State Asset Management PLC (ÁV Rt.), and State Privatization and Property Management PLC (ÁPV Rt.); communication by Péter Mihályi.

The most important advantage, though, is not the 'tangible' fiscal revenue, but the favorable changes described under the next heading.

d) Real owners; injections of capital

Because money has to be paid for the assets of the state, a high proportion of cases involve the immediate appearance of real owners (individual or corporate, domestic or foreign), who exercise real control over the managers. (In the comparatively rare cases of management buy-out, the management and the owners become the same.) Even when a majority is not obtained, a strategic investor's influence will be much stronger than the share held, in many cases even in relation to a majority shareholding by the state. The presence of the new owner is felt particularly strongly where full or partial ownership has passed to a foreign firm or individual.

Privatization by sale produces favorable conditions and strong incentives for reorganization and a new, effective style of corporate governance. This contributes to the fact that privatized Hungarian firms soon surpass state-owned firms in their performance (see *Table 13*).

Table 13: The profitability of privatized companies in 1992

Branch	Gross profitability[a]	
	Privatized companies	Branch average
Mining	1	-8
Metallurgy	-2	-12
Engineering	2	-11
Non-metallic ores	5	-1
Chemicals	15	5
Textiles and garments	9	-2
Timber, paper and printing	6	12
Food, beverages and tobacco	7	-1
Other manufacturing	-2	2
Construction	8	3
Agriculture	0	-4
Commerce	8	1
Accommodation, services	6	6
Transportation, warehousing	5	2

Source: Vanicsek (1995).
Note: [a] Index of gross profitability employed: cash flow (profit plus depreciation) over total assets.

Many state-owned enterprises are in a run-down condition and in great need of a capital injection: they need investment for restructuring. A commitment by the buyer to invest new capital within a short time often appears in the terms of the sales contract. Where there are several potential buyers, the amount of new investment promised often acts as a selection criterion, alongside the price offered. Even if this is not spelled out in the contract, the owners will normally be aware when they buy that the firm needs development, and set about it quickly. Countless examples of this have occurred in Hungarian practice. This is one of the most important advantages over free distribution, which transfers ownership to penniless people unwilling and unable to invest.

e) The shorter side: the privatization supply

One argument often brought against the idea of privatization by sale was that the savings accumulated by the public were too small for them to buy the state's wealth. Disconcerting calculations appeared at the time showing how many decades it would take to sell all the assets, given the low initial stock of savings.

Experience has shown this is not the real bottleneck in the privatization process. There are potential foreign buyers with sufficient purchasing power, and savings have meanwhile been accumulating in the hands of Hungarian entrepreneurs, and more widely the Hungarian public.

The real problem throughout has been to make the privatization supply attractive enough, and it worsens as the privatization process in Hungary continues. Many of the most coveted items in the supply have gone, apart from a few remaining large public utilities, purposely held back. Many of the foreign investors even so far have preferred to make a 'green-field' investment in a new plant. Domestic investors tend to prefer to buy safe, high-yielding Hungarian government bonds with their money, put it in a foreign-currency account at a Hungarian bank, send it abroad illegally, or invest it in a newly established private Hungarian firm, rather than buy shares in firms under privatization. Even if the most favorable credit conditions and the biggest concessions are offered, bordering on free distribution, the demand for the less attractive enterprises is low. This suggests that the viability of many state-owned enterprises is questionable.

f) The purity of privatization

Events are constantly being affected by politics. Every political force that gains governmental power also constitutes a community of interests, intent on helping its clients to gain good positions. Augmenting this are similar endeavors by other political strands and various groups in the bureaucracy. In Hungarian society, as in every living social organism, various kinds of network operate, whose members are intent on helping on each other's careers in the hope of reciprocal assistance.[59] The owners of every newly privatized firm, and new private firms, are glad to bring onto their boards both members of the old nomenclature and members of the new, leading political groupings, for they know such people have valuable connections.

There is widely thought to have been a great deal of corruption during the privatization process. This is presumably true, although no specific exposure of a single case of corruption has been exposed. Certainly the suspicion of corruption and opaqueness in the process have helped cause a further fall in the popularity of privatization, from an already fairly low initial level.[60]

I shall not venture, even with hindsight, a simple yes or no to the question of whether Hungary's has been better or worse on the whole than other privatization strategies. To sum up, I can say only that the gradualism applied to privatization in Hungary, as a spontaneous, wildly proliferating, evolutionary process, presents clearly favorable and unfavorable, attractive and unattractive features. The expression 'gradualism of privatization, Hungarian style' contains a modicum of national pride, and at least as much of self-mockery. But it certainly seems that the strategy works and will result, in the foreseeable future, in the privatization of the enterprises that are viable and that it is not expedient to retain in state ownership. Certainly the process might have been faster, even supposing the same general strategy had been employed, and if the administration at any time had been more forceful and skillful, and shown greater confidence in the decentralized mechanisms. However, even if these weaknesses of Hungarian privatization and the resistance to it mean it is not completed for another few years, it will still have taken place at lightning speed when compared with other changes of ownership relations in world history.

3. New private businesses

Like many other economists, I was convinced from the outset that the key factor in changing property relations, at least in Eastern Europe's smaller countries, was the appearance of new private undertakings.[61] This was different from the ideas of those who wanted to concentrate attention on privatizing the hitherto state-owned enterprises. I argued that even if the new private businesses only accounted initially for a smaller proportion of production, their vigor would make them the real engine of post-socialist transformation.

An appreciable development of Hungary's private sector had begun before the change of political system (*Tables 14* and *15*). It was not alone in this, for East Germany, Poland and Yugoslavia also had sizable private sectors, but the development in Hungary had gone further by 1990 than it had elsewhere. The process was moving along two parallel paths.

One path is development of the legal private sector.[62] The rigid anti-capitalist prohibitions of classical, Stalinist socialism began slowly and almost imperceptibly to ease in the reform-socialist period. The process began to speed up in 1982, when it became possible to found various forms of private companies and conditions for self-employment also became more favorable.

There was a huge increase in the rate at which private businesses appeared after 1990 (see Tables 14 and 15).[63] This brought with it a structural transformation of production. The excessive

Table 14: Number of active earners in Hungary engaged in individual businesses or non-incorporated business associations in 1981–94 (thousands)

Year (1 January)	Self-employed	Family members assisting	Employees	Altogether	As a percentage of all active earners
1981	118.2	61.8	0.3	180.3	3.6
1989	218.4	81.0	48.0	347.4	7.2
1992	466.0	97.4	144.0	707.4	16.7
1994	-	-	-	805.1	21.7

Source: Laky (1995), p. 686.

Table 15: Trends in number of incorporated business associations in Hungary, by main types, 1989–95

Type of association	1989	1992	1994	1995
Enterprises[a]	2400	1733	821	761
Private limited companies	4484	57262	87957	102697
Joint-stock companies (PLCs)	307	1712	2896	3186
Cooperatives[b]	7076	7694	8252	8321

Sources: Central Statistical Office (1994e), p. 115, and (1996b), p. 120.
Notes: The data refer to December of each year.
[a] The term 'enterprise' covers the former socialist-type state-owned enterprises. These were gradually converted into companies during the transition.
[b] Cooperatives include agricultural cooperatives, housing, savings and credit cooperatives, consumer cooperatives, and miscellaneous cooperatives. In April 1995, about a quarter of the cooperatives were engaged in agriculture, a quarter in the real-estate or housing markets, and over a third in manufacturing or construction.

concentration of production lessened; masses of small and medium-sized firms came into being. The relative proportions of the branches changed, with a rise in the weight of the services after decades of neglect.

The other path by which the private sector develops is through the expansion of semi-legal and illegal activity. This was viewed kindly by advocates of the market economy before the political turning-point as the only way, in many fields, of circumventing the restrictions imposed by ideological bias. The 'shadow economy' was a kind of civil-disobedience movement against the bureaucratic constraints. The moral and political standing of the gray and black economy changed increasingly after 1990. It could be interpreted not as acceptable civil disobedience any longer, but as evasion of civic responsibilities, taxes, customs duties and social-insurance contributions.

According to the latest estimate, compiled with particular pains, 30 per cent of 'real' (registered and unregistered) GDP derives from the gray and black economies.[64] Unfortunately, continuity also applies to willingness to pay taxes. Moral norms and behavioral rules instilled over decades alter at a snail's pace. Indeed, if taxpaying morality is altering at all, it seems to be changing in many cases for the worse. Those who infringe regulations had more to fear from the dictatorial state. Moreover the sums at stake have become much greater: tax fraud and utilization of legal loopholes can earn their perpetrators much greater sums. There is not just a handful of tax evaders at work, whom a strict fiscal authority can easily detect. There are not just organized criminals at work, whom the police have to catch. Almost the whole Hungarian population takes part, actively or tacitly. The 'savings' from evading tax and other levies are shared between seller and buyer, employer and employee, and the customs-evading professional smuggler or shopping tourist and the consumer of the smuggled goods. The question of extending taxation to the gray economy is political, not just economic. It would be popular if the police or tax office could catch a few very rich people in the act of tax fraud. But if they start applying more methodical controls—seeing whether traders and service providers give receipts, all employees are registered, or small and medium-scale entrepreneurs' declared incomes square with their lifestyles—they will arouse opposition. No government has attempted to do this, except for one or two hesitant experiments.

Privatization and the genesis of new private enterprise led between them to half of total (recorded and unrecorded) GDP being derived from the private sector by 1992 (*Table 16*), and the proportion has risen further since then. By 1994, the share of the private sector in the recorded GDP amounted to 60 per cent.[65] The private sector's share of employment is even greater.

Table 16: Contributions of total ownership sectors to total GDP, 1980–92

Ownership sector	Contribution to total GDP (%)					
	1980	1985	1989	1990	1991	1992
Public ownership	83	79	74	70	63	50
Private ownership	17	21	26	30	37	50
of which: Domestic	17	21	26	20	34	42
Foreign	0	0	0	1	3	8
Total	*100*	*100*	*100*	*100*	*100*	*100*

Source: Árvay and Vértes (1994), p. 18.
Note: Total GDP is the sum of the contributions of the recorded and unrecorded economy.

Special mention needs to be made of how foreign capital is involved in the Hungarian private sector. Its share of recorded Hungarian GDP was 10.4 per cent in 1994,[66] but the effect of its appearance is disproportionally greater, making a big contribution to modernization of the economy. The volume of foreign direct investment in the 1990s has been far greater in Hungary than in the other post-socialist countries of Eastern Europe.[67] (See *Table 17*.)[68] Statements by foreign investors suggest the attraction was mainly the consolidated state of Hungary's market economy.[69]

Table 17: Foreign direct investment in the post-socialist countries, 1990–94

Country	Cumulative totals (USD mn)			FDI per capita in 1994
	1990	1992	1994	(US$)
Albania	-	20	116	36
Bulgaria	4	102	205	23
Croatia	-	16	104	22
Czech Republic	436	1951	3319	319
Hungary	526	3456	6941	670
Poland	94	495	1602	42
Romania	-	120	501	22
Slovakia	28	210	434	102
Slovenia	7	183	374	185
FYR of Macedonia	-	-	5	3
Eastern Europe	1095	6552	13608	126
Commonwealth of Independent States	-	1761	4622	22
Baltic states	-	111	811	102
Total	*1095*	*8424*	*19041*	*58*

Source: United Nations Economic Commission for Europe (1995), p. 151.
Notes: a Cumulations of inward foreign investment from 1988.
b European countries only.

4. Liberalization and reform of the legal infrastructure

By liberalization I mean all changes that rescind earlier legal restrictions, administrative constraints and bureaucratic regulations on economic activity. Without wholly coinciding with the categories of decentralization and deregulation, the concept largely overlaps with them.

Liberalization of many provinces of economic decision-making has taken place gradually, in many small stages, in Hungary since 1968. The process of price and export liberalization speeded up markedly after 1990 and was concluded in a relatively short time.[70] The government cannot be said to have applied a sudden, shock-like liberalization, if for no other reason than because partial freeing of prices and imports had already occurred, and the bulk of import liberalization was accomplished in the four-year period of 1989–92.[71]

Central wage controls were abolished in 1992, quite soon after the change of political system. Nor was the special tax to curb the running away of wages retained. On the other hand, there was steady development of a central 'interest-arbitration' procedure between the government and the employers' and employees' organizations to influence wage trends. I shall return to this later.

Investment projects before the reform of 1968 were carried out by central state decision and financed out of the central budget. Decentralization of this sphere of decision-making also began decades ago (see *Table 18*). After the change of system, the transformation of property relations went on to institutionalize the distribution of decision-making rights customary in a market economy, whereby the central state authorities only decide projects they finance themselves and have a say in decisions on projects they help to finance.

A measure of liberalization has also occurred in foreign-exchange management, most of it since 1990. The Hungarian forint became partially convertible in 1992 (for the current payment transactions of banks and enterprises), but international capital transactions remained subject to official permit. Under the new Exchange Act, the convertibility of the forint was extended in 1996, although certain restrictions on conversion transactions by individuals and on capital transactions remain. The official exchange rate has hitherto been determined centrally, although a free-market (black) foreign-exchange trading has been tolerated. Periodic devaluations of the forint have been necessitated for years by inflation, but there was no rule of any kind to govern the timing or scale of devaluations before the stabilization program was announced in March

Table 18: The proportion of state-controlled investment, 1968–90

Year	Proportion of total investment spending decided by the state (%)
1968	51
1975	44
1980	46
1985	42
1989	33
1990	29

Sources: 1968: Central Statistical Office (1974), p. 95; 1975: Central Statistical Office (1976), p. 80; 1980: Central Statistical Office (1981), p. 117; 1985, 1989 and 1990: Central Statistical Office (1991), p. 69.

Note: With state-controlled investment, the decision was made at central state level and the funds came from the state budget. Remaining investment was decided at enterprise or cooperative level. It was funded partly from the enterprise or cooperative's own resources, and partly from credit.

1995. Since then, as mentioned before, there has been continual devaluation according to a detailed schedule announced in advance.

Not for a moment has the principle of laissez-faire applied in a pure and extreme form in Hungary. Agencies of the bureaucratic command economy gradually turned into agencies of state supervision and partial regulation. In many instances an earlier bureaucratic authority was abolished, and another, more market-compatible one eventually emerged, resembling more closely the supervisory and regulatory bodies of other market economies. For instance, the following agencies arose: the Economic Competition Office (an anti-trust agency), the Bank Inspectorate, Insurance Inspectorate, Securities Inspectorate, Ministry of Environmental Protection and Regional Development and National Labor Center. A Tax and Financial Office was created for the collection of personal income tax and value-added tax, taxes that were patterned after the tax system in developed market economies.

The process of drafting legislation to conform with a market economy and repealing laws contrary to it began a good few years before the turning-point of 1990. Although transformation of the legal infrastructure has also taken place gradually, in several steps, the earlier start and intensive work done have allowed Hungary in this respect to retain several advantages over the other countries in the region. The most important legislation for the operation of a market economy was in place by 1992–93. The courts and other law-enforcement and judicial organizations, along with the lawyers representing firms and individuals, began to obtain experience in ensuring the implementation of these acts.

I would not like to give the impression that an ideal combination of market and bureaucratic coordination has arisen in Hungary. It is doubtful, of course, whether such a combination exists anywhere. Certainly both the market and the bureaucracy in Hungary today operate with a great deal of friction. Adequate supervision and legal regulation are lacking in areas where they are clearly needed.[72] On the other hand there is still too much bureaucratic intervention in areas where it is superfluous and, in areas where bureaucracy is inevitable, it often works in a sluggish, unprofessional way.

5. Corporatist formations

Trade unions under the socialist system had no great influence on the country's economic policy. They were confined to protecting employees' interests in job-related and enterprise matters. Trade-union leaders were appointed and supervised in their work by the communist party.

Political pluralism provided a chance for trade-union autonomy to develop. The legal successors of the official union movement of the old regime, eager to survive, sought to gain popularity by representing employees' interests as effectively as possible. New unions were created alongside the old, and competition for members among the various alternative unions began. Relatively little attention was paid to unionism by the new parties in parliament except for the socialists, although its influence is substantial, especially in times of heavy economic burdens on employees, with declining real wages and rising unemployment. The successor to the old official union (MSZOSZ) became the strongest of the rival union movements.

National employers' federations were also founded. They, however, have so far had less say than the employees' unions, perhaps because there is still not much interplay between politics and business. The legal and semi-legal methods for business people to influence elections and political power relations by contributing money has not yet developed. The government at any time is more afraid of the employees' than of the employers' organizations.

A central framework for coordinating the views of the government and the employees' and employers' organizations on economic policy came into being in 1988.[73] It is known as the Interest Conciliation Council. Here the union movement has been demanding more and more vehemently that close attention be paid to its views, not only on wage policy, but in the preparation of every other major economic-policy decision. The scope of central coordination of interests is not fully institutionalized, but it is heading in that direction. This adds a major corporatist component to the Hungarian political and economic system. Interplay between the state and unions was increased by the electoral alliance formed before the 1994 general elections by the Socialist Party and the MSZOSZ, several of whose senior officials were elected to parliament, where they have joined the governing Socialist Party's faction.

Closely related to this trend are the changes in the way Hungary's social-insurance system is organized. The pension system and the health-insurance system were both branches of the central bureaucracy of the state, and the so-called social-insurance contribution clearly a state tax. The expenditure of the pension and health-insurance systems was met in practice out of the state budget.

Some separation of the finances of these two great distribution systems from the central government budget had begun before the political change. The profound change, essential from the political and sociological point of view, came with legislation embodying the principle of self-governance for the two social-insurance systems (to cover pensions and health insurance). The law laid down that these two organizations were to be run jointly by representatives of the employers and the employees. For the employers, the employers' federations delegate the representatives, while the representatives of the employees are elected by those entitled to the provision. Under the special election procedures prescribed, the candidates are put up by the trade unions, not political parties. The first such elections brought a sweeping victory for the candidates of the MSZOSZ. Through this 'personal union' the dominant trade-union movement exercises a controlling influence over the two vast apparatuses. This, of course, has further legitimized the movement's demand for a greater say in the country's affairs, and strengthened the corporatist strands in the fabric of social and economic relations.

So far as I know, the course of development in Hungary is unique in this respect. There are extremely strong formal and informal strands binding together the government, the Socialist Party with its majority in parliament, the social-insurance system, and the strongest union federation. Perhaps only the social and economic structure of Israel has shown some similar features.[74]

The acquisition of corporatist traits is leaving its mark on Hungary's economic development. While the country continued on the well-trodden 'Hungarian road', the mutual willingness to compromise shown by the government, unions and employers fitted in well, not least because they concluded no agreement likely to arouse widespread public protest.

It was not surprising that, when the government announced its restrictive stabilization program, it broke the established corporatist conventions. There was no prior agreement with the unions and employers before the program was put forward. Negotiations had been going on in the previous months. The Interest Conciliation Council had met several times and the prospect of concluding a 'social and economic compact' was raised repeatedly. But they could not agree. In the end the government decided to present employees and employers alike with a fait accompli. Since then there have been some efforts on the side of the government to negotiate with the trade unions and other associations representing various interest groups, leading to partial agreements on some points. Still, there is no general 'social compact'. The question is how long this state of 'neither agreement nor confrontation' can be sustained.

V. CONCLUDING REMARKS IN TERMS OF
POLITICAL ECONOMY
AND POLITICAL PHILOSOPHY

1. Positive political economy[75]

This study approaches the history of the Hungarian economy's development and transformation from the angle of positive political economy.[76] The question I have tried to answer is not whether the Hungarian road of post-socialist political and economic transition is good, better or worse than the ones down which governments with other programs have taken their countries. I wanted to know why Hungary's transformation was on a different road. My answer is certainly not comprehensive and may contain mistakes, but I am sure it was justified and important to raise the question.

I have sometimes heard economists, who agreed to act as advisers and then found their advice was not followed, make statements like this: 'My proposals were correct, but these selfish and stupid politicians have subordinated economic rationalism to their own criteria,' or: 'The proposal was correct from an economic point of view, but it was not politically feasible.'

Though psychologically understandable, this reaction has nothing to do with a scientific approach[77] of politics is not an external circumstance for the economy, but one of the main endogenous actors in it. For positive political economy, this is the axiomatic point of departure for analysis. The quest is to find out what makes a proposal politically feasible. What kinds of behavior are typical of the political sphere of the country concerned, and what are the typical solutions to its dilemmas? Or, to go a stage deeper, why have the particular typical political constraints and kinds of behavior evolved? Why are the dilemmas solved in this way, and not in some other?

Economists brought up on welfare economics are inclined to take the welfare function for granted; they expect every government to strive to maximize this function, and criticize a government that departs from the optimum.

This study suggests another approach, to some extent by analogy with the theory of revealed preferences. A specific historical process occurred, in which governments took active part. Can a degree of consistency in time be observed in the actions of the governments? If so, let us construct subsequently the objective function that the political leaders actually maximized, or the preferences revealed in their actions.

By following this line of thought, the study has arrived at two conclusions: (i) there was a consistency in time in the economic policy of the successive, in many respects dissimilar, governments, from the 1960s right up to the spring of 1995; and (ii) they showed clearly discernible preferences. They wanted to avoid conflict. They wanted as far as possible to ensure the uninterrupted survival of the economic élite and continual additions to it of people from the new political forces. They were not prepared to take radical, unpopular action. They aimed at short-term maximization of consumption, accepting as a trade-off the accumulation of social debt.

These revealed preferences go a long way to explaining the macroeconomic proportions that emerged, the constant redistributive concessions, and the gradualism typifying Hungarian development.

The preference system of Hungary's economic politicians was consistent inasmuch as it accepted, at least implicitly, the time-preference, that is, the point in the 'now-or-later' trade-off attractive to them.

On the other hand, I consider fairly inconsistent the position often taken by foreign observers, for instance several staff members of the International Monetary Fund and the World Bank. These economists were enthusiastic over a long period in praising the Hungarian reform, its gradualism, and the concomitant political consensus and calm, including the continuation of this policy after 1990. Hungary was the gradualist success story. Nowadays I have often heard the same economists say something like this: 'We are disillusioned with Hungary. It used to be the model country, but now its results are far worse than those of other, more successful post-socialist countries.'

The disillusioned fail to identify the essential causal connection. Hungary now displays an unfavorable macroeconomic performance precisely because it previously stuck to the road of Hungarian reform and 'gradualism Hungarian style'.

The revealed preferences of Hungarian policy can be deduced not from the programs announced in advance by politicians, but by what occurred. Rhetoric can say one thing and deeds another. Neither is it certain that the politicians, individuals and groups succeeding each other in positions of power really wanted to see what actually ensued. It may be, for instance, that they never fully thought through the 'now-or-later' dilemma. They may have convinced themselves that they were only putting aside certain tasks temporarily, until they had solved some urgent problem. The approach in this study is not intended to interpret the politicians' psychology or the measure of their candor, deliberation and foresight, but the actual routines, conditioned reflexes and decision-making regularities revealed in their deeds.

2. Further remarks on intergenerational time preferences

Although it is not the main purpose of this study to assess past developments, I cannot avoid in these final remarks addressing the question of whether the preferences of successive Hungarian governments deserve approval. The first aspect to clarify is whose

approval is concerned. Can historians or research economists analyzing the period ex post seek to apply their own scale of values?
They can do so, but let this be stated, and let the value system concerned be declared. I have not aimed in this study to judge the past
by my scale of values. What has concerned me more is to try to find
the internal value judgment in the society examined.

Let us again take as an example the problem of 'now or later',
and compare in the light of it the life stories of two Hungarian citizens, A and B.

A was born in 1920 and died in 1993.[78] He was starting out on
his career when the first change of political regime began. By the
time he was 70 he had lived under seven regimes.[79] The rule and
collapse of most were accompanied by war, revolution, repression,
bloodshed, imprisonment and executions. As far as I know,
Hungary set a world record by squeezing seven regimes—six
changes of system—into 47 years of modern history.[80] Well, it was
a benefit to have relative calm in the last 30 years, during the majority of A's adult life. If his material welfare matched the Hungarian
average, it improved greatly to start with and deteriorated relatively little later. He did not live to see the time when a start had to be
made in paying the bill for the earlier policy preference.

B's life differs strongly from A's. He was born in 1970 and
started work in 1993. Two years later, in the spring of 1995, he
began to pay the bill for the short-sighted policies of the previous
regime, and was likely to carry on doing so for a long time. As a
working adult, however, he never felt that policy's relative benefits.

So what did Hungarian development in the last three decades,
with its curious time-preference, mean in terms of material welfare,
security and calm? Let me repeat the question, now using the example: what did it mean to whom?[81] For the older A it was favorable,
more favorable than if he had lived in a communist country which
had set little store by the population's standard of living, and for
that reason applied stronger repression. For the younger B, howev-

er, it was not favorable, because he inherited a bigger social debt than his contemporaries in countries where the political power had applied greater restriction.

Several general conclusions can be drawn from the line of thought so far. Consistent assessment of any past period must be based on normative postulates. Alternative postulates will yield different inter-generational distributive principles. In other words, divergent principles emerge for distributing the advantages and drawbacks, benefits and losses fairly between generations. At this point we touch upon the theoretically extremely difficult issues of interpersonal comparisons of individual utilities and the possibilities and limits of creating a social welfare function.[82] There is a rich, well-expanded literature on the ethics and economic applications of ethical theory for distribution within the same generation, but to my knowledge, dynamic generalization, in other words a normative theory of intergeneration distribution, is still comparatively immature. There are no well-elaborated principles of economic ethics to say what advance the present generation can be allowed to withdraw at the expense of the next, which will have to pay it back. In other words, there are no rules to say what positive or negative legacy the present generation is obliged (or permitted) to bequeath to the future.

When considering long-term economic development, economists, including myself, tend to take as axiomatic the social discount rate that should express the time preference of society. Yet we know what a decisive role this discount rate plays in every theoretical and quantitative model to determine the optimum savings and investment rate and the optimum path of growth.[83]

The problem is that the social discount rate is not given at all. The theory that it finds expression in the prevailing real market rate of interest is strongly disputed.[84] The earlier example of the time-preferences of the two Hungarian citizens shows that behind the dilemma lies a deep ethical problem. It is not at all self-evident how one should 'average' the time preferences of people with different destinies.

Given these difficulties, who authorizes us, as economists taking positions on matters of economic policy, to adjudicate on this dilemma? What right have we to decide what weight to give, in the intergenerational welfare function—even if it is for the retrospective assessment of economic history—to the benefits enjoyed and losses incurred by the different generations? It is especially offensive that most of us, failing even to discern the ethical problem behind our historical judgments, brashly declare that Country X's policy was right and Country Y's was wrong.

Mention of 'authorization' leads to the question of the legitimacy of choice. When examining legitimacy, the analysis should again begin with a positive scientific approach. It is understandable psychologically for generations that have suffered much to disregard the legacy they leave to later generations. It is understandable that A and his contemporaries, having gone through so much suffering, wanted to secure themselves a slightly better, more peaceful life.

Of course most of those in Hungarian society have lived through a stretch of both periods and start to pay off the bill in their lifetime. Relative weighting of present and future value takes place in the thinking of these people themselves, and the spread is certainly wide. If the time preference differs from person to person, people under a democratic political structure have the right to express their preferences as a political choice. Many people try to do that in elections and by other political acts.

This leads to a fundamental question: to what extent can a government be expected to act always in the way the citizens expect it to? I would like now to present this problem not just in relation to the 'now-or-later' dilemma, but in more general terms, with special reference to the post-socialist transformation.

3. With or against the stream?

Communist ideology has a Messianic nature. Sincere believers in it are sure the system they want to apply is the only redeeming social system. The system must be accomplished even though people have not realized what their true interests dictate. Stalinist socialism put the vast majority of Eastern Europeans off Messianic doctrines for life. They want nothing more to do with systems that try to bestow happiness on them by force.

The Kádár regime marked a change in that it tried to confine such forced bestowal of happiness to narrower bounds. In Bolshevik terminology this was 'opportunism', a policy of 'following in the wake of the masses'. The Kádár regime was far from a political democracy, for which the underlying institutions were lacking. But Kádárite politicians resembled those of a parliamentary democracy in trying to form groups of supporters among certain sections of the population and represent their interests. This political endeavor reached fulfillment later, after 1990, when the success of every party and political movement, the seat of every member of parliament, and the acquisition of governmental positions came to depend on the voters.

A Messianic politician feels authorized to impose his or her program by force. The more democratic politics becomes, the more a politician needs mass support to implement a program of any kind.

The Hungarian road of transition to a market economy, displaying the four characteristics described in this study, proved to be a policy that tended to receive mass support to a greater extent (or at least to be less likely to meet resistance) than ideas directed at a radical correction of macro tensions. This policy exacted a great price, however, with succeeding generations pushing before them an ever greater and more perilous quantity of social debt. But must happiness be bestowed on them against their wishes and will?

Here I would like to return to the stabilization program announced in March 1995, in which the government departed from the road taken up to that point, turning away from it in terms of all four characteristics. The program ended Hungary's relative political calm. It aroused passions. The government parties met with sharp resistance even from their supporters. Their political popularity dived.

Justification for the radical program of restriction can be made on several levels. The most obvious argument starts from the current position of the Hungarian economy. The grave macroeconomic tensions and the need to avert economic crisis speak in favor of drastic restriction, rightly, in my view.

Another level of argument reaches its conclusions from the angle of the medium- and long-term transformation of the Hungarian economy and society. The present package is only the first in a succession of measures to remove the barriers to long-term growth caused by the financial disruptions, improve the structures of production and foreign trade, and help to revise the role of the state, including a reform in the welfare sphere. I am convinced that these, too, are correct arguments.

All these arguments, however, fail to resolve a deep political and ethical dilemma: Is it permissible to push through a reform despite opposition from most of the public?

The initial answer comes easily. The government and the political parties and movements behind it should do much better at convincing the public, so that communication between the government and population improves. Preparation for the measures should be more circumspect. Greater consideration must be given to the economic benefit and political cost of each measure, the destabilizing effect of the discontent it engenders. These are justified demands, but it can be questioned whether even the best professional preparation and persuasion can ever make popular a restrictive program that withdraws entitlements.[85] The dilemma cannot be side-stepped.

In my view it is one thing to *understand*, in a sense affected by positive political-economic analysis but also a sympathetic heart, why there is resistance, and another to endorse the resistance. More specifically, it is another matter for a responsible politician to bow to mass pressure, and drift along the stream, when this plainly runs great risks even in the short term, and in the long term aggravates the already large accumulated debt and causes yet greater harm.

We have arrived at a fundamental dilemma in political thinking, which arises not only in Hungary, but in every country where a government and the parties behind it and the legislature face unpopular decisions. I will therefore put the questions in a general way, not one confined to a Hungarian context, and then try to answer them in line with my conscience.

If politicians defy resistance from the majority of the public, swimming against the tide, is this not a return to the Messianic approach of ideological dictators? Is this permissible in a democracy? Can a reform be applied without consensus, or, to use a narrower criterion, without approval from the majority of the public at the time?[86] I believe it is permissible, but only if several conditions are strictly met:

1. The government in all conscience must be convinced there is no alternative. There is an inescapable need for the regulations, although they are opposed by the majority of the public.
2. The government is obliged to remain within the bounds of the constitutional, democratic system of law. This is not self-evident, because the situation, the knowledge that there is a 'state of emergency', may tempt a committed group of reformers to resort to unconstitutional, dictatorial methods.[87]
3. The governing group must make a sincere commitment to subordinate itself unconditionally to the judgment of the public at the next elections. Furthermore, there must be political power relations and institutional guarantees that leave no room for

doubt about the freedom and cleanliness of the next elections. In that case through the elections the public can express retrospectively whether it approves or rejects what the government and parliamentary majority have done without widespread support.

Political direction that is ready to go against the stream and commit itself to unpopular measures, but subordinates itself to these conditions, is acknowledged as 'leadership' in American political jargon. Although I know this kind of reform without consensus departs from the usual 'popularity-maximizing' behavior of many politicians in mature parliamentary democracies, I do not think it can be called anti-democratic in a normative sense, so long as the conditions mentioned are strictly met. Indeed there are difficult situations that require this kind of determined political behavior, and the present Hungarian situation happens to be just such a one.

4. Three scenarios

At the time of writing there is no way of predicting which way Hungary is bound. Several eventualities can be envisaged. I will confine myself here to outlining three clearly defined scenarios.

First scenario: return to the policy of muddling through. After a time, the present government or a reshuffled version of it returns to the well-trodden road. Substantial concessions are made to mass pressure, the stabilization program is toned down and the pace of implementation slowed. Actions urgent from the economic point of view are further delayed. The reduction of state paternalism stalls at its present level. The government resigns itself to a slow rate of growth or even stagnation. With luck the policy does not end in catastrophe. (The bounds of this scenario are exceeded if it does.) It is not impossible to imagine that the policy of muddling through could be continued for a good while after 1995, although it will lose the country its chance of achieving rapid and lasting growth.

There are many forces working to persuade those in power to abandon the course taken in the spring of 1995 and return to the old road. Apart from the ingrained Hungarian habits of decades, parliamentary democracy entices politicians to behave in this way.

It is worth recalling here the example of the United States. American democracy has proved incapable of coping with certain fundamental economic problems, such as the federal budget deficit or health-care reform, because politicians have been unwilling to perform unpopular tasks, especially swift and radical solutions to them. If this is the case in the most mature democracy of all, it is hardly surprising to find the same behavior in several half-mature Eastern European democracies. The experience of several countries shows that the more the political scene fragments and the less the long-term rule of some political grouping becomes institutionalized, the less inclined is the prevailing government to take unpopular actions with a slow political return. Anticipation of political defeat in the foreseeable future is no incentive to embark on altruistic reforms with long-term prospects that entail thinking ahead over decades. Politicians are even more inclined than the general public to think in terms of the well-known Keynesian formula: 'In the long run we are all dead.'

Second scenario: perseverance and political downfall. The present government perseveres with the strict principles of the stabilization program and is ready to carry it out consistently, but fails to obtain the political support to do so. The resistance steadily grows, manifesting itself, perhaps, in a wave of strikes that paralyses the economy or mass protest of other kinds. This further damages the economic situation, making even stricter measures necessary, so that society enters a self-destructive spiral of restriction and resistance. On reaching a critical point, the process leads to the political downfall of the present government policy.

It is not worthwhile in this study to speculate on when and how this might happen. Would it come in 1998, at the next general elections? Or could it occur earlier, when the government parties' members desert them on a critical vote? I do not even include the possibility that the upheaval might bring down parliamentary democracy as well as the government, because I do not think there is a realistic danger of this happening in present-day Hungary.[88]

If the government, adhering to the stabilization program, succumbs politically, its successor is quite likely (though not sure) to adopt a different policy. It may return to the old Hungarian road of muddling through, for instance, or embark on a yet more perilous populist, adventurist policy, but this again points beyond the second scenario.

All who take an active part in the stabilization program, and all who support it in Hungary or abroad, must realize that the program's political downfall cannot be excluded.[89]

Third scenario: Success after delay. Within this scenario there is a variety of alternatives. One is that savage, unpopular stabilization reforms have succeeded in a number of autocratic countries.[90] Protest was met with repression. Sooner or later, the economic results of the reforms arrived, and because there was no more protest, there was no more need for repression. The governments of such countries did not take on the inconveniences of democracy and freedom of speech and association until the reassuring economic results had been obtained. Often cited examples are South Korea, Taiwan and Chile.

There is much debate among analysts of post-socialist transition about what was and what may be the best order in which to take political reform that leads to democracy and economic reform that leads to a market economy.[91] It certainly seems that if political reform is completed sooner or goes faster than economic reform, great political problems posed by the unpopular elements of economic transformation have to be faced.[92] many draw from this is that it was unfortunate to rush the democracy. It would have been better to follow the Chinese strategy of entering a path of fast growth and rising living standards first.

I cannot agree. To my mind, democracy has intrinsic value, a greater and more fundamental value than anything else. Despite the economic troubles and the inconveniences of democracy, I rate Hungary's firm parliamentary democracy as a great achievement. Luckily it rules out the course of suppressing protest by force. So let us confine ourselves to a third scenario in which the events occur in a democratic framework.

It is not unrealistic, in the knowledge of Hungarian conditions, to hope for a relatively favorable succession of events. The government may manage to explain better why and how the stabilization program serves the public's interests. The resistance may not be so vehement. The storm of initial protest may blow itself out and patience come to prevail. The not too distant future may bring favorable trends in the living standards of broad groups in the population, so that the atmosphere improves.

The word 'may' makes the uncertainty plain. Much depends on how the stabilization program's active participants behave, from government, parliament, political parties and interest groups, to employers and employees.

I do not see it as my task to weigh the chances for the three scenarios and the various intermediate and mixed cases, or put subjective odds on the alternatives. I would like to hope that the third scenario prevails, but I am ready to support the stabilization program even if the second scenario threatens. I am convinced that the good of present and future Hungarian generations requires us to find a new road that ensures lasting development.

Notes

1. Reprinted from *Social Research*, Vol. 63, No. 4, Winter 1996, pp. 943–1040. The paper was also published in János Kornai: *Struggle and Hope. Essays on Stabilization and Reform in a Post-socialist Economy*, Cheltenham, UK and Northampton, MA, USA: Edward Elgar, pp. 121–180.
2. My research was supported by the Hungarian National Scientific Research Foundation (OTKA), by Collegium Budapest, Institute for Advanced Study and by the World Bank. Among those with whom I consulted during the research were László Akar, Zsolt Ámon, Rudolf Andorka, Francis Bator, Tamás Bauer, Lajos Bokros, Katalin Bossányi, Michael Bruno, Richard Cooper, Zsuzsa Dániel, Tibor Erdős, Endre Gács, Alan Gelb, Béla Greskovits, Stanley Fischer, Eszter Hamza, György Kopits, Álmos Kovács, Judit Neményi, András Simonovits, Robert Solow, György Surányi, Katalin Szabó, Márton Tardos and László Urbán, all of whom I thank for their valuable comments. My thanks also go to Mária Kovács for helping with the research, to Brian McLean for the excellent translation of the original Hungarian text, and to Julianna Parti for editing it.
3. Yugoslavia set about dismantling the command economy before Hungary did, and in this sense the reform process has a longer history there. Slovenia is the only successor state of former Yugoslavia where the change of political system has been uninterrupted. Ruptures have occurred in all the others due to the conflicts and wars between successor states or ethnic groups.
4. The study is not intended to cover all the essential themes of the Hungarian reform and transformation. Several very important questions are mentioned only in passing or not at all (like inflation, or joining the European Union).
5. There were tumultuous events in East Berlin in 1953 and in Poland in 1956. The peaceful Prague Spring of 1968 was terminated by the tanks of the Warsaw pact. Yet Hungary was the only country where an armed uprising had led to the collapse of the single-party political organization and the formation of a multi-party coalition, even if only for a few days.
6. Based on the verdicts of the courts, 123 death sentences were carried out in reprisals after the 1848–49 Revolution and War of

Independence, 65 after the defeat of the communist regime of 1919, and 189 for fascist acts during the Second World War. See Szakolczai (1994), p. 239.

7. For the history of the taxi-drivers' blockade, see Bozóki and Kovács (1991), Kurtán, Sándor and Vass (1991), and Rockenbauer (1991).

8. See Kornai (1972) and Krugman (1994). The latter uses the expression 'hidden deficit' on pp. 161–9.

9. It is well known from the literature on the subject that the situation is different with state debt incurred to domestic creditors. At the time of repayment, the Hungarian creditors entitled to installments and interest will receive money at the expense of Hungarian citizens paying tax at that time. Here there is a continual redistribution taking place within the Hungarian public, and it does not necessarily entail the dilemma of 'consume now, pay later' for society as a whole.

10. In periods when a populist government ruled in certain Latin American countries, a tendency for the exchange rate to appreciate was apparent in every case.

11. Determining the desirable proportion of investment is one of central issues in growth theory. Its size depends, among other factors, on the period in which consumption is to be maximized and how steep the economy's growth path is to be.
    A satisfactory conclusion has yet to be reached; there is still no theoretical consensus on the problem. Rather than becoming embroiled in a theoretical debate at this juncture, I have chosen a means of expression to which less exception may be taken. All I say is that 'modest' growth would be absolutely necessary. This would seem to suffice for the line of argument in this study, since it allows an idea of the problem of 'investment postponement' to be conveyed.

12. The fall in the proportion of investment would have been justified from an economic point of view if it had coincided with a rise in the efficiency of investment. Unfortunately this was not the case. On the contrary, a great many very costly investment projects of low efficiency were carried out.

13. The average annual number of dwellings removed in the 1991–3 period fell to a quarter of the figure for the period 1976–80 (see Central Statistical Office, 1994b, p. 25).

14. To give a single example, the sum spent on research and development in 1993, at constant prices, was less than a third of the maximum level of such spending in 1987. As a proportion of GDP, the

sum fell from 2.32 per cent to 1.01 per cent (Central Statistical Office, 1989, p. 13 and 1994c, p. 13).

15. I will exemplify the vast scale of such postponed commitments with a single piece of data, the calculation made by the World Bank of the size of Hungary's 'pension debt'. This is the name given to the discounted present value of all pensions to be paid in the future under the laws and regulations that currently apply. It emerged that the pension debt is equivalent to 263 per cent of 1994 GDP. Similar calculations were made recently for seven OECD countries, of which Italy had the highest 'pension debt'. The Hungarian figure is close to the Italian one. See World Bank (1995a), p. 36 and (1995b), p. 127. The idea that the state's 'pension debt' is part of the hidden debt was first suggested by Martin Feldstein.

16. The three items just discussed do not cover the *whole* social debt, which has other components as well. Examples include postponed environmental-protection tasks or postponed repair of environmental damage.

17. The well-known argument for a gradualist transformation over a long period is that if the steady development bears fruit soon enough, it will gain the reform supporters, who will back subsequent, less pleasant measures of reform as well (Roland, 1994a). This really applied initially; the 'golden age' of 1966–75 provided the moral capital for later reform. But in this sense Hungary's early start with reform becomes a drawback. Depletion of the initial moral capital began early as well, and it had largely run out by the time the change of political system arrived.

18. One of the fundamental arguments of the 'big-bang' supporters is that if the 'window of opportunity' opens, you have to reach in. See the account of the debate by Gérard Roland (1994a).

19. In a book I wrote in 1989, before the free elections (Kornai, 1990 [1989]), I recommended to the future Hungarian parliament and government a radical surgery for stabilization and liberalization, similar in many ways to Poland's. This was to cover, among other things, various unpopular measures, including a rise in tax revenues, an end to the budget deficit and strict control on wages. With this part of my proposals I was left more or less isolated; most tone-setting economists in the democratic parties, which were still in opposition, rejected them. The search for popularity and fear of upheaval characteristic of the previous period were deeply embedded in the economists' profession.

The new government's first finance minister, Ferenc Rabár, was prepared to draw up a radical package of stabilization and liberalization
measures. This radicalism of his, along with other conflicts, meant
he soon had to resign.

20. See Bozóki (1994), Bozóki and Sükösd (1992), Dornbusch and
    Edwards (1990), Greskovits (1994), Hausner (1992) and Kaufman
    and Stallings (1991)

21. This also distinguishes the situation from that in Latin America,
    where some countries undergo a cycle of events. Populism rules for
    a time and then falls, but may well return to power later.

22. For a comparison and statistical analysis of welfare spending in
    Hungary and in the OECD countries, see Tóth's article (1994).

23. I call the Hungarian welfare state premature because in my view,
    given the country's medium level of development, serious fiscal
    problems and extremely high level of taxation, it cannot allow itself
    to take on such a burden of state redistribution. Some economists and
    sociologists specializing in welfare issues take just the opposite
    view, for instance Kowalik (1992) and Ferge (1994), arguing that
    because the problems caused by the transition are so grave, these
    post-socialist countries cannot afford not to make great social trans-
    fers.

24. The statement does not apply in reverse. Not all developed countries
    have high proportions of welfare spending. It is notably low, for
    instance, in the United States and Japan. See Tóth (1994).

25. These trends do not apply to the development of the housing sector.
    There the steady rise in the proportion of private building entailed a
    relative reduction in the role of bureaucratic-paternalist distribution.

26. This connection is well known from the literature on the financial
    crises and stabilization attempts of the developing countries: the dis-
    tributive demands push up the budget deficit, thereby contributing to
    inflation and other financial tensions. See Haggard and Kaufman
    (1992a), pp. 273–5.

27. This is not specific to the period of post-socialist transition.
    Governments everywhere use compensation designed to ease restric-
    tive measures of stabilization as a means of dispelling protest (see
    Nelson, 1988).

28. To quote Iván Szabó, the last finance minister of the 1990-94 coali-
    tion government, which described itself as moderately right-wing
    conservative: 'It is strange, but it was a social democratic, rather than

a conservative program that we carried out at the time' (Szabó, 1995, p. 15). On another occasion Szabó remarked that 'over-consumption occurred in the country by comparison with the level of income, of GDP attained. This was the sacrifice the government made for the sake of political stability in the country' (Szabó, 1994, p. 16).

29. Of the analyses of the Hungarian macroeconomic situation, I would emphasize Antal (1994), Békesi (1993, 1994 and 1995), Csaba (1995), Erdős (1994), Köves (1995a and 1995b), Lányi (1994–5), Oblath (1995), and World Bank (1995b).

 For the view of those directing the stabilization program, see Bokros (1995a, 1995b and 1996), and Surányi (1995a, 1995b and 1996).

30. The program's macroeconomic results are undoubtedly remarkable. In 1995, as compared with 1994, the deficit on the current account and the General Finances Statistics (GFS) budget deficit—as a percentage of GDP—decreased by 4 and 3.4 percentage points respectively. What happened in Hungary was clearly an export-led adjustment: the decrease in final consumption was accompanied by a considerable expansion of exports, allowing for some growth in aggregate demand. Thus the external financial and debt crisis was avoided without a recession, and GDP grew by 1.5 per cent in 1995. However, the country had to pay a high price. Inflation speeded up by about 10 percentage points, and real wages decreased by 12.2 per cent. See also Kornai (1996).

31. What made the 12 March stabilization program so urgent were the threats to Hungary on the international financial market. In so far as the program averted a credit crisis and its concomitant catastrophic effects, the present generation is already reaping the benefits, of course. The consumption sacrifice averts the threat of a much deeper fall in consumption.

32. See Gombár (1995), Kéri (1994) and Lengyel (1995).

33. On the political and sociological background of the 1994 elections see Ágh (1995), Gazsó and Stumpf (1995), and Sükösd (1995).

34. Miklós Horthy was the Head of State during the right-wing, ultra-conservative regime in the period 1919–44.

35. On the coalition formed in 1994, see Kis (1994) and Körösényi (1995).

36. This took place much later in all other socialist countries except Yugoslavia.

37. Like many other authors, I made a terminological distinction between the two phases in my earlier writings, notably in my 1992

book The Socialist System. The first I called a 'reform' (as it was directed at modifying the socialist system) and the second a 'post-socialist transition'. I have to concede, however, that in daily political language and professional parlance, the changes since 1990 are called a reform as well.

38. The debate was initially confined almost exclusively to the normative plane: recommendation against recommendation. Later came the first theoretical models. A survey of the debate appears in Funke (1993). Among the participants in the debate at the beginning of the 1990s whose views he sums up are Rudiger Dornbusch, Stanley Fischer, Alan Gelb, Cheryl W. Gray, Michael Hinds, David Lipton, Ronald J. McKinnon, Domenico Nuti, Gérard Roland, Jeffrey Sachs and Horst Sieberst. For a survey of political-economy arguments in the debate see Roland (1994a). A few examples of theoretical models are Aghion and Blanchard (1993), Dewatripont and Roland (1992) and Murrell and Wang (1993).

39. See Sachs (1990 and 1993), and Lipton and Sachs (1990).

40. The study by Brabant (1993) convincingly explains how far from apposite these established expressions are.

41. See Murrell (1990). One of the intellectual sources of the argument was conservative philosophy, for instance Burke (1982) [1790], and other evolutionary theories in economics, for instance Nelson and Winter (1982).

42. I myself would place in this category my first work on the subject of post-socialist transition (Kornai 1990 [1989]), where I recommended a rapid transformation for macro stabilization and liberalization and gradual transformation for privatization and other aspects of social transformation.

43. See Roland (1994b), for instance.

44. See, for example, Brabant (1993), Portes (1994) and Rosati (1994).

45. Limitations of space prevent me from analyzing developments in property relations in the agricultural cooperatives, although they played an important part in the socialist system. They closely resembled the state-owned enterprises. For the same reason I do not cover the privatization of state farms or of state (or local-government) owned housing either.

46. See Kornai (1986).

47. See Szelényi (1994). See also Kende (1994) and Szalai (1994). Nagy (1994a) analyses how the old party elite has developed into the new élite.

48. I spoke out against the idea of free distribution in my book (Kornai, 1990 [1989]). Most Hungarian economists agreed, at least tacitly, and proposals for free distribution were only sporadic, see, for instance, Siklaky (1989). Though espoused briefly, at first by one opposition party and later in the government as well, the idea never gained conviction. Many Western economists, on the other hand, including notable figures like Milton Friedman and Harold Demsetz, recommended rapid, free distribution. The idea was taken up by many economists in several post-socialist countries, notably Poland, Czechoslovakia and Russia.

49. The main exceptions need mentioning. (i) Those deprived of property under the previous regimes or persecuted for their political convictions, religious or ethnic affiliations or class status have received compensation in the form of a special voucher entitling them to modest amounts of state property free of charge. Redemption of these 'compensation vouchers' has been protracted and is far from over. (ii) The law stipulates that specified state property shall be transferred free of charge to the social-insurance system. Partial implementation of this recently began. Ultimately, these exceptions have had little effect on how property relations develop.

50. On Czech privatization see Dlouhý and Mládek (1994) and Federal Ministry of Finance (1992), and on Russian, Boycko, Shleifer and Vishny (1995), these authors being advocates of free distribution. From more critical authors who were not active in initiating or implementing the privatization campaign, see Brom and Orenstein (1994), Hillion and Young (1995) and Stark and Bruszt (1995) in the case of Czech experience, and for analysis of the Russian situation, see Ash and Hare (1994), Bornstein (1994), Nelson and Kuzes (1994), Rutland (1994) and Slider (1994).

51. Of the literature on privatization in Hungary, I would single out Bossányi (1995), Major and Mihályi (1994), Mihályi (1993 and 1994), Mizsei (1992) and Voszka (1992, 1993 and 1994).

52. See Mihályi (1995).

53. According to Crane, based on information provided by the Hungarian privatization agency, 'Over 85 per cent of Hungary's productive capital stock should be in private hands by the end of 1997.' See Crane (1996), p. 14.

54. Official Czech reports suggest the proportion of the former state-owned enterprise sector 'privatized' has risen to about two-thirds

through coupon privatization. However, a majority of the shares have passed from the original coupon-holders into the hands of a few investment funds, where the large state-owned banks wield great influence among the owners (see Portes, 1994, pp. 1186–7 and the study by Stark and Bruszt, 1995). Most privatized firms are heavily in debt to the state-owned banks. So if real bankruptcy proceedings were applied, most of their property would revert to the state. The question is whether genuine private ownership prevails where the primary distribution of property transfers a nominal title of ownership to private citizens, but the state's partial property rights remain in an indirect form. This example shows how superficial it is to describe the state of privatization by a single aggregate percentage.

55. See Stark (1994).
56. See Murrell (1992).
57. See Bossányi (1995).
58. To give an indication of its size, it exceeds Hungary's total investment in 1994.
59. See Stark (1990).
60. According to a survey in 1994, 50 per cent of the adult population thought privatization should be speeded up or continue at the same pace, but 50 per cent thought it should be slowed or halted altogether. See Lengyel (1994), p. 98.
61. See Kornai (1986, 1990 [1989] and 1992a).
62. See Gábor (1979 and 1985), Laky (1984) and Seleny (1993).
63. The extremely rapid growth of self-employment owes partly to the fact the tax burden is lighter on these earnings than on the wages paid to employees.
64. See Árvay and Vértes (1994) and Lackó (1995).
65. Central Statistical Office (1996a), p. 141.
66. *Ibid.*
67. Reform socialist China deserves a special note. The absolute quantity of foreign direct investment entering China is several times as great as Hungary's. However, using relative indices (for example, investment/GDP or investment/per capita GDP), investment in Hungary is still much greater than in China.
68. According to the data supplied by the Hungarian Privatization Agency, the cumulative total through 1994 was US$ 7956 million, which is significantly higher than the figure in Table 17, compiled by an international agency. In 1995 the total increased by the huge

amount of US$ 4570 million (communication by the National Bank of Hungary), giving a cumulative total of US$ 12 526 million for 1990–95.

69. Another important factor is that Hungary has always been an utterly reliable, punctual debtor, never requesting a moratorium on or rescheduling of its debts. This is reassuring to foreign investors.

70. For a numerical presentation of the process of price and import liberalization, see Tables 4, 5 and 6 in Kornai (1995).

71. Several Hungarian economists criticized that the import liberalization as being too fast, particularly in view ofthe failure to implement a drastic devaluation or impose stronger tariff protection at the same time. International experience with import liberalization does not contain an example of application of such an 'own-goal' policy, in which unilateral, radical liberalization was applied without replacing the effect of the administrative restrictions with tariffs, and/or a strong devaluation. See Gács (1994), Köves et al. (1993), Nagy (1994b), and Oblath (1991).

72. Foreign tourists are surprised, for instance, by the 'wild capitalism' practised by taxi-drivers. Unlike most Western cities, Budapest has no clearly regulated system of taxi fares.

73. On the emergence and problems of interest conciliation in Hungary see Greskovits's (1995) instructive analysis.

74. Some years ago an Israeli economist echoed the debate between Stalin and Trotsky in the ironical title of an article: 'Can Socialism Be Built in Half a Country?' The reference is to the trade-union control over half the economy. Though not in a fully developed form, a similar problem has arisen in Hungary.
On the negative effects of the Israeli economy's corporatist features, see Murphy (1993).

75. A survey of the new Western trends in positive political economy is given in Alt and Shepsle (1990).

76. The trend known in Western literature for the last couple of decades as political economy, which examines the interaction of politics and economic policy, has few exponents in Hungary or the post-socialist region as a whole. (The old expression 'pol-econ' denoted a different trend subscribing to Marxist-Leninist doctrine.)
Pioneering work in applying political economy in the modern, Western sense to Hungary was done by Greskovits (1993a,1993b and 1994). I would also like to mention the writings of Bruszt (1992 and 1994a).

77. 'Economic blueprints that treat politics as nothing but an extraneous nuisance are just bad economics', writes Przeworski (1993), p. 134.
78. According to demographic data, Hungarian men who were 50 in 1970 had a further life expectancy of 23 years (Central Statistical Office 1994b, p. 37).
79. 1. To 1944: nationalist-conservative, semi-authoritarian Horthy system. 2. 1944: Occupation by Hitler's army; reign of terror under Hungarian Nazis. 3. 1945 onwards: expulsion of Hitler's army and Hungarian Nazis by Soviet army; beginning of Soviet occupation; formation of multi-party, democratic coalition. 4. 1948 onwards: other parties ousted by communists; Stalinist dictatorship established. 5. 23 October 1956: revolution; formation of multi-party revolutionary government. 6. 4 November 1956 onwards: revolution crushed by Soviet army; Kádár regime takes power, brutally repressive initially, but steadily 'softening' and commencing reforms. 7. 1989–90: collapse of communist system; formation of parties, free elections, formation of new parliament and government.
80. Americans, Britons and Australians contemporary with A underwent no change of regime. These were not changes of the kind occurring in the United States when the Democrats replace the Republicans, or Labor the Tories in Britain. Hungary underwent traumatic changes of regime six times, causing deep upheavals in society.
81. I put this question from the single angle of intergenerational choice, assuming that both individuals' living standard represented the national average. I left open the question of welfare distribution in the period concerned. There will clearly be relative winners and losers within the same age group as well.
82. For a splendid survey of the debate on welfare judgments, social preferences, social choice and public choice, see Sen (1995).
83. For example, in earlier or present, more up-to-date versions of the various 'golden-rule' models. See, for instance, Blanchard and Fischer (1989).
84. See Barro (1974).
85. Greskovits, (1993b and 1994), aptly describes the type of leader engaged in this as suffering from the 'reformer's loneliness'.
86. 'Reform without consensus' is what the study by Sachs (1994) calls the situation just described. I agree with the view expressed here, that the situation is acceptable temporarily, under certain conditions, for want of a better course.

87. I urge the government to be forceful, decisive and consistent, but nothing is further from my intentions than to recommend disregard for the democratic rule of law and constitutionalism. Anyone who reads this into my study or any of my earlier writings misunderstands my position. Unfortunately such a misunderstanding has already occurred. See, for instance, the article by Elliott and Dowlah (1993).

88. However, I cannot exclude this eventuality under similar circumstances in some other post-socialist countries, where parliamentary democracy is less firmly founded than in Hungary.

89. Many foreign observers take too little account in their calculations of this political risk. I consider this especially dangerous and maybe damaging in the case of those whose positions may give them influence over events in Hungary; for instance, those who participate in decisions relating to Hungary in foreign governments or international organizations. It depends on them as well whether the threat to Hungary described in the second scenario is averted. A breakdown of political stability would pull the rug from under economic stabilization, not to mention the direct economic damage caused by radical forms of mass protest.

90. See Collier (1979), Evans (1979), Haggard (1990), Haggard and Kaufman (1989), and Waterbury (1989).

91. See, for instance, Haggard and Kaufman (1992b), pp. 332–42.

92. A few works from the rich body of writing that covers the chances and consequences of autocracy and democracy during the post-socialist transition are: Bruszt (1994a and 1994b), Bunce and Csanádi (1992), Greskovits (1994), Offe (1991) and Przeworski (1991).

REFERENCES

Ágh, Attila (1995), 'Magyar politika jövője' (The Future of Hungarian Politics), *Mozgó Világ*, 21 (2), pp. 17-28.

Aghion, Philippe and Blanchard, Olivier Jean (1993) 'On the Speed of Transition in Central Europe,' *Working Paper*, no. 6, London: European Bank for Reconstruction and Development.

Alt, James E. and Shepsle, Kenneth A. (eds) (1990), *Perspectives on positive political economy*. Cambridge: Cambridge University Press.

Andorka, Rudolf (1994), 'Elégedetlenség, elidegenedés, anómia' (Dissatisfaction, Alienation and Anomie) in István György Tóth (ed.) *Társadalmi átalakulás: 1992-94. Jelentés a Magyar Háztartás Panel III. hullámának eredményeiről* (Social Transformation, 1992-94. Report on the Results of the Third Phase of the Hungarian Household Panel), Műhelytanulmányok, no. 5, Budapest: BKE, KSH, TÁRKI, pp. 83-90.

Antal, László (1994), 'Az örökség. A gazdaság helyzete és a feladatok' (The Legacy. The Situation of the Economy and the Tasks), *Társadalmi Szemle*, 49 (10), pp. 12-21.

Árvay, János and Vértes, András (1994), *A magánszektor és a rejtett gazdaság súlya Magyarországon, 1980-92. Összefoglaló* (The Share of the Private Sector and Hidden Economy in Hungary. Summary). Budapest: Gazdaságkutató Rt.

Ash, Timothy N. and Hare, Paul G. (1994), 'Privatisation in the Russian Federation: Changing Enterprise Behaviour in the Transition Period,' *Cambridge Journal of Economics*, 18 (4), pp. 619-34.

Barro, Robert J. (1974), 'Are Government Bonds Net Wealth?,' *Journal of Political Economy*, 82 (6), pp. 1095-117.

Békesi, László (1993), 'A feladat öt szöglete. Farkas Zoltán interjúja Békesi Lászlóval' (The Five Angles of the Task. An

Interview with László Békesi by Zoltán Farkas), *Társadalmi Szemle*, 48 (3), pp. 3-13.

Békesi, László (1994) 'A társadalom még nincs tisztában a gazdasági helyzettel. Karsai Gábor interjúja Békesi Lászlóval' (The Society is not Aware of the Economic Situation Yet. An Interview with László Békesi by Gábor Karsai), *Figyelő*, July 14, pp. 13-5.

Békesi, László, (1995), 'Mást választhatunk, de "jobbat" aligha' (A Different Program Can Be Chosen, But a 'Better' One Hardly), *Népszabadság*, July 8, pp. 17-8.

Blanchard, Olivier Jean and Fischer, Stanley (1989), *Lectures on macroeconomics*. Cambridge: The MIT Press.

Bokros, Lajos (1995a) 'A leendő pénzügyminiszter huszonöt pontja. Bokros Lajos szakmai cselekvési programjának alapvonalai' (The Twenty Five Points of the Future Minister of Finance. The Fundamental Ideas of Lajos Bokros' Action Programme), *Népszabadság*, February 17, p. 15.

Bokros, Lajos (1995b), 'Az államháztartásról, a stabilizációról. Dr. Bokros Lajos pénzügyminiszter tájékoztatója' (On the State Budget and Stabilization. An Exposition by Dr. Lajos Bokros, the Finance Minister), *Pénzügyi Szemle*, 40 (4), pp. 259-62.

Bokros, Lajos (1996) 'Növekekés és/vagy egyensúly—avagy az 1995. március 12-én meghirdetett stabilizáció tanulságai' (Growth and/or Stabilization—Lessons from the Stabilization Program Announced on March 12, 1995), *Népszabadság*, March 11, p. 8.

Bornstein, Morris (1994), 'Russia's Mass Privatisation Programme,' *Communist Economies and Economic Transformation*, 6 (4), pp. 419-57.

Bossányi, Katalin (1995), 'Aki kapja, marja' (Whoever can seize it, he takes it), *Népszabadság*, Oct. 7, pp. 17 and 21.

Boycko, Maxim; Shleifer, Andrei and Vishny, Robert (1995), *Privatizing Russia*, Cambridge: The MIT Press.

Bozóki, András (1994), 'Vázlat három populizmusról: Egyesült Államok, Argentína és Magyarország' (A Draft of Three Examples of Populism: The United States, Argentina and Hungary), *Politikatudományi Szemle*, 3 (3), pp. 33-68.

Bozóki, András and Kovács, Éva (1991), Politikai pártok megnyilvánulásai a sajtóban a taxisblokád idején' (Statements in the Press by the Political Parties during the Taxi Drivers' Blockade), *Szociológiai Szemle*, no.1, pp. 109–26.

Bozóki, András and Sükösd, Miklós (1992), 'Civil társadalom és populizmus a kelet-európai demokratikus átmenetekben' (Civil Society and Populism in the Process of Democratic Transitions of Eastern Europe), *Mozgó Világ*, 18 (8), pp. 100–12.

Brabant, Jozef M. van (1993), 'Lessons from the Wholesale Transformation in the East,' *Comparative Economic Studies*, 35 (4), pp. 73–102.

Brom, Karla and Orenstein, Mitchell (1994), 'The Privatised Sector in the Czech Republic: Government and Bank Control in a Transitional Economy,' *Europe-Asia Studies*, 46 (6), pp. 893–928.

Bruszt, László (1992), 'Transformative Politics: Social Costs and Social Peace in East Central Europe,' *East European Politics and Societies*, 6 (1), pp. 55–72.

Bruszt, László (1994a), 'Reforming Alliences: Labour, Management, and State Bureaucracy in Hungary's Economic Transition,' *Acta Oeconomica*, 46 (3/4), pp. 313–32.

Bruszt László (1994b), 'Az Antall-kormány és a gazdasági érdekképviseletek' (The Antall Government and the Organizations Representing Economic Interests), in *Kormány a mérlegen, 1990–94* (Appeasing the Government, 1990–94). Eds.: Csaba Gombár, Elemér Hankiss, László Lengyel and Györgyi Várnai. Budapest: Korridor Politikai Kutatások Központja, pp. 208–30.

Bunce, Valerie and Csanádi, Mária (1992), 'The Systematic Analysis of a Non-System. Post-Communism in Eastern Europe,' in *Flying blind: Emerging democracies in East-Central Europe*. Ed.: György Szoboszlai. Budapest: Magyar Politikatudományi Társaság. Évkönyv, pp. 177–203.

Burke, Edmund (1982) [1790], *Reflections on the revolution in France*. London: Pinquin Classics.

Central Statistical Office (1971), *Statisztikai évkönyv 1970* (Statistical Yearbook 1970), Budapest: Központi Statisztikai Hivatal.

Central Statistical Office (1974), *Statisztikai évkönyv 1973* (Statistical Yearbook 1973), Budapest: Központi Statisztikai Hivatal.

Central Statistical Office (1976), *Statisztikai évkönyv 1975* (Statistical Yearbook 1975), Budapest: Központi Statisztikai Hivatal.

Central Statistical Office (1981), *Statisztikai évkönyv 1980* (Statistical Yearbook 1980), Budapest: Központi Statisztikai Hivatal.

Central Statistical Office (1986), *Statisztikai évkönyv 1985* (Statistical Yearbook 1985), Budapest: Központi Statisztikai Hivatal.

Central Statistical Office (1989), *Tudományos kutatás és kísérleti fejlesztés 1988* (Scientific Research and Experimental Development 1988), Budapest: Központi Statisztikai Hivatal.

Central Statistical Office (1991), *Magyar statisztikai évkönyv 1990* (Hungarian Statistical Yearbook 1990), Budapest: Központi Statisztikai Hivatal.

Central Statistical Office (1994a), *Magyar statisztikai zsebkönyv 1993* (Hungarian Statistical Pocket Book 1993), Budapest: Központi Statisztikai Hivatal.

Central Statistical Office (1994b), *Magyar statisztikai évkönyv 1993* (Hungarian Statistical Yearbook 1993), Budapest: Központi Statisztikai Hivatal.

Central Statistical Office (1994c), *Tudományos kutatás és kísérleti fejlesztés 1993* (Scientific Research and Experimental Development 1993), Budapest: Központi Statisztikai Hivatal.

Central Statistical Office (1994d), *Lakásstatisztikai évkönyv 1993* (Yearbook of Housing Statistics 1993), Budapest: Központi Statisztikai Hivatal.

Central Statistical Office (1994e), *Statisztikai Havi Közlemények* (Monthly Statistical Bulletins), No.12.

Central Statistical Office (1995a), *Magyar statisztikai zsebkönyv 1994* (Hungarian Statistical Pocket Book 1994), Budapest: Központi Statisztikai Hivatal.

Central Statistical Office (1995b), *Magyar statisztikai évkönyv 1994* (Hungarian Statistical Yearbook 1994), Budapest: Központi Statisztikai Hivatal.

Central Statistical Office (1996a), *Magyar statisztikai zsebkönyv 1995* (Hungarian Statistical Pocket Book 1995), Budapest: Központi Statisztikai Hivatal.

Central Statistical Office (1996b), *Statisztikai Havi Közlemények* (Monthly Statistical Bulletins), No.5.

Collier, David (ed.) (1979), *The new authoritarianism in Latin America*. Princeton: Princeton University Press.

Csaba, László (1996), 'Gazdaságstratégia helyett konjunktúra-politika' (Trade-Cycle Policy Instead of Economic Strategy), *Külgazdaság*, 39 (3), pp. 36–46.

Dewatripont, Mathias and Roland, Gérard (1992), 'The Virtues of Gradualism and Legitimacy in the Transition to a Market Economy,' *The Economic Journal*, 102 (411), pp. 291–300.

Dlouhý, Vladimír and Mládek, Jan (1949), 'Privatization and Corporate Control in the Czech Republic,' *Economic Policy*, Supplement, no.19, pp. 156–70.

Dornbusch, Rudiger and Edwards, Sebastian (1990), 'The Macroeconomics of Populism in Latin America,' *Journal of Development Economics*, 32 (2), pp. 247–77.

Elliott, John E. and Dowlah, Abu F. (1993), 'Transition Crises in the Post-Soviet Era,' *Journal of Economic Issues*, 27 (2), pp. 527–35.

Erdős, Tibor (1994), 'A tartós gazdasági növekedés realitásai és akadályai' (The Realities of Lasting Economic Growth and Obstacles to It), *Közgazdasági Szemle*, 41 (6), pp. 463–77.

Evans, Peter (1979), *Dependent development: The alliance of multinational, state, and local capital in Brazil*. Princeton: Princeton University Press.

Federal Ministry of Finance (Prague) (1992), 'Coupon Privatization: An Information Handbook,' *Eastern European Economics*, 30 (4), pp. 5–38.

Ferge, Zsuzsa (1994), 'Szabadság és biztonság' (Freedom and Security), *Esély*, no. 5, pp. 2–24.

Funke, Norbert (1993), 'Timing and Sequencing of Reforms: Competing Views and the Role of Credibility,' *Kyklos*, 46 (3), pp. 337–62.

Gábor, R. István (1979), 'The Second (Secondary) Economy. Earning Activity and Regrouping of Income Outside the Socially Organized Production and Distribution,' *Acta Oeconomica*, 22 (3/4), pp. 291–311.

Gábor, R. István (1985), 'The Major Domains of the Second Economy,' in Péter Galasi and György Sziráczky (eds), *Labour market and second economy in Hungary,*. Frankfurt and New York: Campus.

Gács, János (1994), 'Trade Liberalization in the CSFR, Hungary, and Poland: Rush and Reconsideration,' in János Gács and Georg Winckler (eds), *International trade and restructuring in Eastern Europe,* Laxenburg: IIASA and Physica-Verlag, pp. 123–51.

Gazsó, Ferenc and Stumpf, István (1995), 'Pártok és szavazóbázisok két választás után' (Parties and Constituencies after Two Elections), *Társadalmi Szemle*, 50 (6), pp. 3–17.

Gombár, Csaba (1995), 'Száz nap, vagy amit akartok' (One Hundred Days or Whatever You Want), in Csaba Gombár, Elemér Hankiss, László Lengyel and Györgyi Várnai (eds), *Kérdőjelek: a magyar kormány 1994–95* (Inquiry: The Hungarian Government, 1994–95), Budapest: Korridor Politikai Kutatások Központja, pp. 235–59.

Greskovits, Béla (1993a), 'Dominant Economy, Subordinated Politics. The Absence of Economic Populism in the Transition of East Central Europe,' *Working Paper Series*, no. 1, Budapest: The Central European University, Political Science Department.

Greskovits, Béla (1993b), 'The 'Loneliness' of the Economic Policy Maker. An Approach Based on Reviewing the Literature on the Politics of Economic Transition in LDCs, and East Central Europe.' Paper presented at the Radziejowice workshop of the Polish Academy of Sciences on 'Institutionalizing Social Transformations'.

Greskovits, Béla (1994), A tiltakozás és türelem politikai gazdaságtanáról. Latin-Amerika és Közép-Kelet-Európa átalakulásának tapasztalatai alapján (On the political economy of protest and patience. The experience of Central Eastern Europe and Latin America). Manuscript. Budapest: Közép-Európai Egyetem, Politikai Tudományok Tanszéke.

Greskovits, Béla (1995), 'Demokrácia – szegény országban' (Democracy – in a Poor Country), *Társadalmi Szemle*, (50) (5), pp. 3–23.

Haggard, Stephan (1990), *Pathways from the periphery. The politics of growth in the newly industrializing countries*. Ithaca and London: Cornell University Press.

Haggard, Stephan and Kaufman Robert R. (1992b), 'Economic Adjustment and the Prospects for Democracy,' in Haggard, Stephan and Kaufman Robert R. (eds) *The politics of economic adjustment*, Princeton: Princeton University Press, pp. 319–50.

Haggard, Stephan and Kaufman, Robert R. (1989), 'Economic Adjustment in New Democracies,' in Joan M. Nelson and contributors *Fragile coalitions: The politics of economic adjustment*. New Brunswick and Oxford: Transaction Books, pp. 57–78.

Haggard, Stephan and Kaufman, Robert R. (1992), 'The Political Economy of Inflation and Stabilization in Middle-Income Countries,' in (eds) *The politics of economic adjustment*, Princeton: Princeton University Press, pp. 271–315.

Hausner, Jerzy (1992), 'Populist Threat in Transformation of Socialist Society,' *Economic and Social Policy*, No. 29, Warsaw: Friedrich Ebert Foundation in Poland.

Hillion, Pierre and Young, S. David (1995), 'The Czechoslovak Privatization Auction: An Empirical Investigation,' manuscript. INSEAD, May.

Hungarian Government (1994), *A Magyar Köztársaság Kormányának privatizációs stratégiája* (The Privatization Strategy of the Government of the Hungarian Republic), Budapest Magyar Köztársaság Kormánya, November.

Kaufman, Robert R. and Stallings, Barbara (1991), 'The Political Economy of Latin American Populism', in Rudiger Dornbusch and Sebastian Edwards (eds), *The macroeconomics of populism in Latin America*, Chicago and London: The University of Chicago Press, pp. 15–34.

Kende, Péter (1994), 'Politikai kultúra, civil társadalom és elit az 1988 utáni Magyarországon' (Political Culture, Civil Society and Elite in Hungary after 1988), in *Miért nincs rend Kelet-Közép Európában?* (Why is there no order in East Central Europe). Budapest: Osiris and Századvég, pp. 244–357.

Kéri, László (1994), 'Mari néni, a száz nap, meg az egyszerű nép' (Aunt Mary, The One Hundred Days and the People) *Népszabadság*, October 24, p. 13.

Kis, János (1994), 'Veszélyből esély – Kis János a koalícióról' (A Chance Arising out of Danger – János Kis on the Coalition), *168 óra*, 14 June, p. 7.

Kornai, János (1972), *Rush versus harmonic growth*, Amsterdam: North-Holland.

Kornai, János (1986), 'The Hungarian Reform Process: Visions, Hopes and Reality,' *Journal of Economic Literature*, 24 (4), pp. 1687–737.

Kornai, János (1990) [1989], *The road to a free economy. Shifting from a socialist system: The example of Hungary*. New York: W. W. Norton and Budapest: HVG Kiadó.

Kornai, János (1992a), 'The Principles of Privatization in Eastern Europe', *De Economist*, 140 (2), pp. 153–176.

Kornai, János (1992b), *The Socialist System. The Political Economy of Communism*. Princeton: Princeton University Press and Oxford: Oxford University Press.

Kornai, János (1995), 'Eliminating the Shortage Economy. A General Analysis and Examination of the Developments in Hungary' in *Struggle and Hope*, Cheltenham: Edward Elgar, forthcoming.

Kornai, János (1996), 'Adjustment without Recession. A Case Study of Hungarian Stabilization', in *Struggle and Hope,* Cheltenham:Edward Elgar, forthcoming.

Körösényi, András (1995), 'Kényszerkoalíció vagy természetes szövetség' (Forced Coalition or Natural Alliance), in Csaba Gombár, Elemér Hankiss, László Lengyel and Györgyi Várnai (eds), *Kérdőjelek: a magyar kormány 1994–95* (Inquiry: The Hungarian Government: 1994–95), Budapest: Korridor Politikai Kutatások Központja, pp. 260–80.

Köves, András (1995a), 'Egy alternatív gazdaságpolitika szükségessége és lehetősége' (The Necessity and Scope for an Alternative Economic Policy), *Külgazdaság*, 39 (6), pp. 4–17.

Köves, András (1995b), 'Gazdaságpolitikai dilemmák és lehetőségek a Bokros-csomag után' (Economic Policy Dilemmas and Potentials after the Bokros Package), *Külgazdaság*, 39 (11), pp. 4–18

Köves, András; Lányi, Kamilla and Oblath, Gábor, *et al.* (1993), 'Az exportorientált gazdaságpolitika feltételei és eszközei 1993-ban' (The Conditions and Means of the Export Oriented Economic Policy), *Külgazdaság*, 37 (5), pp. 4–22.

Kowalik, Tadeusz (1992), 'Can Poland Afford a Swedish Model? Social Contract as the Basis for Systemic Transformation'. Paper presented at the conference on 'Post-Socialism: Problems and Prospects,' Ambleside, Cumbria, July 3–6, manuscript.

Krugman, Paul (1994), *Peddling prosperity. Economic sense and nonsense in the age of diminished expectations.* New York and London: W. W. Norton and Company.

Kurtán, Sándor; Sándor, Péter and Vass, László (eds) (1991), *Magyarország politikai évkönyve 1991* (Political Yearbook of Hungary, 1991). Budapest: Ökonómia Alapítvány and Economix Rt.

Labour Research Institute (1994), *Munkaerőpiaci helyzetjelentés. A munkaerő-piac keresletét és kínálatát alakító folyamatok.* (Report on the Labour Market: The Processes Shaping Demand and Supply on the Labour Market), Budapest: Munkaügyi Kutatóintézet, April.

Lackó, Mária (1995), 'Hungarian Hidden Economy in International Comparison—Estimation Method Based on Household Electricity Consumption and Currency Ratio,' paper presented at the conference 'Hungary: Towards a Market Economy,' Oct. 20–21, 1995, Budapest, Discussion Paper Series, No. 25, Budapest: Institute of Economics.

Laky, Teréz (1984), 'Mítoszok és valóság: Kisvállalkozások Magyarországon' (Myth and Reality: Small Enterprises in Hungary), *Valóság*, 27 (1), pp. 1-17.

Laky, Teréz (1995), 'A magángazdaság kialakulása és a foglalkoztatottság' (Development of the Private Economy and Employment), *Közgazdasági Szemle*, 42 (7/8), pp. 685–709.

Lányi, Kamilla (1994-95), 'Alkalmazkodás és gazdasági visszaesés Magyarországon és más országokban. I. Tények és magyarázatok. II. Gazdaságpolitika és szelekció' (Adjustment and Economic Recession in Hungary and in Other Countries. I. Facts and Explanations. II. Economic Policy and Selection), *Társadalmi Szemle*, 49 (12), pp. 13–25. and 50 (1), pp. 3–19.

Lengyel, György (1994), 'Vélemények a gazdaságról' (Opinions on the Economy), in István György Tóth (ed), *Társadalmi átalakulás: 1992–94. Jelentés a Magyar Háztartás Panel III. hullámának eredményeiről* (Social transformation, 1992–94. Report on the results of the third phase of the Hungarian household panel survey), Magyar Háztartás Panel, Műhelytanulmányok, no. 5, Budapest: BKE, KSH, TÁRKI, pp. 83-90 and 91–9.

Lengyel, László (1995), 'Egérfogó' (Mousetrap), in Csaba Gombár, Elemér Hankiss, László Lengyel and Györgyi Várnai (eds), *Kérdőjelek: a magyar kormány 1994–95* (Inquiry: The Hungarian Government, 1994–95), Budapest: Korridor Politikai Kutatások Központja, pp. 13–49.

Lindbeck, Assar (1990), '*The Swedish Experience*,' paper presented at the OECD Conference on the Transition to Market Economies in Central and Eastern Europe, November 28–30, Paris, Seminar Paper no. 482, Stockholm: Institute for International Economic Studies, December.

Lipton, David and Sachs, Jeffrey (1990), 'Creating a Market Economy in Eastern Europe: The Case of Poland,' *Brookings Papers on Economic Activity*, no. 1, pp. 75–145.

Major, Iván and Mihályi, Péter (1994), 'Privatizáció – hogyan tovább?' (Privatization – How to Go Further?), *Közgazdasági Szemle*, 41 (3), pp. 214–28.

Mihályi, Péter (1993), 'Plunder – Squander – Plunder. The Strange Demise of State Ownership,' *The Hungarian Quarterly*, 34 (Summer), pp. 62–75.

Mihályi, Péter (1994), 'Privatization in Hungary: An Overview,' in Yilmaz Akyüz, Detlef J. Kotte, András Köves and László Szamuely (eds), *Privatization in the transition process. Recent experiences in Eastern Europe,* Geneva: UNCTAD and Budapest: Kopint-Datorg, pp. 363–85.

Mihályi, Péter (1995), 'Privatisation in Hungary: Now Comes the 'Hard Core',' paper presented at the Fifth World Congress for Central and East European Studies, Warsawa, Aug. 6–11, mimeo.

Ministry of Finance (1996), *Tájékoztató az 1995. évi és az 1996. év eleji gazdasági folyamatokról* (Report on the Economic Processes in 1995 and at the Beginning of 1996). Budapest: Pénzügyminisztérium, March.

Mizsei, Kálmán (1992), 'Privatisation in Eastern Europe: A Comparative Study of Poland and Hungary,' *Soviet Studies*, 44 (2), pp. 283–96.

Murphy, Emma (1993), 'Israel,' in Tim Niblock and Emma Murphy (eds), *Economic and political liberalization in the Middle East,* London and New York: British Academic Press.

Murrel, Peter (1992), 'Evolutionary and Radical Approaches to Economic Reform,' *Economics of Planning*, 25 (1), pp. 79–95.

Murrell, Peter (1990), 'An Evolutionary Perspective on Reform of the Eastern European Economies,' manuscript, College Park: University of Maryland.

Murrell, Peter and Wang, Yijiang (1993), 'When Privatization Should Be Delayed: The Effect of Communist Legacies on Organizational and Institutional Reforms,' *Journal of Comparative Economics*, 17 (2), pp. 385–406.

Nagy, András (1994a), 'Transition and Institutional Change,' *Structural Change and Economic Dynamics*, 5 (2), pp. 315–27.

Nagy, András (1994b), 'Import Liberalization in Hungary,' *Acta Oeconomica*, 46 (1/2), pp. 1–26.

National Bank of Hungary (1994), *Annual Report 1993*, Budapest: National Bank of Hungary.

National Bank of Hungary (1995), *Annual Report 1994*, Budapest: National Bank of Hungary.

Nelson, Joan (1988), 'The Political Economy of Stabilization: Commitment, Capacity and Public Response,' in Robert H. Bates (ed.), *Toward a Political Economy of Development: A Rational Choice Perspective*, Berkeley: University of California Press.

Nelson, Lynn D. and Kuzes, Irina Y. (1994), 'Evaluating the Russian Voucher Privatization Program,' *Comparative Economic Studies*, 36 (1), pp. 55–67.

Nelson, Richard R. and Winter, Sidney (1982), *An Evolutionary Theory of Economic Change*, Cambridge: Harvard University Press.

Oblath, Gábor (1991), 'A magyarországi importliberalizálás korlátai, sikerei és kérdőjelei' (The Limits, Successes and Questions of Import Liberalization in Hungary), *Külgazdaság*, 35 (5), pp. 4–13.

Oblath, Gábor (1995), 'A költségvetési deficit makrogazdasági hatásai Magyarországon' (The Macroeconomic Effects of Budget Deficit in Hungary) *Külgazdaság*, 39 (7/8), pp. 22–33.

Offe, Claus (1991), 'Capitalism by Democratic Design? Democratic Theory Facing the Triple Transition in East Central Europe,' *Social Research*, 58 (4), pp. 864-902..

Portes, Richard (1994), 'Transformation Traps,' *The Economic Journal*, 104 (426), pp. 1178–89.

Przeworski, Adam (1991), *Democracy and the Market: Political and Economic Reforms in Eastern Europe and Latin America. Studies in Rationality and Social Change.* Cambridge: Cambridge University Press.

Przeworski, Adam (1993), 'Economic Reforms, Public Opinion, and Political Institutions: Poland in the Eastern European Perspective,' in Luiz Carlos Bresser Pereira, José María Maravall and Adam Przeworski (eds), *Economic Reforms in New Democracies: A Social-Democratic Approach,* Cambridge: Cambridge University Press, pp. 132–98.

Rockenbauer, Zoltán (1991), 'Társadalmi ünnepek, tüntetések és sztrájkok az 1990-es esztendőben' (National Holidays, Demonstrations and Strikes in 1990), in Sándor Kurtán, Péter Sándor and László Vass (eds), *Magyarország politikai évkönyve 1991* (Political Yearbook of Hungary), Budapest: Ökonómia Alapítvány and Economix Rt., pp. 213–9.

Roland, Gérard (1994a),'The Role of Political Constraints in Transitions Strategies,' *Economics of Transition,* 2 (1), pp. 27–41.

Roland, Gérard (1994b), 'On the Speed and Sequencing of Privatisation and Restructuring,' *The Economic Journal,* 104 (426), pp. 1158–68.

Rosati, Dariusz K. (1994), 'Output Decline during Transition from Plan to Market: A Reconsideration,' *The Economics of Transition,* 2 (4), pp. 419–41.

Rutland, Peter (1994), 'Privatisation in Russia: One Step Forward: Two Steps Back?,' *Europe-Asia Studies,* 46 (7), pp. 1109–31.

Sachs, Jeffrey (1990), 'What is to Be Done?,' *The Economist,* January 13, pp. 19–24.

Sachs, Jeffrey (1993), *Poland's Jump to the Market Economy.* Cambridge and London: The MIT Press.

Sachs, Jeffrey (1994), 'Life in the Economic Emergency Room,' in John Williamson (ed.), *The political economy of policy reform,* Washington, D.C.: Institute for International Economics, pp. 503–23.

Seleny, Anna (1993), 'The Long Transformation: Hungarian Socialism, 1949–89'. Manuscript. Cambridge: Department of Political Science, MIT.

Sen, Amartya (1995), 'Rationality and Social Choice,' *American Economic Review*, 85 (1), pp. 1–24.

Siklaky, István (1989), 'Perújrafelvétel az állami tulajdon ügyében' (Retrial for the Case of the State-Ownership), *Magyar Nemzet*, July 11, p. 5.

Slider, Darrell (1994), 'Privatization in Russia's Regions,' *Post-Soviet Affairs*, 10 (4), pp. 367–96.

Stark, David (1990), 'Privatization in Hungary: From Plan to Market or From Plan to Clan?,' *East European Politics and Societies*, 4 (3), pp.351-92.

Stark, David (1994), 'Recombinant Property in East European Capitalism,' *Public Lecture Series*, No. 8, Budapest: Collegium Budapest, Institute for Advanced Study, December.

Stark, David and Bruszt, László (1995), 'Network Properties of Assets and Liabilities: Patterns of Inter-Enterprise Ownership in the Postsocialist Transformation,' Paper presented at the Workshop on 'Dynamics of Industrial Transformation: East Central European and East Asian Comparisons,' Budapest: Budapest University of Economics, May.

Sükösd, Mihály (1995), '1995: az identitás gondjai' (1995: The Problems of Identity), *Mozgó Világ*, 21 (2), pp. 29–33.

Surányi György (1996), 'Jobban igen, másként nem. Szombati MH-extra Surányi Györggyel, a Magyar Nemzeti Bank elnökével. Pintér Dezső riportja' (It Can Be Done Better, but not in Other Ways. A Saturday Interview of 'Magyar Hírlap' with György Surányi, the President of the Hungarian National Bank. An Interview by Dezső Pintér), *Magyar Hírlap*, January 6, p. 9.

Surányi, György (1995a), 'A gazdaság örökölt struktúrái gúzsba kötik az országot. Válaszol Surányi György, a Nemzeti Bank elnöke' (The Inherited Economic Structures Shackle the Country. György Surányi, the President of the National Bank Answers), *Heti Világgazdaság*, April 29, pp. 47–48.

Surányi, György (1995b), 'Önmagunkkal kell megállapodásra jutni. Beszélgetés árakról, bérekről, kamatokról Surányi Györggyel, az MNB elnökével. Bossányi Katalin interjúja' (It is Ourselves we Have to Come to an Agreement with. A Conversation about Prices, Wages and Interest Rates with György Surányi, President of the National Bank. An Interview by Katalin Bossányi), *Népszabadság*, December 30, pp. 1 and 10.

Szabó, Iván (1994), 'Minden a mézeshetekben dől el' (Everything Depends on the Honeymoon). An interview by György Varga. *Figyelő*, May 26, pp. 16–7.

Szabó, Iván (1995), *168 óra*, March 7, 7 (9), p. 15.

Szakolczai, Attila (1994), 'A forradalmat követő megtorlás során kivégzettekről' (On Those Executed during the Reprisals Following the Revolution), in János Bak, *et al*. (eds), *Évkönyv III, 1956* (Yearbook III, 1956), Budapest: 1956-os Intézet, pp. 237–56.

Szalai, Erzsébet (1994), 'Az elitek metamorfózisa' (The Metamorphosis of Elites), *Magyar Hírlap*, September 14.

Szelényi, Iván (1994), 'Circulation of Elites in Post-Communist Transitions,' *Working Paper Series*, No. 3, University of Michigan, Advanced Study Center, International Institute, August.

Tóth, István György (1994), 'A jóléti rendszer az átmenet időszakában' (The Welfare System in the Transition Period), *Közgazgasági Szemle*, 49 (3), pp. 313–40.

United Nations, Economic Commission for Europe (1993), *Economic Bulletin for Europe 1992*. Vol. 44,. New York: UN ECE.

United Nations, Economic Commission for Europe (1994a), *Economic Survey of Europe in 1993–94*. New York and Geneva: UN ECE.

United Nations, Economic Commission for Europe (1994b), *Economic Bulletin for Europe 1994*. Vol. *46*. New York and Geneva: UN ECE.

United Nations, Economic Commission for Europe (1995), *Economic Survey of Europe in 1994–95*. New York and Geneva: UN ECE.

Vanicsek, Mária (1995), 'A privatizált társaságok hatékonysága' (The Efficiency of the Privatized Companies), *Figyelő* January 26, pp. VI–VII.

Voszka, Éva (1992), 'Not Even the Contrary is True: The Transfigurations of Centralization and Decentralization,' *Acta Oeconomica*, 44 (1/2), pp. 77–94.

Voszka, Éva (1993), 'Variations on the Theme of Self-Privatization,' *Acta Oeconomica*, 45 (3/4), pp. 310–8.

Voszka, Éva (1994), '*Centralization, Renationalization, Redistribution: The Role of the Government in Changing the Ownership Structure in Hungary, 1989–93*,' Discussion Paper, No. 916, London: Centre for Economic Policy Research, February.

Waterbury, John (1989), 'The Political Management of Economic Adjustment and Reform,' in Joan M. Nelson and contributors, *Fragile coalitions: The politics of economic adjustment*, New Brunswick and Oxford: Transaction Books, 1989, pp. 39–56.

World Bank (1995a), *Hungary: Structural reforms for sustainable growth*. First draft. Document of the World Bank, Country Operations Division, Central Europe Department, Report No. 13577-HU, Washington DC: World Bank, February 10.

World Bank (1995b), *Hungary: Structural reforms for sustainable growth*. Document of the World Bank, Country Operations Division, Central Europe Department, Report No. 13577-HU, Washington DC: World Bank, June 12.

World Bank (1995c), *World Tables 1995*. Washington DC: World Bank.

World Economy Research Institute (1994), Warsaw School of Economics. *Poland, International Economic Report 1993–94.* Warsaw, WERI.

Chapter III

Adjustment without Recession:
A Case Study of Hungarian Stabilization[1]

I. INTRODUCTION[2]

On 12 March 1995, Hungary's government and central bank announced a tough program of adjustment and stabilization. (I shall refer to this by the abbreviation ASP 95.)[3] At the time of writing (June 1996) the process of implementing the program has been taking place for 15 months. This study is an attempt to assess and take stock of its results so far.

The terms 'adjustment and stabilization' are applied to economic-policy programs of many different kinds. Along with other components, they usually include measures to reduce inflation. This, however, was not the case with the Hungarian program, which belongs to a class designed mainly to overcome serious current-account and budget disequilibria and avert an external and internal debt crisis.

Fifteen months is a short time. So caution and moderation are called for in applauding the program's early successes, because they could easily slip from our grasp. Indeed, it would be more accurate to entitle the study 'adjustment without recession *so far*',[4] With this warning in mind, it is worthwhile to start to assess the developments up to June 1996.[5] I shall concentrate mainly on experiences that point beyond the specific case of Hungary and may be instructive elsewhere.

The study has the following structure. Section II considers the program's results so far and the costs and sacrifices entailed in applying it. Section III examines the instruments the program employs and the extent to which they can still be used in the future. Finally, Section IV assesses the tasks ahead, the threats to what has been achieved so far, and the prospects for Hungary's development.

II. ACHIEVEMENTS AND COSTS

The main macroeconomic indices appear in *Table 1*. I shall return to these subsequently.

1. Avoiding imminent catastrophe

Many favorable developments have occurred in the post-socialist Hungarian economy of the 1990s. To mention some of the most important ones, liberalization of prices and foreign trade is essentially complete, huge numbers of private firms have been founded, strides have been made in privatizing state-owned enterprises, massive structural transformation has occurred in the composition of production, and foreign trade has been adjusted to conditions after the collapse of Comecon. In 1994, GDP started to grow again, after the deep transformational recession resulting from the change of course in 1990.

However, the developments in Hungary had some disquieting features as well. The socialist system had bequeathed the country a dire macroeconomic heritage, above all a very high foreign debt. In this respect the starting point for the Hungarian economy was worse than for most other post-socialist economies. There were many difficult tasks that the government in office in 1990–94 failed to perform, and the succeeding government, which took office in 1994, vacillated for several months before acting. By 1993, the current-account deficit had already reached 9.0 per cent of GDP. When this recurred in the following year, at 9.5 per cent, there was a real danger that the external finances of the country would get into serious trouble. Partly tied up with this there was a mounting budget deficit, which reached 8.2 per cent of GDP in 1994, according to the national accounts.[6, 7]

Table 1: Macroeconomic indicators in Hungary, 1993–95

	Indicator	1993	1994	1995
1.	GDP (annual growth rate, %)	-0.6	2.9	1.5[a]
2.	GDP per capita (USD)[b]	3745	4,061	4,273
3.	Household consumption (annual growth rate, %)[c]	1.9	-0.2	-6.6[a]
4.	Gross fixed investments (annual growth rate, %)	2.0	12.5	4.3[a]
5.	Exports (annual volume indices)[d]	-13.1	16.6	8.4
6.	Imports (annual volume indices)[d]	20.9	14.5	-3.9
7.	Trade balance (USD mn)[e]	-3267	-3635	-2442
8.	Balance on current account (USD mn)	-3455	-3911	-2480
9.	Net convertible currency debt (USD mn)[f]	14927	18936	16817
10.	Convertible-currency reserves (percentage of annual imports on current account)[f]	59.4	60.2	78.8
11.	Unemployment rate[g] (%)	12.1	10.4	10.4
12.	Employment[h] (employees in percentage of population)	42.2	40.2	39.5
13.	Balance of general government (GFS balance,[i] percentage of GDP)	-5.2	-7.6	-3.6
14.	Inflation (annual consumer-price index)	22.5	18.8	28.2
15.	Gross average earnings[j] (annual growth rate, %)	21.9	24.9	16.8
16.	Net average earnings[j] (annual growth rate, %)	17.7	27.3	12.6
17.	Real wage per wage-earner (annual growth rate, %)	-3.9	7.2	-12.2

Sources: Rows 1-10: Central Statistical Office (1996d) Pages according to rows: 224, 223, 224, 276, 276. 324, 324, 325, 324-25; *Row 11*: National Bank of Hungary (1996a), p. 57, Row 12: Central Statistical Office (1995a), pp. 4-5; *Row 13*: National Bank of Hungary (1996c); Rows 14-17: see Rows 1-10, pages respectively: 313, 75, 77, 86
Notes: [a] Preliminary data.

[b] Converted from Hungarian forints by the annual average of the official commercial exchange rate.

[c] Actual final consumption of GDP by households.

d Export and import data are based on customs statistics. The import data include 1993 arms imports from Russia in repayment of earlier debt.
e Trade-related payments on the current account.
f On 31 December.
g End-year registered unemployed as a percentage of the active (employed and unemployed) population in the previous year.
h On 1 January.
i For more detailed fiscal data and explanations, see Table 4.
j Gross average earnings of full-time employees; 1993-4 indices are calculated from data on organizations with over 20 employees, 1995 indices from data on those with over 10 employees.

The equilibrium problems caused the rise in external and internal debt to accelerate. The growing costs of servicing this debt raised the current-account and budget deficits even more, so that further loans had to be raised to cover them. In the winter of 1994-5 the international financial world, on seeing the unfavorable financial macro indicators, began to lose confidence in Hungary, which had hitherto been a favorite in Eastern Europe for always paying its debts on time. The process I have outlined is well known to be self-propelling. The decline in Hungary's image became manifest in worse credit conditions, which pushed the country even closer to a debt spiral.

In another study of mine[8] I analyzed the historical, political and social reasons why successive governments wavered, why they protracted and postponed the increasingly inevitable radical measures. I shall not repeat these here. Furthermore, only future historians, looking behind the political scenes, will be able to discover what combination of effects eventually brought to an end the habitual conduct of decades, the policy of muddling through. A big part in steeling the Hungarian government to take radical action was certainly played by the deterrent lesson of the Mexican crisis in January 1996. It made oppressive reading to see the guesswork in the international financial press—Which country was going to follow Mexico?—and find Hungary named as prime candidate.

What began in Hungary in March 1995 was *preventive* therapy. Its most important result was to avert a catastrophe that *would* have ensued if the program of adjustment and stabilization had not been initiated. This point I try to convey in *Table 2*, which compares the courses of events in Mexico and Hungary, and *Table 3*, which features the course of crises in some other countries and shows episodes inherently resembling the situation in Hungary before ASP 95.[9]

I would not like to take the analogy too far. Each country has a history that is individual and, strictly speaking, unique. Still, there are some major similarities between the developments in Hungary and the episodes in the other countries featured in *Tables 2* and *3*.[10]

1. Each country suffered adverse phenomena in its trade, with imports running away by comparison with exports. In addition, the trade imbalance led to problems on the current account.
2. In some countries listed, the situation was worsened by the budget deficit.
3. Several analysts believe that one cause of the problems, perhaps the chief one, was the rise in the real exchange rate, and as a result the overvaluation of the domestic currency.
4. The countries had attracted large amounts of credit and investment in various forms; each had long been attractive to lenders and investors, on whose confidence the country's financial situation came greatly to depend.

These are the *antecedents* I would like to underline. They are the respects in which events in Hungary and the other countries in the tables resemble each other. There the similarity ends, however. For the catastrophe that overtook the others *did not occur in Hungary*.

Table 2: Macroeconomic indicators: Hungary compared with Mexico

Indicators	Mexico		Hungary	
	1994	1995	1994	1995
1. GDP (annual growth rate, %)	4.5	-6.2	2.9	1.5
2. Real private consumption (annual growth rate, %)[b]	3.7	-12.9	-0.2	-6.6
3. Industrial production (annual growth rate, %)	4.8	-7.5	9.6	4.8
4. Employment in manufacturing (annual change in number of employees, %)[c]	1.0	-2.9	-9.1	-5.3
5. Real earnings (annual growth rate, %)[d]	4.1	-12.4	7.2	-12.2
6. Inflation[e]	7.1	51.9	18.8	28.2
7. Balance on current account/GDP (%)	-7.8	-0.3	-9.5	-5.4[a]
8. Net external debt/GDP (%)[f]	32.2	36.1	45.9	38.4

Sources: Mexico: The data were collected or calculated by Miguel Messmacher, from the following sources: Rows 1, 3 and 4: 1994: Banco de Mexico (1996), p. f, Tables II-16, II-3 and II-9; *Row 2*: OECD (1996), Table 3; *Row 5*: OECD (1997), p. 58; *Row 6*: Banco de Mexico (1996), Table III-1; *Row 7*: International Monetary Fund (1997), pp. 426-29 and Banco de Mexico (1996), Table IV-1b; *Row 8*: International Monetary Fund (1997), pp. 426-29, 1994: Mexican Ministry of Finance (1995), 1995: Mexican Ministry of Finance (1996). Hungary: Rows 1-2: as for Rows 1 and 3 of Table 1; *Row 3*: Central Statistical Office (1996c), p. 8; Row 4: 1994: Central Statistical Office (1995b), p. 143; 1995: National Bank of Hungary (1996b), p. 56; *Row 5*: as for Row 17 of Table 1; *Row 6*: as for Row 14 of Table 1; Rows 7 and 8: National Bank of Hungary (1996c).

Notes:[a] Preliminary data.

[b] For Hungary actual final consumption of GDP by households.

[c] December/December for Mexico. For Hungary average number of employees; the Hungarian 1995 figure refers to firms with more than 10 employees. Total national unemployment and employment data for Mexico, statistically comparable to the Hungarian data, are not available. For the Hungarian figures see Table 6.1, Rows 11 and 12, which show that the increase of manufacturing unemployment was associated with decreases in other sectors since total employment and the national unemployment rate remained almost unchanged. There is no available information about changes across sectors in Mexico.

d For Mexico, real monthly earnings in manufacturing. For Hungary, real wage per wage earner (see Note j in Table 6.1).

e December/December for Mexico.

f Net external debt for Mexico includes public debt only, for Hungary it includes both public and private foreign debt.

Table 3, A-E
Episodes of crisis and adjustment
in selected Latin American countries

General explanation of the tables.

Year 0 is chosen to be the one with the largest current-account deficit during the period. This year is indicated for each country in the third column. The countries are listed in descending order according to the size of the largest GDP decline. (Chile is first with 14.1 per cent in 1982.) This order is retained in all the tables. The tables were compiled by Miguel Messmacher.

Table 3a: Annual growth rates of GDP (%) (growth positive, decline negative)

Country	Worst current-account deficit	Year of adjust-ment	-4	-3	-2	-1	0	1	2	3	4
Chile	1981	1982	9.9	8.2	8.3	7.8	5.5	-14.1	-0.7	6.4	2.5
Costa Rica	1981	1981	8.9	6.3	4.9	0.8	-2.3	-7.3	2.9	8.0	0.7
Argentina	1981	1981[a]	6.2	-3.3	7.3	1.5	-5.7	-3.1	3.7	1.8	-6.6
Brazil	1982	1983[a]	5.0	6.8	9.1	-4.4	0.6	-2.9	5.4	7.9	7.5
Mexico	1981	1982	3.4	8.3	9.2	8.3	7.9	-0.6	-4.2	3.6	2.6

Source: International Monetary Fund (1995), respective country tables.

Note: a Indicates the year of devaluation.

Table 3b: Current-account balance/GDP (%) (deficit negative, surplus positive)

Country	Worst current-account deficit	Year of adjustment	-4	-3	-2	-1	0	1	2	3	4
Chile	1981	1982	-5.3	-7.1	-5.7	-7.1	-14.5	-9.5	-5.7	-11.0	-8.6
Costa Rica	1981	1981	-7.5	-10.3	-13.8	-13.7	-15.6	-10.4	-9.9	-6.9	-7.4
Argentina	1981	1981[a]	3.2	2.8	-0.5	-2.3	-2.8	-2.8	-2.3	-2.1	-1.1
Brazil	1982	1983[a]	-3.5	-4.8	-5.5	-4.5	-5.9	-3.5	0.0	-0.1	-2.0
Mexico	1981	1982	-2.2	-3.0	-4.0	-5.4	-6.5	-3.4	3.9	2.4	0.4

Sources: International Monetary Fund (1995), pp. 154–5 and respective country pages. For Mexico, 1977–8: World Bank (1995c), pp. 464–6.
Note: [a] Indicates the year of devaluation.

Table 3c: Growth rates of real exchange rates (%) (appreciation negative, depreciation positive)

Country	Worst current-account deficit	Year of adjust-ment	-4	-3	-2	-1	0	1	2	3	4
Chile	1981	1982	-10.6	-6.7	-4.2	-16.0	-7.9	81.9	-3.4	27.4	13.6
Costa Rica	1981	1981	2.2	0.9	2.3	-4.1	239.3	-37.5	-16.3	2.6	1.2
Argentina	1981	1981[a]	-16.0	-34.4	-30.8	-30.4	96.2	168.6	11.4	10.3	-39.9
Brazil	1982	1983[a]	1.1	48.2	-4.4	4.7	6.2	66.0	13.8	4.1	-40.9
Mexico	1981	1982	-5.9	-7.4	-6.9	-10.8	-3.3	96.5	-14.8	-12.3	22.2

Source: International Monetary Fund (1995), respective country tables.

Notes: [a] Indicates the year of devaluation.

Growth rate of real exchange rates =

(1 + rate of change at nominal exchange rate) x (1 + US inflation)/(1 + domestic inflation).

Table 3d: Inflation rate (%) (average annual change of the consumer price index, increase positive)

Country	Worst current-account deficit	Year of adjust-ment	-4	-3	-2	-1	0	1	2	3	4
Chile	1981	1982	91.1	40.1	33.4	35.1	19.7	9.9	27.3	19.9	30.7
Costa Rica	1981	1981	4.2	6.7	8.7	18.4	36.9	89.4	3.0	11.8	15.1
Argentina	1981	1981[a]	176.0	175.5	159.5	100.8	104.5	164.8	343.8	626.7	672.1
Brazil	1982	1983[a]	38.7	52.7	82.8	105.6	97.8	142.1	197.0	226.9	145.2
Mexico	1981	1982	29.0	16.2	20.0	29.8	28.7	98.8	80.8	59.2	63.7

Source: International Monetary Fund (1995), pp. 122–3.
Note: [a] Indicates the year of devaluation.

Table 3e: Annual change in private consumption (%) (growth positive, decline negative)

Country	Worst current-account deficit	Year of adjustment	-4	-3	-2	-1	0	1	2	3	4
Chile	1981	1982	16.6	9.8	14.2	14.4	15.5	-35.6	-8.1	25.2	-5.6
Costa Rica	1981	1981	11.9	9.1	2.0	-2.5	-3.1	-7.9	3.7	7.5	3.1
Argentina[b]	1981	1981[a]	2.5	-1.4	14.0	8.0	-3.8	-6.2	4.1	3.8	-6.8
Brazil	1982	1983[a]	2.3	9.6	6.6	-4.2	3.9	0.7	5.2	2.7	6.8
Mexico	1981	1982	0.3	9.3	9.9	9.4	8.3	-6.5	-7.0	4.4	4.1

Source: World Bank (1995c), pp. 12–13 and 104–5.
Notes: [a] Indicates the year of devaluation.
   [b] In Argentina's case, total consumption.

Though the course of each was different, almost every episode of crisis was typically a cumulative process. These are events similar to fire breaking out in a crowded hall: panic spreads, and everyone rushes for the narrow doorway, meanwhile trampling on each other and blocking the exit.[11] In financial crises, people rush in alarm to withdraw their money and try to get rid of their investments, causing tumultuous capital flight. It is the panic that accelerates and reinforces the crisis, which is why the collapse is so sudden. This panic is what Hungary managed to avoid.[12]

When catastrophe ensues, the most dramatic consequence is the serious fall in production that occurs in a short time, and the concomitant abrupt rise in unemployment (see Tables 2 and 3). This is the brutal process that reduces domestic absorption through a rapid contraction in aggregate demand and rectifies the disproportion between absorption and production. The preventive ASP 95 allowed (or more cautiously, has so far allowed) Hungary to avoid this calamity of recession. It would have been particularly painful in Hungary's case, because the country has still not recovered from the problems caused by the transformational recession after 1990. If Table 1 is compared with Tables 2 and 3, it can be seen that Hungary's production in 1995, far from sinking, even rose to a modest extent, while unemployment remained basically unchanged instead of making a jump.

Hungarian and foreign economists conversant with the history of crises and stabilization efforts have expressed respect for this achievement, but not the Hungarian public, even though it is the greatest success scored by ASP 95. For the man in the street, there is no sense of accomplishment in having averted a catastrophe outside his experience. Indeed some have been irresponsible enough to suggest it would have been better if Hungary had shared Mexico's fate. In the end, runs the argument, the country would have been forgiven its debts and been pulled out of the mire, just as the United States, other developed countries and the international financial institutions rescued Mexico.[13] Apart from the grave doubts about how much help a far more distant Hungary could have expected from the United States, Mexico still paid a dreadful price for the catastrophe, in spite of the help it received.

2. Starting to adjust the macroeconomic proportions

Apart from having short-term preventive effects, ASP 95 has already begun, in several essential ways, to rectify the macroeconomic disproportions that were the deep underlying cause of potential catastrophe. It is hoped that ASP will have beneficial effects in the medium and long term as well. Let me draw attention to the following changes, which were presented numerically in Table 1:

1. The most important change in the current-account deficit, which had remained obstinately at a very high level for two years. It was substantially lower in 1995 than in 1994, its proportion of GDP falling by four percentage points. The net debt/GDP ratio shows significant improvement (see Table 2, Rows 7 and 8).[14]
2. The volume of exports, which had already grown substantially in the previous year, rose by a further 8.4 per cent in 1995. Thus ASP 95 can really count as an export-led adjustment. Meanwhile the volume of imports, having risen appreciably in the previous year, fell by 3.9 per cent (see Table 1).
3. A contraction occurred in domestic absorption, but as I mentioned, without a fall in production, which rose somewhat. This was made possible by the change in proportions itself. On the demand side, there was a rise in the proportion of exports and investment, while that of consumption fell. On the supply side, the proportion of domestic production rose and that of imports fell. This is shown in *Figures 1* and *2*.
4. The budget deficit (GFS balance,[15] in percentage of GDP) has been reduced by 4.0 percentage points.

5.   The profitability of the business sector rose, on average from
     3.8 per cent to 8.2 per cent.[16] The profits of profitable firms
     increased and the losses of loss-makers decreased. The state
     budget's share of total credit placement fell and the share of
     business rose. These circumstances all helped to raise the busi-
     ness sector's prospects of growth.

ASP 95 increased the financial world's confidence in Hungary.
The credit ratings began to rise again, and the barriers to Hungarian
borrowing were removed. The papers of consequence in the world
and the big banks involved in Eastern European investment and
lending gave the program a positive assessment. A credit agreement was finally reached with the IMF and Hungary admitted into
the OECD. These two events put an official seal of approval on
Hungary's improved scores.

3. The price of adjustment

A heavy price had to be paid for adjusting the macroeconomic processes. *Figure 3* shows how inflation accelerated after the
devaluation and other measures decided before the program (for
instance, the increase of energy prices). However, it remained within the range of moderate and controlled inflation, and is now easing
again after its post-ASP 95 peak.

The nominal wage rise far from equalled the rise in the price
level, causing a drastic cut in real wages. Meanwhile several welfare benefits have been reduced or cut with the tightening of budget spending.

These changes will be discussed in the next section in more
detail. Here it is only necessary to note how broad sections of the
Hungarian public made major sacrifices in the approach to a health-
ier macroeconomic equilibrium. Many whose standard of living
had already fallen saw it decline further, while social inequality has

increased. The sense of security has weakened in much of the population, mainly, of course, among the direct financial losers by the program. Disillusion and bitterness have taken hold.

Figure 1: Factors contributing to the change in the volume of aggregate demand

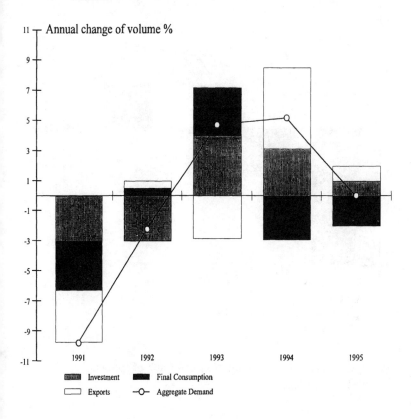

Source: Communication from the National Bank of Hungary.
Note: The underlying figures for 1995 are not consistent with the figures in Tables 1 and 2, because they are based on a different preliminary estimate, although the changes point in the same direction.

Figure 2: Factors contributing to the change in the volume of aggregate supply

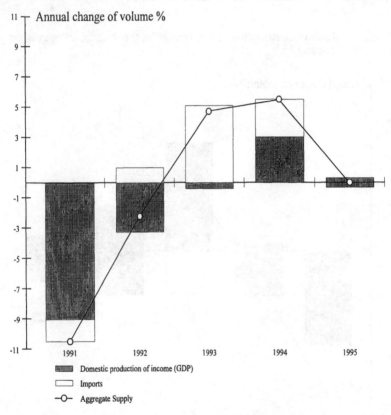

Source: Communication from the National Bank of Hungary.
Note: See note to Figure 1.

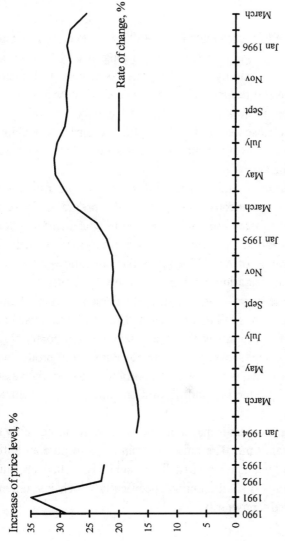

Figure 3: Consumer price level

Increase of price level, %

Rate of change, %

Sources: 1991-3: Central Statistical Office (1995g), p. 286, 1994-5: National Bank of Hungary (1996b), p. 67, 1996: Central Statistical Office (1996b), p. 63.
Note: Data for 1990-93 show growth of the average price level of a given year from the average price level of the earlier year. Data for 1994-6 show growth of the average price level of a given month from the average price level of the month 12 months earlier.

III. THE INSTRUMENTS OF THE PROGRAM

The choice of instruments for ASP 95 was severely restricted by the fact that Hungary does not have a long history as a market economy. It is an economy that entered on a post-socialist transformation after several decades of socialism. This difference of history is worth bearing in mind, even though Hungary's situation and problems show close similarities with other countries at a similar level of economic development, including several Latin American countries, for instance.

The government and central bank have used instruments of several kinds simultaneously in applying the program. The economic policy has been *heterodox*, with orthodox instruments of financial stabilization augmented by several unorthodox methods. One notable feature of ASP 95 is that it has *not* followed the dogmatic formula of restoring equilibrium simply by contraction, that is indiscriminate narrowing of aggregate demand, which would have brought a serious fall in production. The aim instead has been an adjustment that minimizes the albeit inevitable temporary slowdown in growth, and seeks to avoid an absolute fall in production. The approach to the desired macro proportions has been by way of reallocation of production and absorption, not absolute contraction.[17]

A separate problem is that some of the instruments can only be used for a certain time. The most they can do is to give an initial boost to the adjustment process; they cannot be relied on later. During the survey, I shall mention specifically which instruments can only be used temporarily.

1. Exchange-rate and foreign-trade policy

During the period before to ASP 95, the government and central bank had devalued the forint (HUF) from time to time, but retained a fixed exchange rate between devaluations. There were two problems with this exchange-rate policy. One was that the real exchange rate of the forint was rising in spite of the nominal depreciation. This trend accelerated notably in certain periods, for example in 1991–2 (*Figure 4* and see the studies by Halpern and Oblath).[18] The other problem was the unpredictability of the exchange-rate policy. No one knew beforehand when a devaluation would occur or how big it would be. Long overdue exchange-rate adjustments would be put off time and again. This made it hard for investors to make considered business calculations. Before the program was announced, deflationary expectations had been mounting and speculative attacks against the forint emerging.

To overcome these two problems, ASP 95 included the following measures:

As an initial step, the forint was devalued by 9 per cent. A *foreign-exchange regime with a pre-announced crawling peg* was introduced with immediate effect, under which the central bank announces for a longer period (6–12 months) in advance the pace at which it will devalue the forint.[19] This began with a monthly rate of 1.9 per cent, which was reduced gradually in the later stages. The monthly rate of devaluation for 1996 will be 1.2 per cent.

In setting the rate, monetary policy-makers attempt to retain more or less the real exchange rate produced by the initial devaluation, and prevent the real appreciation of the forint. The announced rate of nominal devaluation rests on a careful forecast of the rate difference between domestic and foreign inflation.[20] This entails gauging in advance on the expenditure side what nominal wage increase can be 'squeezed in' beneath the planned upper limit of inflation, given the likely trend in Hungarian productivity.

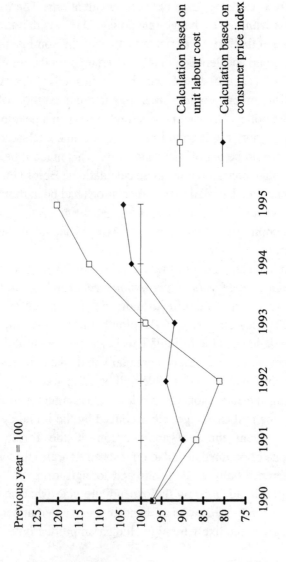

Figure 4: Real exchange rate

Previous year = 100

Source: Szentgyörgyvári and Baár (1996), p. 2.
Note: An index larger than 100 means a real depreciation, and an index smaller than 100 a real appreciation compared with the previous year.

The pre-announced crawling peg needs to be coupled with an appropriate interest-rate policy. If the rate is not high enough, it becomes worth investors' while to start converting their forint holdings into foreign exchange on a mass scale and withdrawing them from Hungary. This would cause the exchange rate to collapse.

It is certainly an achievement that the announced exchange rate has been fully adhered to so far. The central bank has allowed itself a band of plus or minus 2.5 per cent around the announced rate. It would intervene if the exchange rate on the inter-bank currency market moves out of this band. In the event, the market rate has never exceeded the intervention band. Rates on the black (or rather Grey) currency market in the street, catering for the general public and foreign visitors, do not deviate from the official rates either. In private savings, there is a trend away from savings in foreign exchange towards savings in forints. Starting 1 January 1996 the Hungarian currency became convertible in current transactions.[21] This combination of circumstances has dampened the speculation in this sphere, and greatly increased confidence in the forint and the credibility of monetary policy.

The initial and subsequent continuous devaluations have caused a very drastic nominal depreciation of the forint. The exchange rate in November 1995 represented a nominal depreciation of 30.6 per cent over the rate twelve months earlier. The real effective exchange rate, as is shown in Figure 4, changed much less, of course, since inflation accelerated. There are several accepted methods of measuring this. If inflation is measured by the industrial wholesale-price index, the real effective exchange rate decreased by 5.5 per cent over the above mentioned period. Discounting seasonal effects and taking unit labor costs as a basis, the decrease was 17.1 per cent over the first ten months of 1995 (compared with the same period of 1994).[22] I will leave open here the problems of measurement methodology. Whatever the case, there was a nominal depreciation in excess of inflation, which substantially improved the competitiveness of Hungarian production in export markets.[23]

Apart from the devaluation and the new exchange-rate policy, ASP 95 tried other instruments designed to adjust foreign trade. An 8 per cent import surcharge was imposed, augmenting the effect of existing tariffs. The program refrained from restricting imports by such administrative means as further quotas. However, it seemed expedient to curb temporarily (as is allowed by the international agreements) the runaway import demand with an import surcharge effective for a period of two years. This also yields substantial extra budget revenue.[24]

So to some extent, the program is asymmetrical: it lays great emphasis on curbing import demand. However, this takes place in a differentiated way, because it seeks mainly to curb the import demand induced by consumption. The import surcharge is refunded to those who use the products imported for investment or for export production. This underlines still more that ASP 95 is designed to encourage investment and export-led growth.

Nonetheless, it must be admitted that the economic policy borders on protectionism in this respect. Special treatment of imports can only be justified by the threat of a balance-of-payments crisis. If the same course were pursued permanently, it would cause distortion of relative prices and slow down the improvement of efficiency. So later, when the results have been consolidated, the country will have to move towards reducing tariffs and opening up even more widely, for this is the road that leads to *lastingly* rapid growth.

There are various debates going on about the exchange-rate policy for the future. One issue concerns the connection between exchange-rate policy and policy designed to reduce inflation. Some people in Hungary, as in many other countries, advocate using real appreciation as an instrument for slowing down inflation.[25] This would be a big mistake, in my view. Inflation is a grave problem, but so long as it is kept under control and within a moderate range, it remains bearable. On the other hand, if real appreciation of the forint causes the trade and current-account balances start to worsen and confidence begins to erode again, the country will be back on the brink of a debt crisis. A tendency to real appreciation, alongside other factors, can be found among the culprits in all the countries where a payments and debt crisis has occurred.[26] This is confirmed by Table 3c, where every crisis episode was preceded by real appreciation. For Hungary, as for the other small open economies, export-led growth represents the true, permanent escape from the struggles of today. The competitiveness of the economy must be promoted by various instruments, of which more will be said later. However, this is certainly the aspect that the exchange-rate policy must promote in the first place.

2. Income policy

In the framework of the adjustment, it was unavoidable to have a sharp reduction in consumption. The orthodox recipe is to achieve this by a thoroughly painful course of treatment. There is a serious fall in production, accompanied by a large increase in unemployment, which forces real wages down, through the mechanism of the labor market. This occurs after a long delay, because of the rigidity of wages and the frictions in labor-market adjustment. Indeed a much larger unemployment increment is needed to achieve the wage level necessary in macroeconomic terms than would be the case if there were a mechanism free of friction and delay. Empirical writings on the 'wage curve'[27] suggest as a rule of thumb that unemployment must double to cause a 10 per cent fall in wages. It is not worth trying to decide how far this empirical regularity, based mainly on observations of regional differences within a particular country, would apply to Hungary today. However, the figure certainly demonstrates that without state intervention, only a very substantial rise in the already high unemployment rate

of over 10 per cent would have led to the new proportions of consumption, investment and exports desirable in macroeconomic
terms.

Instead, ASP 95 applied other, non-orthodox means of forcing
down real wages, with the help of direct state intervention. Central
wage controls ceased in Hungary in 1992. Year after year there are
talks between the employees' and the employers' organizations and
the government about pay, employment, and other current aspects
of economic policy. Even if agreement is reached, it is not binding.
Such talks duly took place early in 1995, but they dragged on fruit-
lessly. The announcement of ASP 95 fell like a thunderbolt. The
employers gave reluctant support. The unions took various stances.
The reactions in various trades at various times ranged from strong
protests, strikes and street demonstrations to relatively resigned
acquiescence. The Hungarian heterodox program, unlike, for example, the Israeli stabilization, does not rest on a declared agreement
reached with the unions.[28]

The government imposed unilateral limits on nominal pay
rises in organizations funded by the budget (in public administration, the armed forces, education and health) and in firms still
owned predominantly by the state. For brevity's sake, I shall not
give details here of the differentiated nominal pay increases
allowed in the state sector as interpreted in this broader sense; in
general, the limit was 15 per cent nominal wage increase for 1995.
Certainly this rise was substantially slower than the sudden increase
in the level of consumer prices. The government did not interfere in
private-sector pay. However, as the state and private sectors largely share a common pool of labor, private employers followed more
or less the same wage policy as the state employers.

As Table 1 has shown, real wages fell by more than 12 per
cent. This can also be taken to mean that the employed made a big
sacrifice in real wages to maintain the existing employment level.
There have been cases in labor-market history, on an enterprise or

national scale, of employees voluntarily making such sacrifice out of solidarity. Under ASP 95, this sacrifice was compelled by two factors. One was state intervention, and the other the force of surprise. It is a well-known proposition of macroeconomics that the agents in the economy react differently to inflation depending on whether it is in line with expectations or unanticipated. They tailor wage demands to the former in advance, but they cannot adjust to the latter in time, since their scope for action is blocked, or at least impeded by existing wage contracts.[29] This effect too has certainly contributed to the very sudden fall in real income.

It can be stated that income-policy intervention, like exchange-rate policy, has been one of the keys to ASP 95's efficacy so far. However, it is doubtful how long these elements of income policy can be maintained. Certainly the state sector will decline in relative size, which in itself will narrow the scope for applying instruments similar to the 1995 intervention. The chance of increasing resistance to such an income policy cannot be ruled out either.

Nor is it just that the *scope* is narrowing. Thought should also be given to how *desirable* these instruments are. The criteria of a fair distribution of income speak against them. The incomes targeted have been the ones easiest to target, which affronts those who lose by the policy, and offends others' sense of justice as well.

3. Fiscal policy

The budget deficit showed a tendency to increase in the period before ASP 95 (*Table 4*). There were fears that the country might enter a debt spiral. On the fiscal side, this would have meant the deficit would grow because of the budget's increasing interest burden, the interest rate would grow because of the crowding-out effect of the growing borrowing requirement of the budget, which would increase the interest burden further, and so on.[30]

Table 4: Fiscal balance and gross debt of the general government (% of
GDP)

Indicators	1992	1993	1994	1995[a]
1.Primary GFS balance of the general government	2.1	-1.6	-2.7	1.7
2.Borrowing requirement of the general government				
SNA system[b]	-6.9	-5.5	-8.2	-6.6
GFS system	-6.0	-5.2	-7.6	-3.6
3.Gross debt of the general government	79.2	90.0	87.6	87.7
Consolidated gross public debt[c]	65.2	83.4	82.5	86.5
Domestic	12.1	23.2	23.5	24.5
Foreign	53.1	60.2	59.0	62.0
International reserves	15.7	21.9	20.2	32.9

Source: National Bank of Hungary (1996c), and direct communication by
the National Bank of Hungary.

Notes: The general government alongside the central government includes
the extra budgetary funds, social security and health insurance funds and
local governments. The main differences between the System of National
Accounts (SNA) and the General Financial Statistics (GFS) methods are
the following: Under SNA, privatization income and repayment of state
loans do not feature as revenue, so that the borrowing requirement is not
lessened by the amount of them, as it is under the GFS system. The SNA
system considers foreign borrowing as revenue, while the GFS system
accounts it as financing.

[a] Preliminary data.

[b] Adjusted GFS balance (without privatization revenues and without lending minus repayments).

[c] The consolidated gross public debt includes the total debt (domestic and
foreign) of the general government and the foreign debt of the National
Bank of Hungary.

ASP 95 has halted this tendency and begun to reverse it. The
most important change is that the real value of expenditure in the
primary budget has fallen significantly, while the real value of revenue has remained roughly the same. As a consequence, the primary budget deficit has passed into surplus.[31] This provides a source
from which the great burden of debt on public finances can be

reduced and the self-generating spiral of public debt can be broken.[32]

The changes in the fiscal sphere have included some measures that reduce certain universal welfare entitlements or apply a means test to them, as follows:

1. Higher education has ceased to be free. Although the fees imposed cover only a fraction of tuition costs, they go some way to applying the principle that those who will enjoy a lifetime's higher income thanks to their degree should contribute to the educational investment. Regrettably, a system of loans for students has still not been instituted.
2. In line with the principle of need, the scope of entitlement to maternity benefits and family allowance has been reduced.
3. Dental care has ceased to be generally and fully free of charge. The provision remains free for specified exceptional groups (such as children and young people, the elderly, and the needy). The budget subsidy on pharmaceuticals has fallen and become more targeted.
4. The period of active life has been lengthened by raising the general retirement age. (Hungary has been one of the countries where the retiring age is very low: 55 for women and 60 for men.)

Very few practical steps have been taken to reform the welfare sector.[33] It was unfortunate that one or two of the measures were introduced too hastily, without sufficient preparation.[34] Even so, there is symbolic significance in the fact that such measures have been taken at all. The changes over the last three decades had all been in the same direction, creating successive new entitlements year by year that added to the welfare commitments of the state. The system of entitlements at any time was politically taboo. There was no political force willing to tackle painful reforms.[35] It has now

been shown that change is possible, which opens the way to ideas
for reform in this field as well. A start has been made in devising
and debating proposals for reforming the welfare sector although,
regrettably, the process is still only at the very beginning.[36]

International experience shows that fiscal reforms are more
sustainable if they are based more on reducing expenditure than on
increasing revenue.[37] This applies all the more to Hungary, as a
country with one of the highest ratios of state spending to GDP in
the world (*Table 5*). ASP 95 took this radical approach. The
decrease in the budget deficit in 1995 was achieved by making
spending cuts of HUF 3 for every additional HUF 1 of fiscal revenue.[38]

Most of the fiscal reform is still ahead, including concomitant
reassessment of the role of the state. Many functions that the state
has hitherto performed by bureaucratic means, at taxpayers'
expense, must be transferred—completely or partially—to the market, to for-profit and non-profit bodies, and to the voluntary organizations of a civil society.

4. Monetary policy and savings

The financial administration and the central bank, in opting for
the exchange-rate regime described in Section III/1, substantially
reduced the room for maneuver in monetary policy. The chosen
regime in effect sets a *fixed* exchange rate at a given time, or only
allows the exchange rate to move within a narrow band around a
fixed mean. Although the fixed exchange rate continuously
changes over time, this does not alter the fact that the present system belongs to the fixed, not the flexible, floating category of
regimes. Furthermore, it means that the central bank has no way of
setting quantitative monetary targets for itself. It has to adapt to the
conditions of money supply and demand.

Table 5: Fiscal balance and gross debt of the general government (% of GDP)

Country	Year	Consolidated general government expenditure		
		current	capital	total
Lithuania	1993	22.0	2.6	24.6
Kazakstan	1993	-	-	23.5
Estonia	1993	30.2	2.0	32.2
Russia	1993	-	-	32.9
USA	1992	36.3	2.5	38.8
Romania	1992	37.0	4.4	41.4
United Kingdom	1991	39.7	4.1	43.8
France	1992	46.2	4.6	50.9
Czech Republic	1993	41.4	6.8	48.2
Canada	1991	48.3	2.2	50.5
Germany[a]	1992	45.7	4.9	50.6
Ukraine	1993	50.4	1.7	52.1
Austria	1992	46.8	5.5	52.3
Belgium	1992	50.7	3.1	53.8
Netherlands	1992	52.7	3.8	56.5
Norway	1990	53.2	3.5	56.7
Hungary	1994	55.1	6.7	61.8
Denmark[a]	1993	58.9	2.8	61.8
Sweden	1993	67.6	3.3	71.0

Sources: Horváth (1996), p. 11. Primary sources: International Monetary Fund (1994a); for Lithuania and Estonia, International Monetary Fund (1994b); for Kazakstan, International Monetary Fund (1994c); for Ukraine, International Monetary Fund (1994d); for Russia, International Monetary Fund (1994e); for Hungary, calculated on the basis of publications by the Ministry of Finance; source of GDP for Germany and Austria: World Bank (1995c).

Note: [a] Data are provisional or preliminary.

258 János Kornai

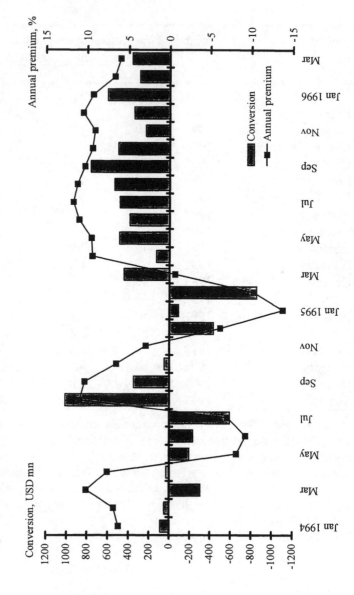

Figure 5: Premium on conversion

Source: Information provided by the National Bank of Hungary.

Note: On the conversion graph, a negative sign represents a net conversion from Hungarian currency to hard foreign currency; and a positive sign a net conversion in hard foreign currency to Hungarian currency.

On the premiums graph, the premiums are calculated on an annual basis. The premium is the excess on the return of the Hungarian government's three month treasury bill over the nominal depreciation of the Hungarian currency, and the average interest rate of hard foreign currencies. (The basket of foreign currencies is determined according to the proportions of Hungarian foreign trade.) It is a proxy for the real return on government securities.

For 1994 and 1995, the calculations are based on *ex post* actual data, while the figures for the first quarter of 1996 are *ex ante* estimates.

Even so, some instruments remain: altering the compulsory reserve rates, changing the rate of interest paid on compulsory or voluntary deposits by commercial banks, open market transactions, and so on. Certainly it is worrying to think that the central bank, with its constitutional duty to combat inflation, has lost its leading role in this respect. The front-line battle concerns the budget deficit and the running away of incomes.

Although the monetary policy was tight, ASP 95 set out to reallocate lending, rather than reduce lending overall. Compared with the previous year, 1995 was one in which the budget received relatively fewer resources and the business sector relatively more. This redirection of lending is among the unorthodox features of the program.

One of the most fortunate occurrences in the monetary sphere was somewhat unexpected. While economic policy reduced household income, household savings increased. Net lending by households rose from HUF 294 billion in 1994 to HUF 391 billion in 1995. Adjusted for inflation the increase of savings was three per cent.[39] There were certainly several factors at work. For a while, real interest rates rose enough to encourage saving.[40] There may also have been an inducement to save in the growing general feeling that the future holds many uncertainties and people can no longer rely on help from a paternalist state. This has been brought home by several changes: from full employment and chronic labor shortage to mass unemployment, hardening of the earlier soft budget constraint and the associated constant threat to business survival, and the reduction in the universal commitments of the welfare state. The idea was put forward by Martin Feldstein[41] that the spread of state care will reduce private savings. Debate has continued in the West about how far this hypothesis can stand its ground. Now, the laboratory of post-socialist transition provides a new way of testing the hypothesis, with a process in the opposite direction. It is too soon to draw far-reaching conclusions from the Hungarian figures for 1995. Hungarian savings may still fluctuate a great deal in response to many other factors (above all interest rates and incomes). In any case it will certainly be instructive to follow the process by comparative studies across countries.

It is of great importance to the internal and external equilibrium of the Hungarian economy that household saving rates should fluctuate as little as possible and total household savings, in real terms, grow reliably. If the household saving rate should fall again, one of the harmful effects would be on aggregate demand, and ultimately on the current account. There are several ways in which savings can be helped to grow:

First, it would be desirable to have as little fluctuation as possible in the real return on household savings, so that they remain lastingly positive. *Figure 5* shows the failure to achieve such stability over many years. The trend was reversed after the first successes of ASP 95. Instead of capital flight (largely concealed), foreign capital began to flow into the country. Part of this is not intended as long-term real investment, some investors tend to buy short-term government securities and treasury bills only. These are extremely attractive investments, because the present exchange-rate regime almost eliminates the exchange-rate risk, and such

Hungarian securities offer a sizeable, secure real return. This influx has already pushed the previously high rates of interest appreciably downwards. From the point of view of household savings, it would not be desirable for the interest level to fall too far.[42]

Second, reforms must continue to narrow the range of bureaucratic public services financed from taxation (or compulsory contributions, levied like taxes) and enhance the role of decentralized pension funds, health-insurance funds and building societies. As these reforms make themselves felt by reducing taxes and contributions, as well as by narrowing the range of free services and transfers, they will encourage private savings. This is also needed for the expansion of the decentralized capital market, where institutional investors can play a greater part.

5. Privatization

A new surge of privatization did not feature in the ASP 95 package. On the contrary, the financial administration emphasized several times that the economy's grave disequilibrium must be overcome even if there are no substantial revenues imminent from privatization. They rightly underlined that the practical implementation of privatization must not be subordinated to short-term fiscal considerations.

Preparations for privatizing several key branches had been taking place for a long time. The legislation governing these was drawn up, and the legal and organizational infrastructure for regulating the natural monopolies prepared after much delay and procrastination. Once these tasks had been completed, the process speeded up suddenly. In the second half of 1995, within the space of a few months, the privatization of the energy sector and telecommunications made a great stride forward. Several large state-owned banks and a number of sizeable manufacturing companies were also privatized. The financial results of the accelerated privatization of 1995 (as well as those of the overall privatization process in earlier years) are shown in *Table 6*.

Table 6: Annual flow of foreign direct investment into Hungary, 1990–95 (USD million)

Form of investment	1990	1991	1992	1993	1994	1995
Inward foreign capital in cash	311	1459	1471	2339	1147	4453
of which privatization income	8	329	519	1202	104	3024
Inward foreign capital in kind	589	155	170	142	173	117
Total inward flow of FDI	900	1614	1641	2481	1320	4570

Sources: Direct communication by the State Privatization and Property Management PLC (ÁPV Rt.), except for the figure for privatization revenue in 1995, which was communicated by the National Bank of Hungary.

Most of the buyers were large Western firms. The contracts made with them call for strong development of these key branches. To take one example, one of the most grievous manifestations of the shortage economy for decades was the telephone shortage, with several hundred thousand families waiting for years for a phone in their homes. Since the beginning of privatization—from 1994 to the first quarter of 1996—650 000 new lines have been installed. The concession contract stipulates a mandatory annual increase of 15.5 per cent in the number of telephone lines, which so far has always been outstripped by the telecommunication company.[43] In a few years the telephone service will have changed from a sellers' to a buyers' market.

It is especially worth noting that this is not just a case of new foreign owners setting about development tasks under privatization agreements. Large international concerns that acquired property in Hungary earlier are making successive new investments, and these will contribute to modernizing the Hungarian economy.

This study does not set out to analyze the experiences with privatization in Hungary.[44] I shall confine myself to the macroeconomic side-effects. Foreign direct investment in 1995, including sums paid in connection with privatization, came to about USD 4.6 billion (see Table 6). The scale of the sum can be gauged accurately from the fact that in 1994, the worst year of external disequilibrium, the deficit on the current account was USD 3.9 billion. This fell in 1995 to USD 2.5 bn, due to the factors already discussed (see Table 1).

There was a debate about how to utilize this windfall income. There were plenty of applicants, and great pressure was applied to use the money in a 'popular' way, in other words to consume it. Economic common sense prevailed at last, and it was decided to use the proceeds of privatizing the key branches to reduce Hungary's state debt. Given how large the debt burden is, the saving of interest in this way seems to be the safest, and when all is said and done, the most effective investment. Furthermore, a reduction in Hungary's indebtedness has numerous favorable external effects on the country's financial ratings and acts as a stimulus to investment.

IV. WHAT COMES NEXT?

To a large extent it will be the political, rather than the economic sphere that determines subsequent development. Will the government, its each and every member and its parliamentary majority be prepared to persevere with the present economic policy? Will they not be tempted to change course, especially when they see the 1998 general elections approaching? What attitude will various groups in society take to the achievements and costs of adjustment and stabilization? What power relations will emerge between the program's supporters and opponents? Indeed most of the tasks entailed by it will extend beyond 1998. What will be the political composition of the next government and parliamentary majority, and what economic policy will it pursue? I have simply posed some questions here, to signify my appreciation of how vitally important the answers are to assessing the future. Even so, I leave the task of answering such questions to other studies, confining myself here to economic and economic-policy forecasts and recommendations in the narrow sense.

1. A prolonged process

ASP 95 was an example of 'shock therapy' on a small scale, and it brought a rapid improvement in certain macroeconomic indicators. International experience, however, shows that such results are fragile, and can easily slip from economic policy-makers' grasp.

Interactions of several kinds take place between the various problems in the economy. In some cases, easing one economic difficulty may help to reduce another. Let me give two instances of such a favorable interaction, one might say a 'virtuous circle'. As the budget deficit lessens, the fall in the government's aggregate demand for credit has a 'crowding in' effect. This makes more funds available for private lending, which is conducive to the acceleration of growth. This in turn increases budget revenue, which further reduces the budget deficit. At the same time, the reduction in the state borrowing requirement reduces the demand for foreign credit, so improving the country's external debt position. The interest premium paid on the debt is reduced. This means it is worth going substantially further in reducing Hungary's budget deficit.

The other example of a virtuous circle is the climate of business opinion. In the space of a few months, ASP 95 increased confidence among entrepreneurs and investors, at home and abroad. One of Hungary's business research institutes has been putting the same questions every quarter about the business situation and prospects to top company managers since 1987. According to their report,[45] the situation in manufacturing was assessed more favorably in January 1996 than at any time in the previous decade. This is corroborated by the new surge of foreign investment, mentioned in connection with privatization. The confidence itself becomes a growth factor, and the continuing or, in the best case, accelerating growth in turn reinforces the optimism.

However, there also exist unfavorable interactions—'vicious circles'—that must be taken into account. Let me give a few examples of these. Mention was made, in earlier parts of the study, of maintaining the real exchange rate which, at a given rate of inflation, requires nominal depreciation at the same pace. The depreciation becomes built into the inflationary expectations, which contributes to upholding the inertial inflation. It is extremely hard to improve the country's trading position, prevent a growth of indebtedness, and *concurrently* achieve disinflation. To take other examples, the forcing of growth by fiscal means may aggravate the budget deficit, and conversely, attempts to reduce the budget deficit at any price, by large tax increases, for example, may cause recession. What is a remedy for one ill turns out to exacerbate another.

Experience in Latin American countries with similar problems shows that the struggle may even last for one or two decades. First one, then another economic tension intensifies, and the therapy applied for the ill of the moment causes a further problem to arise. Some countries have relapsed time and again into one of their original difficulties after successful partial stabilizations. Either production falls drastically, or the balance on the current account deteriorates, or inflation speeds up, or more than one problem arises. Chile, possibly the most successful Latin American country from the economic point of view, moved in 1978 from high inflation to the moderate rate of 20–40 per cent a year. It was another 17 years before the country finally reached single-digit inflation in 1995, but in the meantime, production continuously rose at an imposing rate of 4.8 per cent a year.[46] The chance of this happening sooner in Hungary cannot be excluded, but it cannot be relied upon either. It would be unfortunate to delude ourselves and others into thinking that a single great action like ASP 95 can suffice to right matters in two or three years.

One of the great dangers is complacency: 'The situation's a bit better now, there's no need to be as strict as before.' This is an enticing idea to any politician in government. There are already signs of it in Hungary. For instance, the total national wage bill jumped again at the beginning of 1996, imports began to resume their rise, and investment activity seemed to be slowing down. We have to be constantly prepared to combat the adverse phenomena immediately they appear.

The antecedents of ASP 95 are thought-provoking in this respect. Some researchers who studied the political economy of reforms[47] take the view that politicians are not prepared to take unpopular action until a crisis has actually *occurred*. The Hungarian ASP 95, as I emphasized earlier, is preventive in nature, which partly supports and partly refutes the hypothesis. It was the immediate threat, if not the crisis itself that triggered the program. The question is how imminent the crisis has to be before politicians can summon up the courage to act. Is it too much to expect that they could keep the economy in good repair simply by discernment of the economic situation, without a crisis looming or occurring?

I confess I am uncertain about the answer. Even consolidated, stable countries like the United States or France tend to protract and postpone long overdue fiscal reforms because their consequences would be unpopular.

2. Selecting priorities

Returning to Hungary's problems, one difficulty is to choose the correct economic-policy priorities and assign the right relative importance to the various parallel tasks. There has been much argument about this. In my view there is no universal rule, valid at all times in every country (or more narrowly, every post-socialist country). If a country has rapid inflation, or even hyperinflation, the prime task must undoubtedly be to reduce it, at least to the annual rate of 30–40 per cent. There is enough evidence to show this is a prerequisite for healthy development.[48] What is less clear is how to choose the priorities when the inflation rate has come down to the moderate range.

In the moderate band of inflation, disinflation becomes very costly. In most cases it has not been achieved without a substantial rise in unemployment and a serious fall in production. So the lesser of two evils seems to be to allow the moderate inflation to continue. Care and strict control are needed to prevent it from running away. The emphasis, though, must shift to attaining the conditions for balanced, lasting growth. This includes reducing the budget deficit, cutting state expenditure, halting the increase in external indebtedness (and where necessary, improving the debt/GDP ratio), and promoting exports and investment. All these developments will contribute to the acceleration of growth, which should also be encouraged in other ways. As a by-product or side-effect of such measures, inflation may gradually slow down, so long as they are joined by the right price and income policy and monetary policy. In my view it would be unwise under such circumstances to impose an urgent and radical curb on inflation at the expense of all the other tasks.

The economies of the post-socialist countries may prove to be interesting experimental laboratories in this respect as well. The various governments have different points of departure and different economic policies. There are, and no doubt will remain some countries where the financial administration uses real appreciation of the exchange rate to reduce the inflation rate. I would argue against doing this in Hungary. I continue to recommend caution, warning against real appreciation of the forint and the threat of a renewed deterioration in the balance of trade.[49]

3. A reassuring sign: rising productivity

Readers will gather that I feel the Hungarian economy is vulnerable in several respects. I have tried to point to the dangers, but there is one fundamentally important aspect of the Hungarian economy that fills me with confidence: the rise in labor productivity. Mention was made earlier of auspicious signs that the competitiveness of Hungarian exports is improving. This arises partly from the movement in the exchange rate, but even more important is the efficiency of the underlying real process. The trend in productivity is the key to growth (and for a small, open economy like Hungary's, export-led growth).

Table 7 compares productivity over time in several post-socialist countries.[50] Hungary shows the most favorable trend in this respect. There are several contributing factors. Although property relations were transformed more slowly than in countries that conducted so-called mass privatization (distributing fragmented property rights free of charge), Hungary's privatization process[51] was more inclined to generate genuine owners. Ownership has gone mainly to private persons or already operating businesses that can exercise real control over management and apply the profit motive. This has also helped to bring about a radical restructuring in many firms.

Table 7: Labor productivity in post-socialist countries: an international comparison

Country	Average labour productivity					
	(real GDP/employment, 1989 = 100)					
	1989	1990	1991	1992	1993	1994
Bulgaria	1.00	0.97	0.88	0.89	0.88	0.91
Czech Republic	1.00	0.97	0.88	0.89	0.88	0.91
Hungary	1.00	0.98	0.92	1.05	1.11	1.16
Poland	1.00	0.92	0.91	0.98	1.00	1.07
Romania	1.00	0.95	0.83	0.77	0.81	-
Russia	-	1.00	0.89	0.74	0.66	0.57
Slovakia	1.00	0.98	0.95	0.93	0.92	0.96

Source: Calculations from McHale (1996), Table 1, on the basis of the following sources: European Commission (1995), EBRD (1995), and various issues of the OECD publications *Short-Term Economic Indicators and Transition Economies*.

The budget constraint in Hungary has really hardened. This was promoted by legislation compatible with a market economy and conducive to financial discipline: the new Acts on bankruptcy, banking and accounting. Although some stipulations in the Bankruptcy Act, initially formulated in an extreme way, caused serious problems for a time, the mistakes were quickly remedied. The ultimate result is a process of natural selection that allows the truly fit, efficient and profitable businesses to survive.[52]

Connected to the above changes is the elimination of the phenomenon of 'unemployment on the job' that evolved under the socialist system. The larger part of this painful process—accompanied by human suffering, the tormented feelings of losing one's job—has already taken place in Hungary, while, as it seems, many other post-socialist countries try to put it off.

One common explanation for all the changes listed so far is the very high rate of foreign direct investment. Hungary has received about half the foreign capital investment entering Eastern Europe. Apart from its benefits in macro-financial terms, this has helped to introduce new products, technologies and management methods and tighten labor discipline and organization.

A steady rise in labor productivity is not enough by itself to produce lasting growth in the economy. There must also be a favorable development in several other areas, some of which have been detailed in this study. However, theory demonstrates and the broad experience of international economic history confirms, that the rise in labor productivity is one of the most important conditions (perhaps *the* most important) for healthy, steady economic growth. It is among the factors that give cause for confidence in the future of the Hungarian economy, despite the many difficulties it faces.

Notes

1. Reprinted from *Central and Eastern Europe in the 1990s,* ed.: Salvatore Zecchini. Dorndrecht: Kluwer Academic Publishers and OECD, 1997, 123–152. The paper was also published in *Struggle and Hope. Essays on Stabilization and Reform in a Post-socialist Economy,* Cheltenham, UK and Northampton, MA, USA: Edward Elgar, 1997, pp. 180–215.

2. My research was supported by the Hungarian National Scientific Research Foundation (OTKA). The first version of this study was presented at the OECD-CCET Colloquium 'Economic Transformation and Development of Central and Eastern Europe: What Lessons from the 1990s?', 29–30 May 1996, Paris. I benefited from the consultations with László Csaba, Zsuzsa Dániel, Rudiger Dornbusch, John McHale, Csaba László, Judit Neményi, Gábor Oblath, Jeffrey Sachs, György Surányi, Georg Winckler and Charles Wyplosz; some of these colleagues also read the first draft of this paper. I thank them for their valuable comments.

3. Work on some parts of ASP 95 had begun under the previous finance minister, László Békesi. The program was then drawn up under the direction of the new finance minister, Lajos Bokros, and the new president of the National Bank of Hungary, György Surányi. ASP 95 was announced to the country on television by Prime Minister Gyula Horn, accompanied by the finance minister and the president of the central bank.

   For a year, Bokros played a prominent part in devising, explaining and implementing the program, and it came to be known colloquially as the Bokros Package. I have preferred to use a 'non-personal' name here because responsibility for the program was accepted throughout by the prime minister, and because the government, the majority in parliament and the central bank remain collectively responsible for what occurs under it—achievements and mistakes alike. Lajos Bokros resigned in February 1996, however, the new finance minister and the government committed themselves to continuing to implement the program.

4. Indeed it takes two or, more probably, three years before the effects of such a program can be fully assessed. A study by Alesina and

271

Perotti (1995), for instance, terms a fiscal adjustment successful if the public debt/GDP ratio shows a material improvement (of at least five per cent) in the third year after the firm measures were taken.

5. Attempts at an overall assessment have been largely confined so far to articles in the Hungarian daily and weekly papers and internal reports by the government and the central bank. These I have tried to use in my study. See, for instance, National Bank of Hungary (1996a) and Ministry of Finance (1996a). Among the more detailed studies see Köves (1995b) and Oblath (1996).

6. The sources of the data are: National Bank of Hungary (1995), pp. 172 and 234, and see also *Tables 1, 2* and *4*.

7. Of the analyses of the Hungarian macroeconomic situation that built up in 1993–5, I would emphasize Antal (1994), Békesi (1993), (1994), and (1995), Csaba (1995), Erdős (1994), Köves (1995a) and (1995b), Lányi (1994–1995), Oblath (1995), and World Bank (1995b).

    For the view of those directing ASP 95, see Bokros (1995a), (1995b), and (1996), and Surányi (1995a), (1995b), and (1996).

    For my own views see Kornai (1995a) that was written before the announcement of ASP 95, see also Kornai (1995b) and (1996a), written during the implementation of the program.

8. Kornai (1996a)

9. Of the literature on the Latin American crises and protracted financial disequilibria, I relied mainly on Cooper (1992), Dornbusch and Fischer (1993), Dornbusch, Goldfajn and Valdés (1995), Dornbusch and Werner (1994), Krugman (1991), Little *et al.* (1993), Sachs (1996), and Sachs, Tornell and Velasco (1995).

10. For the sake of brevity I did not include all indicators demonstrating similarities in *Tables 2* and *3*.

11. See Kindleberger (1978).

12. Economists watching the events in Mexico with concern, including myself, avoided alarming the public and hesitant politicians with threats of catastrophe. There was a danger that such warnings would become self-fulfilling prophecies by arousing panic. It was hard to reassure the Hungarian public and the international business world, in other words to avoid arousing panic, while mobilizing efforts to avert the crisis.

13. These views are reported in the article by Kocsis (1995).

14. The balance on current account does not contain the balance of medium- and long-term capital flows. Therefore a very important item,

namely foreign direct investment, does not appear in the current account. However, while the large inflow of foreign direct investment does not improve the current account, it does show up in the improvement of the country's net external debt. When calculating *net* foreign debt, reserves are part of the asset side, and capital inflow contributes to the reserves. Therefore it is feasible to have a negative current account and at the same time a reduction of net external debt.

15. For an explanation of the General Financial Statistics (GFS) methodology, see the note to Table 4.

16. The index number mentioned in the text is a quotient with the business sector's 'own resources for investment purposes' as numerator and GDP as denominator. The definition of own resources for investment purposes is depreciation plus pre-tax profit minus company taxation. The source of the data is Ministry of Finance (1996a), p. 20. Szentgyörgyvári and Baár (1996), p. 18 take another definition: profitability before tax equals difference between total income and total costs, divided by total income. Taking the average for the whole business sector, this was –3.2 per cent in 1992, rising to 3.3 per cent in 1994, and to 7.2 per cent in 1995.

17. This idea was central to my economic-policy proposals, published in Hungary in the summer of 1994, before the definitive version of ASP 95 was devised. See Kornai (1995a).

18. See Halpern (1996) and Oblath (1995).

19. For the analysis of this exchange rate regime see Kopits (1995).

20. Foreign inflation means here the average inflation for a basket of currencies that reflects the actual composition of Hungary's foreign trade.

21. The convertibility of the Hungarian forint meets the criteria of 'current-account convertibility' in Article VIII of IMF's 'Articles of Agreement'. Furthermore, it meets the OECD's convertibility requirements for certain capital transactions.

22. National Bank of Hungary (1996a), p. 25.

23. The study by Szentgyörgyvári and Baár (1996) provides an excellent survey of measurement of the real exchange rate and competitiveness, and the Hungarian situation and problems in this respect.

24. Analyses showed that imports of certain products, such as private cars, had increased particularly. So extra consumer tax was imposed on these (alongside the import surcharge).

25. Under the present exchange-rate regime, this would amount to having a pre-announced rate of nominal depreciation much lower than

the expected rate of inflation. The pre-announced exchange rate would act as a nominal anchor, pulling the rate of inflation down.

26. See the literature quoted in Note 8 in connection with the crises. There are also lessons for Hungary in the conclusions reached in the study by Dornbusch, Goldfajn and Valdés (1995), pp. 251–2, 'A policy of bringing down inflation by slowing the rate of depreciation below the rate of inflation ... is a common way of creating overvaluation. Because the real exchange rate is sticky downward, overvaluation is not easily undone by wage-price deflation and thus, ultimately, leads to collapse and devaluation ... The temptation to use the exchange rate to obtain early results on disinflation without much unemployment is all too obvious as a shortcut, but the results are often illusory. After the collapse, inflation will be higher than it was at the outset.'

27. See, for example, Blanchflower and Oswald (1994).

28. See Bruno (1993).

29. On the effects of unanticipated inflation, see Sachs and Larrain (1993), pp. 349–52.

30. The best account of the debt position in Hungarian public finance can be found in Borbély and Neményi (1994) and (1995).

31. A thorough analysis of the fiscal policy of ASP 95 appears in the study by Oblath (1996), pp. 81–4 and 95–7.

32. The index of gross debt of the general government over GDP remained practically unchanged, while the index of consolidated gross public debt over GDP has risen somewhat (see Table 4). A substantial reduction in both these indices would be desirable, so as to bring the country's macroeconomic situation closer to the norms required for EU membership.

33. The specific expenditure-reducing changes listed above had relatively little effect on the fiscal situation in 1995. Their effect will really be felt in 1996, and still more in 1997.

34. It was a regrettable mistake that some of the measures in their original form conflicted with the principles of constitutionalism, and were therefore rejected by the Constitutional Court.

35. See Section 3.3 in Kornai (1996a).

36. See World Bank (1995a). Among those to comment on welfare-sector reform have been Andorka, Kontradas and Tóth (1995), Augusztinovics (1993), Augusztinovics and Martos (1995), Ferge (1995), (1996a) and (1996b), and myself (see Kornai, 1996b)). See also Note 33 in Kornai 1996b).

37. See Alesina and Perotti (1995) and Giavazzi and Pagano (1990) and (1996).
38. Own calculation on the basis of data from the National Bank of Hungary (1996b), p. 110.
39. Net lending by households equals gross money savings less increment in borrowing by households. (All three figures are flow variables.) The source of the figures is Ministry of Finance (1996b), Table 14.
40. A contribution to the rise in total household savings expressed in forints was made by the fact that continuous depreciation of the forint increases the forint value of deposits held in foreign exchange.
41. See Feldstein (1974).
42. Speculative short-term inflows of capital can cause other grave problems as well. The conversion of hard currency increases the inflationary pressure, and sterilized intervention (absorption of excess liquidity due to inflow of foreign capital) is extremely expensive. It is not possible to count on the resulting extra foreign-exchange reserves, which may evaporate as easily as they arrived. It is difficult to gauge what would be the ideal interest level and return on state securities. Even if this were known, the central bank could still only exert an indirect influence, after a long lag, on the narrow credit and capital markets, which continue to operate with a great deal of friction. On this, see Darvas (1996), Darvas and Simon (1996), Dornbusch, Goldfajn and Valdés (1995), and Sachs (1996).
43. Information provided by the telecommunication company Matáv.
44. On this, see Laki (1993), Major and Mihályi (1994), Mihályi (1993), (1994), and (1995), and Voszka (1992), (1993), and (1994). See furthermore Section 4 in Kornai (1996a).
45. See Kopint-Datorg (1996).
46. The sources of the data are International Monetary Fund (1995), pp. 122–3, 288–91, and for 1995: International Monetary Fund (1996), p. 65, and International Monetary Fund (1997), pp. 184-9.
47. See, for instance, Drazen and Grilli (1993).
48. See Bruno and Easterly (1995), Fischer, Sahay and Végh (1996), and Végh (1992).
49. Darvas and Simon (1996) take a similar position.
50. On the comparative productivity of post-socialist countries, see McHale (1996).
51. See Section 4 in Kornai (1996a).

52. Regrettably, the tendencies are not unequivocal. Firms in grave
    financial difficulties are bailed out far less frequently than before, but
    some of the business sector's financial woes tend nowadays to take
    the form of 'non-performing bank loans', and in most cases the
    banks so far have been rescued from insolvency. (Even so, it must be
    admitted, they can rely less confidently on state assistance than they
    could in the past, following the liquidation of a few non-viable
    banks.) Nevertheless, it certainly cannot be said that Hungary has left
    the syndrome of a soft budget constraint behind.

REFERENCES

Alesina, Alberto and Roberto Perotti (1995), *Reducing Budget Deficits*, prepared for the conference 'Growing Government Debt—International Experiences', Stockholm, 12 June, mimeo.

Andorka, Rudolf, A. Kondratas and István György Tóth (1995), 'A jóléti rendszer jellemzői és reformjának lehetőségei' (Characteristics of the Welfare System and Ways of Reforming It), *Közgazdasági Szemle*, 42 (1), 1–29.

Antal, László (1994), 'Az örökség. A gazdaság helyzete és a feladatok' (The Legacy. The Situation of the Economy and the Tasks), *Társadalmi Szemle*, 49 (10), 12–21.

Augusztinovics, M. (1993), 'Egy értelmes nyugdíjrendszer' (An Intelligent Pension System), *Közgazdasági Szemle*, 40 (5), 415–31.

Augusztinovics, M. and B. Martos (1995), 'Számítások és következtetések nyugdíjreformra' (Calculations and Deductions for a Pension Reform), *Közgazdasági Szemle*, 42 (11), 993–1023.

Banco de Mexico (1996), *Indicadores Economicos*, November.

Békesi, László (1993), 'A feladat öt szöglete. Farkas Zoltán interjúja Békesi Lászlóval' (The Five Angles of the Task. Interview with László Békesi by Zoltán Farkas), *Társadalmi Szemle*, 48 (3), 3–13.

Békesi, László (1994), 'A társadalom még nincs tisztában a gazdasági helyzettel. Karsai Gábor interjúja Békesi Lászlóval' (Society Is Still Unclear about the Economic Situation. Interview with László Békesi by Gábor Karsai), *Figyelő*, 14 July, pp. 13–15.

Békesi, László (1995), 'Mást választhatunk, de "jobbat" aligha' (We Can Choose Something Else, but Hardly Something Better), *Népszabadság*, 8 July, pp. 17–18.

Blanchard, Olivier Jean and Stanley Fischer (1989), *Lectures on Macroeconomics*, Cambridge, Mass.: MIT Press.

Blanchflower, David G. and Andrew J. Oswald (1994), *The Wage Curve*, Cambridge, Mass. and London: MIT Press.

Bokros, Lajos (1995a), 'A leendő pénzügyminiszter huszonöt pontja. Bokros Lajos szakmai cselekvési programjának alapvonalai' (The 25 Points of the Finance Minister Elect. Main Outlines of Lajos Bokros's Action Program), *Népszabadság*, 17 February, p. 15.

Bokros, Lajos (1995b), 'Az államháztartásról, a stabilizációról. Dr. Bokros Lajos pénzügyminiszter tájékoztatója' (On the State Budget and Stabilization. Exposition by Dr. Lajos Bokros, Finance Minister), *Pénzügyi Szemle*, 40 (4), 259–62.

Bokros, Lajos (1996), 'Növekedés és/vagy egyensúly—avagy az 1995. március 12-én meghirdetett stabilizáció tanulságai' (Growth and/or Stabilization—Lessons from the Stabilization Program Announced on 12 March 1995), *Népszabadság*, 11 March, p. 8.

Borbély, László András and Judit Neményi (1994), 'Az államadósság növekedésének összetevői 1990–1992-ben' (The Factors behind the Growth in the State Debt, 1990–92), *Közgazdasági Szemle*, 41 (2), 110–26.

Borbély, László András and Judit Neményi(1995), 'Eladósodás, a külső és belső államadósság alakulása az átmenet gazdaságában (1990–1993)' (Indebtedness and the Development of External and Internal State Debt in the Transition Economy, 1990–93), in Tamás Mellár (ed.), *Rendszerváltás és stabilizáció. A piacgazdasági átmenet első évei* (Change of System and Stabilization. The First Years of Market Economic Transition), Budapest: Magyar Trendkutató Központ, pp. 123–66.

Bruno, Michael (1993), *Crisis, Stabilization, and Economic Reform: Therapy by Consensus*, New York: Oxford University Press.

Bruno, Michael and William Easterly (1995), *Inflation Crises and Long-Run Growth*, NBER Working Paper series, No. 5209, Cambridge: National Bureau of Economic Research, Harvard University, August.

Central Statistical Office (1995a), *A nemzetgazdaság munkaerőmérlege* (The Labour Balance of the National Economy), January 1, Budapest: Központi Statisztikai Hivatal.

Central Statistical Office (1995b), *Magyar statisztikai évkönyv 1994* (Hungarian Statistical Yearbook 1994), Budapest: Központi Statisztikai Hivatal.

Central Statistical Office (1996a), *Statisztikai Havi Közlemények* (Monthly Statistical Bulletins), No. 4.

Central Statistical Office (1996b), *KSH Statisztikai Hírek* (CSO Statistical News), 2 April.

Central Statistical Office (1996c), *A KSH jelenti* (The CSO Reports), No. 1.

Central Statistical Office (1996d), *Magyar statisztikai évkönyv 1995* (Hungarian Statistical Yearbook 1995), Harvard University Press.

Cooper, Richard N. (1992), *Economic Stabilization and Debt in Developing Countries*, Cambridge, Mass. and London: MIT Press.

Csaba, László (1995), 'Gazdaságstratégia helyett konjunktúra-politika' (Trade-Cycle Policy Instead of Economic Strategy), *Külgazdaság*, 39 (3), 36–46.

Darvas, Zsolt (1996), *Exchange Rate Premia and the Credibility of the Crawling Target Zone in Hungary*, Discussion Paper series No. 1307, London: Centre for Economic Research, January.

Darvas, Zsolt and András Simon (1996), *Tőke beáramlás, árfolyam- és pénzpolitika* (Capital Inflow, Exchange Rate and Monetary Policy), mimeo, Budapest: Magyar Nemzeti Bank, February.

Dornbusch, Rudiger and A. Werner (1994), 'Mexico: Stabilization, Reform and No Growth', *Brookings Papers on Economic Activity*, no. 1, pp. 253–315.

Dornbusch, Rudiger and Stanley Fischer (1993), 'Moderate Inflation', *The World Bank Economic Review*, 7 (1), 1–44.

Dornbusch, Rudiger, I. Goldfajn and R.O. Valdés (1995), Currency Crises and Collapses', *Brookings Papers on Economic Activity*, no. 2, pp. 219–93.

Drazen, A. and V.Grilli (1993), 'The Benefit of Crises for Economic Reforms', *American Economic Review*, 83 (3), 598–607.

EBRD (1995), *Transition Report*, London: European Bank for Reconstruction and Development.

Erdős, Tibor (1994), 'A tartós gazdasági növekedés realitásai és akadályai' (The Realities of Lasting Economic Growth and Obstacles to It), *Közgazdasági Szemle*, 41 (6), 463–77.

European Commission (1995), *Employment Observatory: Central and Eastern Europe*, no. 7.

Feldstein, Martin (1974), 'Social Security, Induced Retirement, and Aggregate Capital Accumulation', *Journal of Political Economy*, 82 (5), 905–26.

Ferge, Zsuzsa (1995), 'A magyar segélyezési rendszer reformja, 1.' (Reform of the Hungarian System of Cash Benefits, 1), *Esély*, no. 6, pp. 43–62 .

Ferge, Zsuzsa (1996a), 'A magyar segélyezési rendszer reformja, 2.' (Reform of the Hungarian System of Cash Benefits, 2), *Esély*, no. 1, pp. 25–42.

Ferge, Zsuzsa (1996b), 'A szociálpolitika esélyei' (The Prospects of Social Policy), *Vigilia*, 61 (7), 528–35.

Fischer, Stanley, Ratna Sahay and Carlos A. Végh (1996), 'Stabilization and Growth in Transition Economies: The Early Experience', *Journal of Economic Perspectives*, 10 (2), 45–66.

Giavazzi, F. and M. Pagano (1990), 'Can Severe Fiscal Contractions be Expansionary? Tales of Two Small European Countries', *NBER Macroeconomics Annual*, pp. 75–116.

Giavazzi, F. and M. Pagano (1996), 'Non-Keynesian Effects of Fiscal Policy Changes: International Evidence and the Swedish Experience', *Swedish Economic Policy Review*, May, forthcoming.

Halpern, László (1996), *Real Exchange Rates and Exchange Rate Policy in Hungary*, Discussion Paper series, No. 1366, London: Centre for Economic Policy Research, March.

Horváth, Piroska (1996), *Vizsgálatok az állami redisztribúció tanulmányozásához* (Examinations towards a Study of State Redistribution), mimeo, Budapest.

Hungarian Government (1994), *A Magyar Köztársaság Kormányának privatizációs stratégiája* (The Government of the Republic of Hungary's Privatization Strategy), Budapest: Magyar Köztársaság Kormánya, 11 November.

International Monetary Fund (1994a), *International Financial Statistics Yearbook 1994*, Washington DC: International Monetary Fund.

International Monetary Fund (1994b), *IMF Economic Review*, No. 7.

International Monetary Fund (1994c), *IMF Economic Review*, No. 16.

International Monetary Fund (1994d), *IMF Economic Review*, No. 17.

International Monetary Fund (1994e), *IMF Economic Review*, No. 18.

International Monetary Fund (1996), *International Financial Statistics*, April.

International Monetary Fund (1997), *International Financial Statistics*, February.

Kindleberger, Charles P. (1978), *Manias, Panics, and Crashes: A History of Financial Crisis*, New York: Basic Books.

Kocsis, Gy. (1995), 'Mégis, kinek a bőrére?' (Even So, Who's Paying?), *Heti Világgazdaság*, October 28, p. 100.

Kolodko, G.W. (1993), *From Output Collapse to Sustainable Growth in Transition Economies. The Fiscal Implications*, Working Papers No. 35, Warsaw: Institute of Finance.

Kolodko, G.W. and W.W. McMahon (1987), 'Stagflation and Shortageflation: A Comparative Approach', *Kyklos*, 40 (2), 176–97.

Kopint-Datorg (1996), *Konjunktúrateszt-eredmények a feldolgozóiparban, az építőiparban és a kiskereskedelemben, 1995. IV. negyedév* (Activity Test Results in Manufacturing, Construction and the Retail Trade, 1995, 4th Quarter), Budapest: Kopint-Datorg.

Kopits, G. (1995), 'Hungary's Preannounced Crawling Peg', *Acta Oeconomica*, 47 (3/4), 267–86

Kornai, János (1959) [1957], *Overcentralization in Economic Administration*, Oxford: Oxford University Press.

Kornai, János (1971), *Anti-Equilibrium*, Amsterdam: North-Holland.

Kornai, János (1972), *Rush versus Harmonic Growth*, Amsterdam: North-Holland.

Kornai, János (1979), 'Resource-Constrained versus Demand-Constrained Systems', *Econometrica*, 47 (4), 801–19.

Kornai, János (1980), *Economics of Shortage*, Amsterdam: North-Holland.

Kornai, János (1986), 'The Hungarian Reform Process: Visions, Hopes and Reality', *Journal of Economic Literature*, 24 (4), 1687–737.

Kornai, János (1990) [1989], *The Road to a Free Economy. Shifting from a Socialist System: The Example of Hungary*, New York and London: W. W. Norton.

Kornai, János (1992a), 'The Principles of Privatization in Eastern Europe', *De Economist*, 140 (2), 153–76.

Kornai, János (1992b), 'The Postsocialist Transition and the State: Reflections in the Light of Hungarian Fiscal Problems', *American Economic Review*, Papers and Proceedings, 82 (2), 1–21.

Kornai, János (1992c), 'Visszaesés, veszteglés vagy fellendülés' (Recession, Stagnation or Recovery), *Magyar Hírlap*, 14 December, pp. 12–13.

Kornai, János (1992d), *The Socialist System: The Political Economy of Communism*, Princeton: Princeton University Press and Oxford: Oxford University Press.

Kornai, János (1993a), 'The Evolution of Financial Discipline under the Postsocialist System', *Kyklos*, 46 (3), 315–36.

Kornai, János (1993b), 'Transformational Recession: A General Phenomenon Examined through the Example of Hungary's Development', *Economie Appliquée*, 46 (2), 181–227.

Kornai, János (1995a), 'Lasting Growth as the Top Priority: Macroeconomic Tensions and Government Economic Policy in Hungary', in *Struggle and Hope*, Cheltenham: Edward Elgar, pp. 45-87.

Kornai, János (1995b), 'The Dilemmas of Hungarian Economic Policy: An Analysis of the Stabilization Program', in *Struggle and Hope*, Cheltenham: Edward Elgar, pp. 100-120.

Kornai, János (1996a), 'Paying the Bill for Goulash Communism: Hungarian Development and Macro Stabilization in a Political Economy Perspective', in *Struggle and Hope*, Cheltenham: Edward Elgar, pp. 121-179.

Kornai, János (1996b), 'The Citizen and the State: Reform of the Welfare System', in *Struggle and Hope*, Cheltenham: Edward Elgar, pp. 239-254.

Köves, András (1995a), 'Egy alternatív gazdaságpolitika szükségessége és lehetősége' (The Need and Scope for an Alternative Economic Policy), *Külgazdaság*, 39 (6), 4–17.

Köves, András (1995b), 'Gazdaságpolitikai dilemmák és lehetőségek a Bokros-csomag után' (Economic Policy

Dilemmas and Potentials after the Bokros Package), *Külgazdaság*, 39 (11), 4–18.

Krugman, Paul (1991), 'Financial Crises in the International Economy' in Martin Feldstein (ed.), *The Risk of Economic Crisis*, Chicago and London: University of Chicago Press, pp. 85–128.

Laki, Mihály (1993), 'Chances for the Acceleration of Transition: The Case of Hungarian Privatization', *East European Politics and Societies*, Fall, 7 (3), 440–51.

Lányi, Kamilla (1994–5), 'Alkalmazkodás és gazdasági visszaesés Magyarországon és más országokban. I. Tények és magyarázatok. II. Gazdaságpolitika és szelekció' (Adjustment and Economic Recession in Hungary and Other Countries. I. Facts and Explanations. II. Economic Policy and Selection), *Társadalmi Szemle*, 49 (12), 13–25. and 50 (1), 3–19.

Little, I.M.D., Richard N. Cooper, W. Max Corden and Sarath Rajapatirana (1993), *Boom, Crisis and Adjustment. The Macroeconomic Experience of Developing Countries*, Oxford: Oxford University Press (for World Bank).

Major, Iván and Péter Mihályi (1994), 'Privatizáció – hogyan tovább?' (Privatization – How to Go Further?), *Közgazdasági Szemle*, 41 (3), 214–28.

McHale, John (1996), *Equilibrium Employment Rates and Transformational Slumps*, mimeo. Cambridge, Mass.: Harvard University, March.

Mexican Ministry of Finance (SHCP) (1995), *Informe sobre la Situacion Economica, las Finanzas Publicas y la Deuda Publica*, Fourth Quarter, Mexico City.

Mexican Ministry of Finance (SHCP) (1996), *Informe sobre la Situacion Economica, las Finanzas Publicas y la Deuda Publica*, Fourth Quarter, Mexico City.

Mihályi, Péter (1993), 'Plunder—Squander—Plunder. The Strange Demise of State Ownership', *The Hungarian Quarterly*, 34 (Summer), 62–75.

Mihályi, Péter (1994), 'Privatization in Hungary: An Overview', in Yilmaz Akyüz, Detlef J. Kotte, András Köves and László Szamuely (eds), *Privatization in the Transition Process. Recent Experiences in Eastern Europe*, Geneva: UNCTAD and Budapest: Kopint-Datorg, pp. 363–85.

Mihályi, Péter (1995), *Privatisation in Hungary: Now Comes the 'Hard Core'*, paper presented at Fifth World Congress for Central and East European Studies, Warsaw, 6-11 August, mimeo.

Ministry of Finance (1996a), *A gazdaság helyzete 1995–96 fordulóján* (The Economic Situation at the Turn of 1995–6), Budapest: Pénzügyminisztérium, February.

Ministry of Finance (1996b), *Tájékoztató az 1995. évi és az 1996. év eleji gazdasági folyamatokról* (Report on the Economic Processes in 1995 and Early 1996), Budapest, Pénzügyminisztérium, March.

National Bank of Hungary (1995), *Annual Report 1994,* Budapest: National Bank of Hungary.

National Bank of Hungary (1996a), *Az 1995. évi gazdasági és pénzügyi folyamatokról* (The Economic and Monetary Processes in 1995), Budapest: Magyar Nemzeti Bank, February.

National Bank of Hungary (1996b), *Havi Jelentés* (Monthly Report), No. 2.

National Bank of Hungary (1996c), *Előterjesztés és jelentés az 1996. évi rendes közgyűlésnek a Magyar Nemzeti Bank 1995. évi üzlettervéről* (Presentation and Report to the 1996 Annual General Assembly on the 1995 Business Plan of the National Bank of Hungary), Budapest: Magyar Nemzeti Bank, April.

Oblath, Gábor (1995), 'A költségvetési deficit makrogazdasági hatásai Magyarországon' (The Macroeconomic Effects of the Budget Deficit in Hungary) *Külgazdaság*, 39 (7/8), 22–33.

Oblath, Gábor (1996), 'Makrogazdasági folyamatok' (Macroeconomic Processes), in *Konjunktúrajelentés. A világgazdaság és a magyar gazdaság helyzete és kilátásai 1996 tavaszán* (Business Activity Report. The Situation and Prospects of the World Economy and the Hungarian Economy), Budapest: Kopint-Datorg, No. 1, pp. 79–118.

OECD (1996), *OECD Economic Outlook*, December.

OECD (1997), *Economic Indicators*, January.

Sachs, Jeffrey D. (1996), *Economic Transition and the Exchange Rate Regime*, mimeo, Cambridge: Harvard Institute for International Development, Harvard University.

Sachs, Jeffrey D. and Felipe B. Larrain (1993), *Macroeconomics in the Global Economy*, New York: Harvester Wheatsheaf.

Sachs, Jeffrey D., Aaron Tornell and Andres Velasco (1995), *The Collapse of the Mexican Peso: What Have We Learned?*, Discussion Paper No. 1724, Cambridge: Harvard Institute of Economic Research, Harvard University, May.

Surányi, György (1995a), 'A gazdaság örökölt struktúrái gúzsba kötik az országot. Válaszol Surányi György, a Nemzeti Bank elnöke' (The Inherited Economic Structures Shackle the Country. György Surányi, President of the National Bank, Replies), *Heti Világgazdaság*, 29 April, pp. 47–8.

Surányi, György (1995b), 'Önmagunkkal kell megállapodásra jutni. Beszélgetés árakról, bérekről, kamatokról Surányi Györggyel, az MNB elnökével. Bossányi Katalin interjúja' (We Have to Come to Terms with Ourselves. Conversation about Prices, Wages and Interest Rates with György Surányi, President of the National Bank. Interview by Katalin Bossányi), *Népszabadság*, 30 December, pp. 1 and 10.

Surányi, György (1996), 'Jobban igen, másként nem. Szombati MH-extra Surányi Györggyel, a Magyar Nemzeti Bank elnökével. Pintér Dezső riportja' (It Can Be Done Better, but not in Other Ways. A Saturday Supplement Interview with György Surányi, President of the Hungarian National Bank. Report by Dezső Pintér), *Magyar Hírlap*, 6 January, p. 9.

Szentgyörgyvári, Artúr and Ilona Baár (1996), *A magyar nemzetgazdaság nemzetközi versenyképessége 1995-ben, kitekintés 1996-ra és 1997-re* (The International Competitiveness of the Hungarian Economy in 1995, and the Outlook for 1996 and 1997), mimeo, Budapest: Magyar Nemzeti Bank, April.

Végh, Carlos A. (1992), 'Stopping High Inflation', *IMF Staff Papers*, 39 (3), 626–95.

Voszka, Éva (1992), 'Not Even the Contrary is True: The Transfigurations of Centralization and Decentralization', *Acta Oeconomica*, 44 (1/2), 77–94.

Voszka, Éva (1993), 'Variations on the Theme of Self-Privatization', *Acta Oeconomica*, 45 (3/4), 310–18.

Voszka, Éva (1994), *Centralization, Renationalization, Redistribution: The Role of the Government in Changing the Ownership Structure in Hungary, 1989–93*, Discussion Paper series 916, London: Centre for Economic Policy Research, February.

World Bank (1995a), *Hungary: Structural Reforms for Sustainable Growth. First Draft*, Document of the World Bank, Country Operations Division, Central Europe Department, Report No. 13577-HU, Washington DC: World Bank, February 10.

World Bank (1995b), *Hungary: Structural Reforms for Sustainable Growth*, Document of the World Bank, Country Operations Division, Central Europe Department, Report No. 13577-HU, Washington DC: World Bank, June 12.

World Bank (1995c), *World Tables 1995*, Washington DC: World Bank.

World Bank (1995d), *Magyarország. Szerkezetváltás és tartós növekedés* (Hungary: Structural Change and Lasting Growth). Washington DC: World Bank, November.

LIST OF BIOGRAPHIES

BOKROS, LAJOS (1954–)

Hungarian economist and banker, who held high posts in the National Bank of Hungary (1991-95) and commercial banking before becoming finance minister in the Horn government in 1995. Faced with a Hungarian economy on the brink of a balance-of-payments and credibility crisis, he introduced the stringent 'Bokros' package of austerity measures, which was vindicated by the subsequently strong performance of the Hungarian economy. Bokros resigned in 1996. Since then he has served as a director of the World Bank in Washington D.C.

FRIEDMAN, MILTON (1912–)

Appointed Professor of Economics at the University of Chicago in 1949 and the leading member of the Chicago School, Friedman was awarded the Nobel Prize for Economics in 1976. He was a pioneer in developing the idea of human capital. His work on the consumption function led to the formulation of his permanent-income hypothesis. With his methodological stance of positive economics, his libertarian ideology, and his formulation of the natural rate of unemployment, he helped to emphasize the limitations of Keynesianism. With Anna Schwartz, he wrote a monumental *Monetary History of the United States 1867–1960* (1963), which provided much of the basis for his development of the quantity theory of money and revival of the pre-Keynesian faith in the automatic stability of the economic system.[1]

GALBRAITH, JOHN KENNETH (1908–)

Canadian-born American economist and social critic, who became a Harvard economics professor in 1949. Galbraith was an itinerant scholar and researcher, in and out of government and academic institutions in the US and elsewhere. His major theme was that industrial societies, notably America's, no longer resembled the descriptive model of conventional economic theory. In *The Affluent Society* (1958), Galbraith criticized the contrivance of demand by large-scale business, as leading to instability, inflation and unbalanced production that ignores social needs such as public goods and services. The *New Industrial State* (1967) summarizes much of his thought on the giant firms.[1]

HAYEK, FRIEDRICH A. von (1899–1992)

Born and educated in Vienna, Hayek held chairs at the London School of Economics and the universities of Chicago, Freiburg and Salzburg. In 1974 he was jointly awarded the Nobel Prize with Gunnar Myrdal, for his pioneering work on the theory of money and economic fluctuations, on the functional efficiency of different economic systems, and the extension of his field of study to include the legal framework of the economic system. In *Prices and Production* (1931) he integrated monetary theory with the Austrian theory of capital. In the 1930s, Hayek had analysed the problems of rational economic planning under socialism, foreseeing that its rationality would founder on the problem of acquiring and applying all the dispersed knowledge it required. With *The Road to Serfdom* (1944), he moved to fields of legal and political philosophy, analysing the problem of liberty, which he summed up in *The Constitution of Liberty* (1960).[1]

KEYNES, JOHN MAYNARD (1883–1946)

British economist, who entered the civil service in 1906. However, he resigned from the Treasury and resumed teaching at Cambridge, as well as pursuing a career in the City. His early, more practical work (for instance on the gold standard) led him to a new, highly influential theoretical framework for public policy (*Treatise on Money*, 1930, and especially *General Theory of Employment, Interest and Money*, 1936). Keynes was also a major contributor to the Bretton Woods Conference (1944), which set up the International Monetary Fund. A director of the Bank of England, he was created Lord Keynes of Tilton in 1942. The *General Theory* is undoubtedly Keynes's most significant work, regarded by many as a turning point in the history of economic thought. The policy problem which occupied Keynes in the 1930s was mass unemployment. This led him to focus attention on what determined the level of output, rather than on what determined the general price level (the major concern of contemporary economic theory).[1]

LANGE, OSCAR (1904–1965)

Polish socialist economist, who taught in several American universities and held a chair at the University of Chicago. He was one of the founders of econometrics and an advocate of Keynesian economics. Though he made significant contributions in numerous fields (welfare economics, utility functions, stability conditions), he is best remembered for his part in the debate in the 1930s on whether rational economic calculation could take place in a planned economy. He argued this was possible, for the prices which were required as indices of scarcity could be calculated outside the market system, although to obtain his system of prices, Lange required the creation of an institution that was an analogue of a market. His *Political Economy*, though incomplete (English translation 1963) is the first major synthesis of Marxist economics.[1]

LIBERMAN, Yevsei (1897–1981)

Russian economist, university professor. In 1962 he published 'Plan, Profit Premium' in Pravda, which opened the academic and political debate on the best ways to improve the planning or administration of Soviet industry by linking the reward of state enterprises to profits earned on the capital assets they used rather than to the increase in gross output over the previous year. Liberman argued that paying a rate of interest, or rather its equivalent, for capital (new plants and equipment) instead of receiving them free from the state would induce the managers to economize in its use. The managers would therefore have an incentive to maximize their profits rather than to hold large stocks of equipment or materials, or to hoard labour.[2]

MISES, LUDWIG von (1881–1973)

Von Mises, a leading member of the Austrian school of economists, was a professor of economics at Vienna and New York universities, and author of numerous works on economics and government. *The Theory of Money and Credit* (1934) extended the subjective value revolution to monetary analysis. In the first German edition of 1912, Mises predicted the Great Depression and developed the Austrian School's theory of the business cycle. *Socialism* (1936) was probably the most comprehensive analysis written by an economist. In *Epistemological Problems of Economics* (1960) and *Theory and History* (1957) he developed the position that economic theory is logically independent of reality in the sense in which logic and mathematics are independent. Reality for the social sciences is always unique and unrepeatable history.[1]

SIK, OTA (1919–)

Czechoslovak economist; he started to write on the forms of market that could advantageously be incorporated into a centrally planned society in the early 1960s. He came into prominence in 1968 as a Deputy Finance Minister in the Dubcek government, after which he taught economics at the University of Basle, Switzerland, and wrote *Der Dritte Weg* (The Third Road), published in Hamburg in 1972. In this book Sik discussed the mechanics of capital accumulation, provision for

ensuring initiative and founding new enterprises, and the organization of a system of collectivized ownership of capital
using the market mechanism.[2]

SCHUMPETER, JOSEPH ALOIS (1883–1950)

Austrian economist who taught at Chernowitz and later Graz.
After the First World War, he was a finance minister in the
Austrian Republic, but soon gave this up in favour of chairs at
Bonn, then at Harvard (1932). Schumpeter was a fertile, ver-
satile writer. *Capitalism, Socialism and Democracy* (1942)
and *History of Economic Analysis* (published posthumously in
1954) give only a small indication of this. In his *Theory of
Economic Development* (1912) and *Business Cycles* (1939) he
analysed the capitalist system and put forward the theory that
innovations made by entrepreneurs are the strategic factor in
economic development and the trade cycle.[1]

WALRAS, LÉON (1834–1910)

Born in France, Walras was the first holder in 1870 of the chair
of Political Economy in the University of Lausanne in
Switzerland. He is remembered for his independent development of the marginal utility approach to the theory of value in
1873, and more still, for his development of the theory of general equilibrium, in which all the markets in an economy are
examined, and in which all prices of goods and factors and all
goods' outputs and factor supplies are simultaneously determined. He set out this approach in the first edition of *Elements
d'economie politique pure* (1874–7), laying the groundwork
for a unified model comprising theories of exchange, production, capital formation and money. In subsequent revisions, he
strengthened the logic of the model by applying the principle
of the maximizations of utility in all sectors. He developed a
pioneer model, albeit with primitive mathematical tools.
Although the model and its properties have been repeatedly
refined and polished, the general conception behind them
remains untouched.[2]

Notes:

[1]Based on *The Dictionary of Modern Economics*. General editor David W. Pearce. Cambridge, MA: The MIT Press, 1981

[2] Based on Everyman's Dictionary of Economics. Compiled by Arthur Seldon and F.G. Pennance. London: J.M. Dent and Sons Ltd.1975.

SELECTED BIBLIOGRAPHY

Aghion, P. 1993. "Economic Reform in Eastern Europe: Can Theory Help?" *European Economic Review* 37: 525–32.

Aghion, P. and O. Blanchard 1993. *On the Speed of Transition in Central Europe.* London: EBRD, Working Paper No. 6, July.

Antal, L. 1979. "Development with Some Digression. The Hungarian Economic Mechanism in the Seventies," *Acta Oeconomica* 23: 257–73.

Aslund, A. and R. Layard (eds.) 1993. *Changing the Economic System in Russia.* New York: St Martin's Press.

Bardhan, P.K. and J.E. Roemer (eds.) 1993. *Market Socialism. The Current Debate.* Oxford University Press.

Barr, N. (ed.) 1994. *Labor Market and Social Policy in Central and Eastern Europe.* Oxford University Press.

Bauer, T. 1987. "Reforming or Perfectioning the Economic Mechanism," *European Economc Review* 31: 132–38.

Begg, D. and R. Portes 1993. "Enterprise Debt and Financial Restructuring in Central and Eastern Europe," *European Economic Review* 37: 396–407.

Blanchard, O. 1997. *The Economics of Post-Communist Transition.* Oxford University Press.

Blanchard, O., K.A. Froot and J.D. Sachs 1994. *The Transition in Eastern Europe*, vol. 1 *Country Studies*, vol. 2 *Restructuring.* NBER, University of Chicago Press.

Blanchard, O., R. Dornbush, P. Krugman, R. Layard and L. Summers 1991. *Reform in Eastern Europe.* Cambridge, MA: The MIT Press.

Boeri, T. 1994. "Transitional Unemployment," *Economics of Transition* 2: 1–25.

Bornstein, M. 1989. *Comparative Economic Systems: Models and Cases*, sixth edition, Homewood, Illinois: Irwin.

Boycko, M., A. Shleifer and R. Vishny, 1995. *Privatizing Russia.* Cambridge, MA: The MIT Press.

Brabant, J. M van (ed.) 1980. *Socialist Economic Integration. Aspects of Contemporary Economic Problems in Eastern Europe.* Cambridge University Press.

Brabant, J. M van (ed.) 1991. *Economic Reforms in Centrally Planned Economies and their Impact on the Global Economy,* in association with the United Nations. London and Basingstoke: Macmillan.

Brus, W. and K. Laski 1989. *From Marx to the Market: Socialism in Search of an Economic System.* Oxford: Clarendon Press.

Brus: W. 1972. *The Market in a Socialist Economy.* London: Routledge and Kegan Paul.

Campbell, R. W. 1991. *The Socialist Economies in Transition: A Primer on Semi-Reformed Systems.* Bloomington and Indianapolis: Indiana University Press.

Chavance, B. 1994. *The Transformation of Communist Systems. Economic Reform Since the 1950s.* Boulder and Oxford: Westview Press.

Csaba, L. (ed.) 1991. *Systemic Change and Stabilization in Eastern Europe.* Aldershot: Dartmouth.

de Melo, M. and A. Gelb 1996 "A Comparative Analysis of Twenty Eight Transition Countries in Europe and Asia," *Post-Soviet Geography and Economics* 37: 265–85.

Diamond, L. and M.F. Plattner 1995. *Economic Reform and Democracy.* Baltimore: John Hopkins University Press.

EBRD 1998. *Transition Report 1997.* London.

Elster, J., C. Offe and U.K. Preuss 1998. *Institutional Design in Post-Communist Societies.* Cambridge University Press.

Fischer, S. and A. Gelb 1991. "The Process of Socialist Economic Transformation," *Journal of Economic Perspectives* 5: 91–105.

Frydman, R. and A. Rapaczynski 1994. *Privatization in Eastern Europe: Is the State Withering Away?* Budapest: Central European University Press.

Gomulka, S. 1994. "Economic and Political Constraints During Transition," *Europe-Asia Studies* 46: 89–106.

Hare, P., H.K. Radice and N. Swain (eds) 1981 *Hungary: A Decade of Economic Reform*. London and Boston: Allen and Unwin.

Hare, P.G. and R.J. Davis (eds.) 1997. *Transition to the Market Economy. Critical Perspective to the World Economy* Vols 1–4. London: Routledge.

Kaser, M. (ed.) 1985, 1986. *The Economic History of Eastern Europe 1919–1975*. Oxford: Clarandon Press.

Kornai. J. 1980. *Economics of Shortage*. Amsterdam: North Holland.

Kornai, J. 1986. The Soft Budget Constraint, *Kyklos* 39: 3–30.

Kornai, J. 1990. *The Road to a Free Economy. Shifting from a Socialist System: The Example of Hungary*. New York: W.W. Norton.

Kornai, J. 1992, *The Socialist System. The Political Economy of Communism*. Oxford University Press.

Kornai, J. 1995. *Highway and Byways. Studies on Reform and Postcommunist Transition*. Cambridge, MA: The MIT Press.

Kornai, J. 1997. *Struggle and Hope. Essays on Stabilization and Reform in a Post-Socialist Economy*. Cheltenham: Edward Elgar.

Kornai, J. 1998. *From Socialism to Capitalism*. London: Centre for Post-Collectivist Studies.

Kornai, J., S. Haggard and R.R. Kaufman (eds.) 2000. *Reforming the State: Fiscal and Welfare Reform in Post-Socialist Countries*. Cambridge University Press.

Lavigne, M. 1995. *The Economics of Transition. From Socialist Economy to Market Economy*. London: Macmillan.

Maskin. E.S. 1996. "Theories of the Soft Budget Constraint," *Japan and the World Economy* 8: 125–33.

McKinnon, R.I. 1991. *The Order of Economic Liberalization: Financial Control in the Transition to a Market Economy.* Baltimore: John Hopkins University Press.

McKinnon, R.I. 1994. "Gradual versus Rapid Liberalization in Socialist Economies: The Problem of Macroeconomic Control," in M. Bruno and B. Pleskovic (eds) *Proceedings of the World Bank Annual Conference on Development Economics.* Washington, DC.

Mihályi, P. 1993. "Property Rights and Privatization. The Three-Agent Model (A Case Study on Hungary)?" *Eastern European Economics* 31: 5–64.

Murrell, P. 1991. "Public Choice and the Transformation of Socialism," *Journal of Comparative Economics* 15: 203–10.

Nelson, J.M. (ed.) 1989. *Fragile Coalitions: The Politics of Economic Adjustment.* New Brunswick and Oxford: Transaction Books.

Nelson, J.M., C. Tilly and L. Walker (eds.) 1997. *Transforming Post-Communist Political Economies.* Washington, DC: National Academy Press.

North, D. 1990. *Institutions, Institutional Change and Economic Performance.* Cambridge University Press.

Nuti, D.M. 1992. "Market Socialism: The Model that Might Have Been but Never Was," in A. Aslund (ed.) *Market Socialism or the Restoration of Capitalism?* Cambridge University Press.

Rutkowski, M. 1998. "A New Generation of Pension Reforms conquers the East. A Taxonomy in Transition Economies," *Transition* vol. 9, No. 4.

Sachs, J. 1993. *Poland's Leap to the Market Economy.* Cambridge, MA: The MIT Press.

Saltman, R.S. and J. Figueras 1998. "Analysing the Evidence on European Health Care Reforms," *Health Affairs* 17: 85–108.

Schaffer, M. 1998. "Do Firms in Transition Economies Have Soft Budget Constraints? A Reconsideration of Concepts and Evidence," *Journal of Comparative Economics* 26: 80–103.

Schleifer, A. 1997. "Government in Transition," *European Economic Review* 41: 385–410.

Stark, D. and L. Bruszt 1998. *Postsocialist Pathways: Transforming Politics and Property in East Central Europe.* Cambridge University Press.

Steinfeld, E. 1998. *Forging Reform in China.* Cambridge University Press.

Tanzi, V. 1993. "The Budget Deficit in Transition," *IMF Staff Papers* 40: 697–707.

Williamson, J. (ed.) 1994. *The Politcal Economy of Policy Reform.* Washington, DC: Institute for International Economics.

Woo, W. T. and J. Sachs (eds.) 1997. *Economics in Transition: Comparing Asia and Eastern Europe.* Cambridge, MA: The MIT Press.

World Bank 1996. *From Plan to Market: World Development Report 1996.* Oxford University Press.

THE AUTHOR

JÁNOS KORNAI was born on 21 January, 1928 in Budapest, Hungary.

Since his appointment in 1986 as Professor of Economics at Harvard University he has divided his time between Budapest and Cambridge, Massachusetts. He has been a Permanent Fellow of Collegium Budapest, Institute for Advanced Study since its creation in 1992. From the beginning of his academic career in 1955 he has been associated with the Institute of Economics of the Hungarian Academy of Sciences, first as a research fellow, and later as a research professor. He has been Visiting Professor at the London School of Economics, at the universities of Stanford, Yale, Princeton and Stockholm, and Fellow at the Princeton Institute for Advanced Study.

He has received honorary doctorates from the universities of Paris, London, Amsterdam, Budapest, Poznan, Wroclaw, and Torino. He is a Member of the Hungarian Academy of Sciences and the European Academy, Foreign Member of the American, British, Swedish, Finnish, and Russian Academies, and Honorary Member of the American Economic Association. He has been awarded the State Prize and the Széchenyi Prize in Hungary, the Humboldt Prize in Germany, and the Seidman Award in the USA. He served as President of the Econometric Society in 1978 and President of the European Economic Association in 1987. He became Officer of the Ordre National de la Légion d'Honneur in 1997.

He is a member of the Board of the National Bank of Hungary, the Hungarian central bank.

János Kornai's general field of research is socialist economies and the post-socialist transition.

His first book, *Overcentralization of Economic Administration*, written in 1955-6, was a critique of the socialist system, the first book by a citizen of a communist country suggesting decentralisation reforms. In the late 1950s, he was among those initiating the use of mathematical methods in socialist planning. He elaborated the theory of two-level planning with Tamás Lipták and directed the first large-scale economy-wide multi-level planning project. Experiencing the limits of planning led him to an increasing interest in theoretical foundations. *Anti-Equilibrium* (1971), a controversial essay criticising Walrasian neoclassical economics, suggested new approaches to studying chronic non-Walrasian states, price- and non-price signals. In his personal intellectual development, this book was a preparation for the task that followed: enquiry into the nature of socialist systems. Issues like chronic shortage, forced growth, the soft budget constraint syndrome, bureaucratisation, and conflicts between socialist principles and efficiency became his main concern. His findings were summarized first in *Economics of Shortage* (1980), and later in *The Socialist System. The Political Economy of Communism* (1992), which presents a synthetic analysis of the political, social and economic attributes of the system.

After the collapse of socialism in Eastern Europe part of his attention turned to economic policy. *The Road to a Free Economy* (1989) which was translated into 17 languages, was the first book to draw up the main tasks of post-socialist transition. It proposed radical, rapid stabilization, with gradual privatization. Many of his subsequent writings dealt with macroeconomic aspects and the interaction between politics and economic policy in the period of post-socialist transition. These writings address issues which are at the centre of public debate and legislative activity in all the post-socialist countries, and use Hungary—the country with which he is most familiar—as a case study with which to demonstrate the more general problems. His writings had an impact on the formulation of the 1995 adjustment and stabilisation program, which he endorsed publicly as soon as it was announced. He studied the specific features of the programme, monitored its results and shortcomings, and published his recommendations in a series of articles, dealing, among other things, with the public controversy concerning the use of the 'windfall' revenues from privatisation, the plans to institute a disinflationary policy, and the dangers of relaxing fiscal and wage discipline. Some of his papers analysed problems of hardening the budget constraint, which proved one of the key issues of the transformation to a market economy. His paper on fiscal policy pointed out that the final period of East European socialism had brought a 'premature welfare state'. These writings of his were published in two volumes, *Highway and Byways* (1995) and *Struggle and Hope* (1997).

His recent work has centred on issues concerning the redefinition of the role of the state in a post-socialist society in general, and reforming the state's activities in the area of social policy in particular—in other words, reconsidering the role and scope of the welfare state, especially reform of the pension system and the health sector. At present he is working on a book containing a thorough analysis of and his recommendations for the health sectors in the post-socialist countries, an extension of his 1998 book on the reform of the health sector in Hungary.

His works have been translated into Arabic, Bulgarian, Chinese, Czech, Croatian, English, Estonian, French, German, Greek, Hebrew, Italian, Japanese, Polish, Portuguase, Rumanian, Russian, Serbian, Singhalese, Slovak, Spanish, Tamil, Ukrainian and Vietnamese.

Books

Overcentralization in Economic Administration. Oxford: Oxford University Press, 1959. Also published in Hungarian. Second edition in English: 1994.

Mathematical Planning of Structural Decisions. With contributions from Tamás Lipták and Péter Wellisch. Amsterdam: North Holland; Budapest: Akadémiai Kiadó, 1967, second, extended edition in 1975. Also published in Hungarian, Slovak, German, and Polish.

Anti-Equilibrium. Amsterdam: North Holland, 1971. Also published in Hungarian, Romanian, German, Japanese, Polish, and Croatian.

Rush versus Harmonic Growth. Amsterdam. North Holland, 1980. Also published in Hungarian, Czech, Spanish, and Chinese.

Economics of Shortage. Amsterdam: North-Holland, 1980. Also published in Hungarian, Czech, French, Polish, Chinese and Russian.

Growth, Shortage and Efficiency. Oxford: Basil Blackwell; Berkeley and Los Angeles: University of California Press, 1982. Also published in Hungarian, Estonian, Chinese, and Polish.

Contradictions and Dilemmas. Budapest: Corvina, 1985; Cambridge: MIT Press, 1986. Also published in Hungarian, Japanese, Chinese, Vietnamese, and Estonian.

Visions and Reality, Market and State: New Studies on the Socialist Economy and Society. Budapest: Corvina; Hemel Hempstead and New York: Harvester Wheatsheaf; New York: Routledge, 1990. Also published in Hungarian.

The Road to a Free Economy. Shifting from a Socialist System: The Example of Hungary. New York: W. W. Norton, 1990. Also published in Hungarian, Russian, Czech, Slovak, French, Italian, Spanish, Polish, Ukrainian, Estonian, Serbian, Japanese, Tamil, Singhalese (Sri Lanka), and Chinese.

The Socialist System. The Political Economy of Communism. Princeton: Princeton University Press; Oxford: Oxford University Press, 1992. Also published in Hungarian, German, French, and Bulgarian.

Highway and Byways. Studies on Socialist Reform and Postsocialist Transition. Cambridge: MIT Press, 1995. Also published in Hungarian, Arabic, Bulgarian, German, Polish and Slovak.

Struggle and Hope. Essays on Stabilization and Reform in a Post-Socialist Economy. Cheltenham, UK: Edward Elgar Publishing, 1997. Also published in Hungarian, Bulgarian, Polish and Slovak.

On Health Care Reform. Budapest: Közgazdasági és Jogi Könyvkiadó, 1998. In Hungarian.

Volumes Published in
"Atlantic Studies on Society in Change"

* Vols. no. I through XXXVI refer to the series *War and Society in East Central Europe*

No. 12   *From Hunyadi to Rákóczi: War and Society in Late Medieval*
Vol. III   *and Early Modern Hungary.* Edited by János M. Bak and
           Béla K. Király. 1982.

No. 13   *East Central European Society and War in the Era of*
Vol. IV   *Revolutions: 1775-1856.* Edited by B. K. Király. 1984.

No. 14   *Essays on World War I: Origins and Prisoners of War.*
Vol. V   Edited by Samuel R. Williamson, Jr. and Peter Pastor. 1983.

No. 15   *Essays on World War I: Total War and Peacemaking, A Case*
Vol. VI   *Study on Trianon.* Edited by B. K. Király, Peter Pastor, and
           Ivan Sanders. 1982.

No. 16   *Army, Aristocracy, Monarchy: War, Society and Government*
Vol. VII   *in Austria, 1618-1780.* Edited by Thomas M. Barker. 1982.

No. 17   *The First Serbian Uprising 1804-1813.* Edited by Wayne S.
Vol. VIII Vucinich. 1982.

No. 18   *Czechoslovak Policy and the Hungarian Minority 1945-1948.*
Vol. IX   Kálmán Janics. Edited by Stephen Borsody. 1982.

No. 19   *At the Brink of War and Peace: The Tito-Stalin Split in a*
Vol. X   *Historic Perspective.* Edited by Wayne S. Vucinich. 1982.

No. 20   *Inflation Through the Ages: Economic, Social, Psychological*
           and Historical Aspects. Edited by Edward Marcus and
           Nathan Schmuckler. 1981.

No. 21   *Germany and America: Essays on Problems of International*
           Relations and Immigration. Edited by Hans L. Trefousse.
           1980.

No. 22   *Brooklyn College: The First Half Century.* Murray M.
           Horowitz. 1981.

No. 23   *A New Deal for the World: Eleanor Roosevelt and American*
           Foreign Policy. Jason Berger. 1981.

No. 24   *The Legacy of Jewish Migration: 1881 and Its Impact.* Edited
           by David Berger. 1982.

No. 25   *The Road to Bellapais: Cypriot Exodus to Northern Cyprus.*
           Pierre Oberling. 1982.

No. 26   *New Hungarian Peasants: An East Central European*
           Experience with Collectivization. Edited by Marida Hollos
           and Béla C. Maday. 1983.

No. 27 *Germans in America: Aspects of German-American Relations in the Nineteenth Century.* Edited by Allen McCormick. 1983.

No. 28 *A Question of Empire: Leopold I and the War of Spanish Succession, 1701-1705.* Linda and Marsha Frey. 1983.

No. 29 *The Beginning of Cyrillic Printing — Cracow, 1491. From the Orthodox Past in Poland.* Szczepan K. Zimmer. Edited by Ludwik Krzyżanowski and Irene Nagurski. 1983.

No. 29a *A Grand Ecole for the Grand Corps: The Recruitment and Training of the French Administration.* Thomas R. Osborne. 1983.

No. 30 *The First War between Socialist States: The Hungarian*
Vol. XI *Revolution of 1956 and Its Impact.* Edited by Béla K. Király, Barbara Lotze, Nandor Dreisziger. 1984.

No. 31 *The Effects of World War I, The Uprooted: Hungarian*
Vol. XII *Refugees and Their Impact on Hungary's Domestic Politics.* István Mócsy. 1983.

No. 32 *The Effects of World War I: The Class War after the Great*
Vol. XIII *War: The Rise Of Communist Parties in East Central Europe, 1918-1921.* Edited by Ivo Banac. 1983.

No. 33 *The Crucial Decade: East Central European Society and*
Vol. XIV *National Defense, 1859-1870.* Edited by Béla K. Király. 1984.

No. 35 *Effects of World War I: War Communism in Hungary, 1919.*
Vol. XVI György Péteri. 1984.

No. 36 *Insurrections, Wars, and the Eastern Crisis in the 1870s.*
Vol. XVII Edited by B. K. Király and Gale Stokes. 1985.

No. 37 *East Central European Society and the Balkan Wars, 1912-*
Vol. XVIII *1913.* Edited by B. K. Király and Dimitrije Djordjevic. 1986.

No. 38 *East Central European Society in World War I.* Edited by B.
Vol. XIX K. Király and N. F. Dreisziger, Assistant Editor Albert A. Nofi. 1985.

No. 39 *Revolutions and Interventions in Hungary and Its Neighbor*
Vol. XX *States, 1918-1919.* Edited by Peter Pastor. 1988.

310   Atlantic Studies on Society in Change

with the Polish Institute of Arts and Sciences of America, New York. 1991.

No. 74   *Hungarian Economy and Society during World War Two.*
Vol. XXIX Edited by György Lengyel. 1993.

No. 75   *The Life of a Communist Revolutionary, Béla Kun.* György Borsányi. 1993.

No. 76   *Yugoslavia: The Process of Disintegration.* Laslo Sekelj. 1993.

No. 77   *Wartime American Plans for a New Hungary. Documents*
Vol. XXX *from the U.S. Department of State, 1942-1944.* Edited by Ignác Romsics. 1992.

No. 78   *Planning for War against Russia and Serbia. Austro-*
Vol. XXXI *Hungarian and German Military Strategies, 1871-1914.* Graydon A. Tunstall, Jr. 1993.

No. 79   *American Effects on Hungarian Imagination and Political Thought, 1559-1848.* Géza Závodszky. 1995.

No. 80   *Trianon and East Central Europe: Antecedents and*
Vol. XXXII *Repercussions.* Edited by Béla K. Király and László Veszprémy. 1995.

No. 81   *Hungarians and Their Neighbors in Modern Times, 1867-1950.* Edited by Ferenc Glatz. 1995.

No. 82   *István Bethlen: A Great Conservative Statesman of Hungary, 1874-1946.* Ignác Romsics. 1995.

No. 83   *20th Century Hungary and the Great Powers.* Edited
Vol. XXXIII by Ignác Romsics. 1995.

No. 84   *Lawful Revolution in Hungary, 1989-1994.* Edited by Béla K. Király. András Bozóki Associate Editor. 1995.

No. 85   *The Demography of Contemporary Hungarian Society.* Edited by Pál Péter Tóth and Emil Valkovics. 1996.

No. 86   *Budapest, A History from Its Beginnings to 1996.* Edited By András Gerő and János Poór. 1996.

No. 87   *The Dominant Ideas of the Nineteenth Century and Their Impact on the State.* Volume 1. *Diagnosis.* József Eötvös. Translated, edited, annotated and indexed with an introductory essay by D. Mervyn Jones. 1997.

No. 88   *The Dominant Ideas of the Nineteenth Century and Their Impact on the State. Volume 2. Remedy.* József Eötvös. Translated, edited, annotated and indexed with an introductory essay by D. Mervyn Jones. 1997.

No. 89   *The Social History of the Hungarian Intelligentsia in the "Long Nineteenth Century," 1825-1914.* János Mazsu. 1997.

No. 90   *Pax Britannica: Wartime Foreign Office Documents*
Vol.XXXIV *Regarding Plans for a Post Bellum East Central Europe.* Edited by András D. Bán. 1997.

No. 91   *National Identity in Contemporary Hungary.* György Csepeli. 1997.

No. 92   *The Hungarian Parliament, 1867-1918: A Mirage of Power.* András Gerő. 1997.

No. 93   *The Hungarian Revolution and War of Independence, 1848-*
Vol. XXXV *1849. A Military History.* Edited by Gábor Bona. 1999.

No. 94   *Academia and State Socialism: Essays on the Political History of Academic Life in Post-1945 Hungary and East Central Europe.* György Péteri. 1998.

No. 95   *Through the Prism of the Habsburg Monarchy: Hungary in*
Vol.XXXVI *American Diplomacy and Public Opinion during World War I.* Tibor Glant. 1998.

No. 96   *Appeal of Sovereignty in Hungary, Austria and Russia.* Edited by Csaba Gombár, Elemér Hankiss, László Lengyel and Györgyi Várnai. 1997.

No. 97   *Geopolitics in the Danube Region. Hungarian Reconciliation Efforts, 1848-1998.* Edited by Ignác Romsics and Béla K. Király. 1998.

No. 98   *Hungarian Agrarian Society from the Emancipation of Serfs (1848) to Re-privatization of Land (1998).* Edited by Péter Gunst. 1999.

No. 99   *"The Jewish Question" in Europe. The Case of Hungary.* Tamás Ungvári. 2000.

No. 100   *Soviet Military Intervention in Hungary, 1956.* Edited by Jenő Györkei and Miklós Horváth. 1999.

No. 101   *Jewish Budapest.* Edited by Géza Komoróczy. 1999.

No. 102   *Evolution of the Hungarian Economy, 1848-1998.* Vol. I. *One and a Half Centuries of Semi-Successful Modernization, 1848-1989.* Edited by Iván T. Berend. 2000.

No. 103   *Evolution of the Hungarian Economy, 1848-1998.* Vol. II. *Paying the Bill for Goulash-Communism.* János Kornai. 2000.

No. 104   *Evolution of the Hungarian Economy, 1848-1998.* Vol. III. *Hungary: from Transition to Integration.* Edited by György Csáki. 2000.

No. 105   *From Habsburg Agent to Victorian Scholar: G. G. Zerffi (1820-1892).* Tibor Frank. 2000.

No. 106   *A History of Transylvania from the Beginning to 1919.* Vol. I. Edited by Zoltán Szász and Béla Köpeczy. 2000.

No. 107   *A History of Transylvania from the Beginning to 1919.* Vol. II. Edited by Zoltán Szász and Béla Köpeczy. 2000.

No. 108   *A History of Transylvania from the Beginning to 1919.* Vol. III. Edited by Zoltán Szász and Béla Köpeczy. 2000.

No. 109   *Hungary: Governments and Politics, 1848–1999.* Edited by Mária Ormos and Béla K. Király. 2000.

No. 110   *Hungarian Minority in the Voivodina.* Edited by Enikő A. Sajti. 2001.

No. 111   *Hungarian Successes.* Edited by László Somlyódy. 2001.

No. 112   *Hungary and International Politics in 1848–1849.* Edited by Domokos Kosáry.

No. 113   *Social History of Hungary from the Reform Era to the End of the Twentieth Century.* Edited by Gábor Gyáni, György Kövér and Tibor Valuch. 2000.

No. 114   *Hungarian Social-democracy, the Fiercest Foe of the Communists.* Edited by Róbert Gábor and Vilmos Vass. 2000.